Deep Waters

Deep Waters

The Textual Continuum in American Indian Literature

CHRISTOPHER B. TEUTON

UNIVERSITY OF NEBRASKA PRESS | LINCOLN AND LONDON

Parts of chapter 1 originally appeared in "Theorizing American Indian Literature: Applying Oral Concepts to Written Traditions," in *Reasoning Together: The Native Critics Collective*, edited by Daniel Justice, Christopher B. Teuton, and Craig Womack (Norman: University of Oklahoma Press, 2008). © 2008 University of Oklahoma Press, Norman, publishing division of the university.

A version of chapter 2 was originally published as "Interpreting Our World: Authority and the Written Word in Robert J. Conley's *Real People* Series," *Mfs: Modern Fiction Studies* 53, no. 3 (2007): 544–68.

Publication of this volume was assisted by The Virginia Faulkner Fund, established in memory of Virginia Faulkner, editor in chief of the University of Nebraska Press.

Library of Congress Cataloging-in-Publication Data

Teuton, Christopher B.
Deep waters: the textual continuum in American Indian literature / Christopher B. Teuton.
    p.   cm.
Includes bibliographical references and index.
ISBN 978-0-8032-2849-8 (cloth: alk. paper)
ISBN 978-1-4962-0768-5 (paper: alk. paper)
1. American literature—Indian authors—History and criticism. 2. Indians in literature. 3. Oral tradition in literature. 4. Vision in literature. 5. Indian philosophy—United States. 6. Indians of North America—Intellectual life. I. Title.
PS153.I52T46 2010
810.9'897—dc22
2010008266

Set in Quadraat & Quadraat Sans
Designed by Ray Boeche

For schemes and dreams,
And my band on the run.

Contents

Acknowledgments

The University of Denver and its Center for Multicultural Excellence provided generous research funding during the writing of this book. Thanks to Fernando Guzman in particular for his support of my work. My colleagues in the DU English Department have been encouraging, especially Ann Dobyns, Clark Davis, Scott Howard, and Maik Nwosu. Robert Warrior, Craig S. Womack, Daniel Heath Justice, Roberta Hill, and Kenneth M. Roemer offered useful feedback on this manuscript. Friends back home in Cherokee country have kept me grounded. I want to thank Sequoyah Guess, Richard Allen, Chief David Comingdeer and his family, and my fellow members of the Echota Ceremonial Grounds for their commitments to Cherokee community. I want to thank my mom for her love, my dad for always answering the phone when I needed to talk, and my brothers Billy, Mark, and Danny for their friendship. My brother Sean is an admired colleague as well as a friend. Thanks for sharing this journey, brother. My friend and mentor Craig Werner taught me how to trust myself as a writer and a teacher. I can only aspire to guide others as he has guided me. Melissa, Markus, and Azalea are my inspiration and joy. All my work flows through their love. *Wado.*

Introduction

Diving into Deep Waters

My elders say this is how our world was created. Before there was this solid earth on which we live, the place we call Elo-hi, there was only Galunlati, the Sky World, which exists high above the arch of the Sky-Vault. A long time ago, before humans, the ancient animals grew crowded in there; they needed more space to live and grow. These animals were similar to those we know today. There was Rabbit, Bear, Possum, Bat, and all the others. But the animals were larger than they are now, and they could talk. In the ancient time they were still changing; this was before their forms were finally shaped by their thoughts and actions.

In council all the animals discussed what should be done about their collective problem, and they all had a voice in the process. Many spoke, but in the end they decided together to explore the vast world of water far below the Sky-Vault.

Many strong and swift ones volunteered to search the waters, but one by one they came back to Galunlati, exhausted and without news of a place they could live. Finally little Dayunisi, Beaver's grandchild, also known as the water beetle, volunteered to search the waters. She was small and weak in comparison to the other animals, but Dayunisi bravely set off from Galunlati and dutifully explored the surface of the waters. She searched all over but found no land. So she dove underneath the surface, down into the dark blue depths. The other animals watched from above. She was gone a long time, and the animals began to worry. Finally, they gave up on her, thinking there was no way such a little creature could hold her breath so long. They began to mourn her passing, but as they praised her courage here comes Dayunisi with a handful of mud in her hand. She places that dark mud on the surface of the dark blue water, and with the help of others it begins to spread out in all directions, growing and drying. And it becomes the world on which we now stand, the world that is in between the Sky World and the Under World, our beloved Elohi.

This story, the Cherokee creation story, reminds me what stories do: enable us to create our worlds. I have heard this story, and I have told it. I have read this story, read about it, and found it referenced in dozens of works, including those by James Mooney, Charles Hudson, Theda Perdue, Robert J. Conley, and Thomas King. I have written it. I have seen it in the form of an animated cartoon by Joseph Erb, and I have seen it depicted by a Hollywood actor. I have a painting of it in my home. I have talked about it with family and friends. I tell it to my children. I think about it. And I feel it, as I once did when I lay in the middle of a creek deep in the Smoky

Mountains and watched out of the corners of my eyes Dayunisi skitter across and dive into the water all around me. This story shapes me. I never tire of its beauty and its meanings; it is both a story and a constant source of reflection on the responsibilities of being. These two aspects of its reality are inextricable.

The Cherokee creation story is richly theoretical, with evocative metaphors and symbolism that invite interpretation. The world does not begin with humans at the center of existence, but with animals, our teachers and sources of sustenance, who through their complex relations afford us mirrors by which we may understand ourselves and our world. The creation of Elohi is made possible by the values that arise when creatures recognize their shared stake in survival. Communal solidarity, egalitarian discussion and consensus, and individual self-sacrifice for the welfare of the whole are necessary conditions for finding and developing that new space on which the community may grow. Most important, these values are acted on individually, but within a social context, for all persons, no matter their gifts or abilities, are integral to the welfare of the group, and some of the most unlikely of us may become heroes.

Among its meanings the creation story is an allegory about the creation of new knowledge on which a community may stand, grow, and live. The Upper World in Cherokee thought is the place of order and stability, but also the place of static forms. As the animals found out, there is not much room for growth there. The Under World is the place of chaos and mystery, but also a source of powerful energy and change. We may visit this place, but it is not hospitable to human society. The middle place, Elohi, is where we humans seek a dynamic balance between these opposing forces of order and chaos through our application of knowledge that may draw the best qualities from each. The mud that Dayunisi brings to the surface represents not only land, but raw, experiential knowledge and energy that must be accounted for and shaped in order for the world to spread and grow.

As a Cherokee literary scholar I like to conceptualize the critical process as modeled by Dayunisi's journey. Like Dayunisi, the critic leaves the ordered world of stable, static knowledge. She leaves behind theories and methods that, though having their place, have begun to inhibit the individual's movement and the growth of the community's world. She takes a risk diving down into the Under World; she could drown in those deep waters where chaos lives. But the process of change demands that the depths be plumbed for new forms, new methods, and new theories drawn from new interpretations of experience. The act of returning with this fertile mud offers the hope that with the help of the whole community, our collective possibilities may grow. Like Dayunisi, each of us brings his or her own viewpoint, experience, and unique skills to the task of creating this knowledge. We depend on each other to help articulate and extend what we've found and brought to the surface, for if we do not, we are left simply with a handful of mud, and our new world remains unlivable.

Deep Waters: The Textual Continuum in American Indian Literature brings to the surface and introduces a theory of Native American signification organized around three interrelated theoretical concepts: the *oral impulse*, the *graphic impulse*, and the *critical impulse*. This book demonstrates how crucial twentieth- and twenty-first-century literary texts develop a sustained and illuminating critique of the relationship between tradition and modernity through their conceptual and thematic explorations of Indigenous traditions of oral and graphic forms of communication. Native American literature, I argue, continues a sophisticated Indigenous critical practice that explores the roles of the individual and the community in the context of survivance, balance, harmony, and peace, among other tribally specific values.[1] The center of the book consists of extended readings of four texts that embody this critical and cultural project in different ways. Two of the writers I consider, N. Scott Momaday (Kiowa) and Gerald Vizenor (Anishinaabe), are well known to students of Native literature, while Ray A. Young Bear (Meskwaki) and Robert J. Conley (Cherokee) have received relatively little critical attention.

The critical vocabulary of my study critiques and decenters the standard definitions of *orality* and *literacy* that provide a structuring binary common to Native American literary studies. After exposing the ideological nature of oral-literate theoretical definitions of orality and literacy, I draw on the work of Jacques Derrida to critique the way writing as recorded speech has been valued as the most technologically advanced, clearest, most efficient mode of signifying. As Derrida argues convincingly, no form of communication is inherently more clear, present, or "truthful" than another. The privileging of writing as recorded speech has led to the perception that context-dependent forms of signification, such as Native American oral and graphic traditions, are less culturally advanced. This privileging has contributed to the historical and political subjugation of Native communities by characterizing them as oral, nonliterate peoples. In doing so it has blinded scholars to the ways oral and graphic traditions function in interdependent ways in the expression of Indigenous knowledge.

Seen in this context it is not surprising that the writers I study view the theoretical issues surrounding orality and literacy as a central concern of their work.

As a starting point I explore the ways oral and graphic forms of communication functioned relationally in three Indigenous cultures. Examining Mesoamerican writings, Diné sandpainting, and Haudenosaunee wampum belts, I propose a theory of Indigenous signification that values both oral and graphic means of recording thought, but privileges neither. Building on an interdisciplinary body of scholarship, I argue that Native cultures and literature share three basic commitments: (1) to develop new knowledge in relation to a dynamically changing group experience; (2) to maintain necessary knowledge for posterity and to share that knowledge; and (3) to critique both the contents of and the process leading to that knowledge. As Native signification critiques the relationship between what I call the *oral impulse* and the *graphic impulse* (the terminology of the impulse is borrowed from the African American novelist Ralph Ellison's notion of a *blues impulse*), it draws on a sensibility, which I refer to as the *critical impulse*, which is not dependent on a particular form of expression (Ellison 1964, 78).

Deep Waters begins with an extended discussion of the origin and significance of the three impulses. The oral and graphic build on the premise that oral discourses are living forms of cultural knowledge, kept alive in the memory of members of a group; graphic discourses record tradition for posterity, to live beyond the lives of those who record them. The oral impulse emphasizes a relational and experiential engagement with the world through sound-based forms of communication. Although oral modes of communication are not inherently more "present" than graphic forms, they offer the potential for a more direct social engagement, if only because a speaker and a listener must be within earshot of one another. The oral impulse is the impulse communities and individuals feel as the need to create and maintain knowledge in relatively direct response to one another and to a rapidly changing world. The graphic impulse, on the other hand, expresses a desire for the permanent recording of cultural knowledge in formats that will allow for recollection and study. In contrast to oral discourses, graphic discourses aspire to be expressed in lasting formats. Graphic discourses change in time, as do oral discourses, but they do so more slowly and in response to the oral discourses with which they engage.

At best the oral and graphic impulses complement one another, but when either discourse infringes upon the functions of the other the resulting imbalance can threaten the survival of the community. Without the counterbalancing effects of the graphic impulse to create a sense of cultural and epistemological continuity, oral traditions will codify as they attempt to do the discursive work of graphic discourses. Where once an oral tradition represented a group's fluid intellectual engagement with the world, it now risks becoming mystical dogma disconnected from the contemporary lived experience of a community. Similarly, when cut off from the oral impulse the graphic impulse may overreach its cultural roles and become abstract, theoretical in the narrow sense, freezing community knowledge in objectifying, unchanging, authoritative forms.

Aware of both the insights and the blindness of the oral and the graphic impulses, the critical impulse is always balancing, but never creating a static balance. As within the chronotopes of Rabbit, Monkey, Raven, Coyote, and Spider, the critical impulse is always undercutting, always making messes, always disrupting things when they seem to be functioning well enough. But it is precisely when things *seem* stable, *seem* natural, that they must be questioned by an infusion of knowledge from discourses that will undercut smug satisfaction. The critical impulse arises out of a context of community consciousness, and it responds to the oral and graphic communicative needs of a community for survivance. Aside from basic material needs, cultural survivance depends on a community's vibrant, active engagement with the worldview its members continually construct. The ultimate purpose of critical discourse is to question the assumptions and authority of dominant cultural discourses, wherever they may be on the textual continuum. They appear in every format: an authoritative oral story may be counteracted with another oral story or with a graphic text; a graphic text may be undercut by another graphic text or with an oral story. Regardless of how it manifests, the critical impulse disrupts textual authority by critiquing dominant texts in new contexts and forms that counteract the static tendencies to which both graphic and oral discourses are prone. When fluid stability is achieved the critical impulse is integrated within those textual events. Critical discourses are fluid and ever changing; that is the nature of their power and function. They are the life force of cultural production and survivance.

The dynamic balance between oral and graphic discourses on the textual continuum was ultimately disrupted by Euro-American colonialism and the privileging of alphabetic writing. However, oral, graphic, and critical discourses continue to be expressed in Indigenous communities, just as wampum, sandpainting, and the Aztec calendar continue to serve their communities. Contemporary oral, graphic, and critical discourses may be expressed in any number of cultural forms, from the visual art of Norval Morriseau to James Luna's performance pieces, from Vine Deloria Jr.'s legal polemics and John Trudell's music to Sequoyah Guess's stories. Each of these artistic forms has discursive power. In the current postcolonial context, however, the critical impulse is expressed most strikingly in dominant discursive forms that are in greatest need of counterbalancing on the textual continuum. Because writing is unrivaled as the discursive mode with which Native Americans have faced colonialism, it is through this very medium that graphic dominance is most actively disrupted. Writing has been a tool of both colonialism and survivance. By incorporating the oral impulse within a historically graphic mode of communication, American Indian literature negotiates the tensions between the oral and the graphic, inviting readers and their communities to enliven their own critical impulses in the process.

The history of Native American literature shows a preoccupation with juxtaposing oral and graphic forms of expression. From William Apess's sermons revealing Christian hypocrisy to Charles Eastman's literary transcription of Santee Sioux oral discourse, Native American writers have been dialogically engaging oral discourse in their literary works as a means of challenging Euro-American colonialism and its imposition of values through writing. This tradition continues, for as Michael D. Wilson argues, "Indigenous writers of contemporary fiction are generally less concerned with assimilation than they are about the power of appropriating and revising nonindigenous forms to create a literature of resistance"

(2008, 3). Indigenous writers infuse graphic texts with oral forms, creating more dialogic, open texts that require readers to engage the social narratives that shape the identities of their characters (40–41). Contemporary fiction also incorporates oral themes, ideas, and motifs as structuring devices, such as reciprocity, balance, and the figure of twins. In subtle but important ways the relationship between the oral and the graphic is central to contemporary Native fiction.

In his discussion of Jana Sequoya Magdaleno's and David Treuer's claims that the oral tradition in Native American novels represents signs of cultural authenticity rather than expressions of a living cultural tradition, Michael D. Wilson argues that oral traditions may provide useful "patterns" for narratives of colonial resistance (2008, xiv). It is true that some may read Native novels as "authentic representations of indigenous culture" and encounter them "as a kind of literary tourism or readable anthropology" (xiii). However, cultural content is secondary to the formal aspects of oral discourse as a mode of interpreting experience that is socially located and dialogic. That is what empowers these postcolonial works. Some Native writers may use oral tradition as a "prop," but others, Wilson argues, develop "the entire trajectory of their novels either on specific oral stories or on narratives derived from concepts of orality, such as the use of multiple narrators that suggest subjectivity both in points of view and in the grain or nuance of the spoken voice" (xiii). Oral discourse in Native novels, then, may act as a critical intervention in a graphically dominated postcolonial context, offering models of how to engage and interpret the social narratives that affect characters and, by extension, readers.

Deep Waters demonstrates through critical readings of key

contemporary narratives that Native American writers have been identifying and exploring the effects of the legacy of imbalances between the oral, graphic, and critical impulses and their effects on Native American life. Embedding images of dialogue and storytelling (both key elements of the oral impulse) in their ostensibly graphic texts, the works of the writers I discuss explore the relationships between the oral and the graphic in ways that open spaces within which the critical impulse can flourish.

In chapter 1 I explain the textual continuum in depth and offer examples of how the oral and graphic impulses have functioned in Native American traditions of signification. In the remaining four chapters I address a diverse range of canonical and less well-known Native American writers and narrative texts, analyzing their self-conscious examination of the purposes and roles of oral and graphic traditions. In chapter 2 I present a reading of the classic *The Way to Rainy Mountain* (1969), N. Scott Momaday's most philosophically and structurally complex work. I demonstrate how Momaday's narrator confronts the colonialism of literate-based epistemological frameworks by reclaiming his Kiowa self in an embrace of Kiowa oral traditional knowledge. In chapter 3 I offer a reading of another canonical work, Gerald Vizenor's controversial trickster novel, *Bearheart: The Heirship Chronicles* (1990). One of the most influential and least critically understood Native American texts, *Bearheart*, I argue, does not advocate the subversion of all values, but aims to invigorate the critical impulse as trickster discourse by undercutting graphically dominant value systems that evade the fluidity of oral epistemologies. In chapter 4 I offer in-depth readings of Ray A. Young Bear's *Black Eagle Child: The Facepaint Narratives* (1992) and *Remnants of the First Earth* (1996), two of the most conceptually erudite and culturally rooted narrative works of Native American literature ever published. Universally admired but virtually ignored by critics for the structural, mythical, and social complexity of his writing, Young Bear's paired prose works portray the act of writing as a form of artistic mediation, a heuristic through which his protagonist, Edgar Bearchild, works out complicated sociocultural changes in a Native community. In chapter 5 I examine one of the most ambitious series of Native American novels, Robert J. Conley's *Real People* series, reprinted by the University of Oklahoma Press in 2000. Charting Cherokee life from pre-contact times through forced removal to Indian Territory in 1839, Conley's works of popular fiction foreground the tensions between oral traditions and Cherokee writing while re-creating historical narratives as a means of reclaiming tribal histories. I argue that these writers and their texts are redefining the concept of literary interpretation from within social, community-based concepts.

Through their exploration of the discursive relationships between oral and graphic forms, the history of Native textual expression as well as contemporary American Indian literature have been teaching listeners and readers about the role of interpretation in American Indian experience. Interpretation, these works have been telling us, is not strictly an individualistic affair, but is also a socially located and socially constructed process on the textual continuum. It is time we critics dive like Dayunisi into deep waters.

Deep Waters

1

The Oral Impulse, the Graphic Impulse, and the Critical Impulse

Reframing Signification in American Indian Literary Studies

On a warm July afternoon north of Tahlequah, Oklahoma, the capital of the Cherokee Nation, I sit with Sequoyah Guess and Sam Still under a shady canopy of trees telling stories. Sequoyah and Sam, Cherokee language teachers and cultural traditionalists, are teaching me the language of my family's kinship. As my nephew, Matt, divides his time stalking birds with his blowgun and tending the fire that keeps the mosquitoes off us, my elders share the language with me through conversation.

The sun slides under the Sky-Vault and talk turns to the one Sequoyah Guess's family still calls "Grandpa," the famed nineteenth-century Cherokee linguist Sequoyah. A sixth-generation direct descendant of his namesake, Sequoyah Guess knows well the differences between the written history of Sequoyah's work with the Cherokee syllabary and the oral stories that recount his accomplishments. Commonly referred to as the "American Cadmus," Sequoyah, whose English name was George Guess, is thought to be the only person in human history to have created a written language from scratch, albeit through "idea diffusion" (Diamond 1999, 228). Although he was illiterate, Sequoyah saw the value in writing and created his "talking leaves," a system that culminated in the eighty-five signs of the Cherokee syllabary. When interviewed by Jeremiah Evarts, Sequoyah was asked "why and how he invented the alphabet," to which he replied that "he had observed, that many things were found out by men, and known in the world, but that this knowledge escaped and was lost, for want of some way to preserve it. He had also observed white people write things on paper, and he had seen books; and he knew that what was written down remained and was not forgotten" (Foreman 1938, 28). "Things on paper," I imagine, is not a reference to Romantic poetry but to treaties or, even more likely, trade accounts. Sequoyah saw his people's need to record their knowledge in writing and so he created the system.

By the light of the fire Sequoyah Guess explains the contrasts between the Sequoyah of record and the man his family recalls. The first Sequoyah's father, a man named Guess, was not English but a Cherokee. His mother, Wuteh, married Guess, who left for whence he came soon after Sequoyah's birth. Sequoyah's original name was Jisquaya, or There's a Bird Inside, which was given to him because there was a bird in his family's home when he was born. Before he became a farmer he was a mercenary and fought with a group of warriors for hire. He was a traditionalist and a Cherokee patriot, not an advocate of acculturation. The syllabary project took him nearly twenty years to complete, not twelve, as scholars commonly claim. Sequoyah was willing to risk all that he had for this project. He neglected his farm to such an extent that people began to make fun of him, changing his name from Jisquaya to Sequoyah, meaning There's a Pig Inside. Most important, Sequoyah did not create or invent the Cherokee syllabary. His family claims that he developed the syllabary from a much older language, one used by an ancient priesthood called the Ani-Kutani.

Though the Cherokee have seven clans today, the old ones say we once had eight. The Ani-Kutani were the eighth clan, sacred medicine people who wielded tremendous power in their maintenance of the ceremonial cycles and rituals that ordered the Cherokee year and society. They were the most powerful clan, and they governed the Cherokee. But their power corrupted them, and they began taking greater and greater liberties with their fellow Cherokee. The priest Nicotani (whose very name became synonymous with the priests) led a group of Ani-Kutani to kidnap Cherokee wives. The Cherokee rose up against the priests, and a civil war ensued. The Ani-Kutani were destroyed, every remaining member of the clan killed. The vengeful Nicotani cursed the Cherokee, and with his last breath unleashed a powerful form of witchcraft that is with the Cherokee to this day, an ever present temptation to control others through spiritual medicine.

This moment in Cherokee history is looked back upon somberly. Although the Cherokee populace won its freedom from hierarchical control, with the destruction of the Ani-Kutani they lost the great body of their spiritual traditions and sacred knowledge. What remains of that ancient tradition, it is said, are remembered pieces of what once was a complete cosmology and ritual system. Since the civil war with the Ani-Kutani, Cherokee culture has carried deep within it an anxiety regarding the means of communication that was the guarantor of their authority, the source of their knowledge, and the impetus for their arrogance: writing.

It is argued that pre-contact North American Indians had many forms of expressing thought graphically, but they did not have the technology of writing, defined as recorded speech. In that context this story of Cherokee writing is bound to face skepticism, if not outright dismissal; the lack of corroborating documentary evidence makes it apocryphal. However, Cherokees have been telling this story for a long time, and it gains its authority and meaning within a Cherokee cultural context.[1] Rather than trying to prove the veracity of the story using Western historiographic methods, I want to imagine what this story means from a Cherokee cultural perspective. Weaving together the story of the Ani-Kutani, Sequoyah, and the Cherokee relationship with writing, I use what Robert Warrior calls "synchronicity," an "imaginative tool" that "helps in a consideration of the gaps of what documentary history doesn't reveal." As Warrior argues, in many cases of Native American historical investigation a researcher will need to "grasp from the shreds and shards of evidence significant aspects of a Native intellectual patrimony" (2005, 6). Considering oral traditional stories allows me to reinterpret the historical record, coming to new conclusions regarding the ways knowledge was encouraged to exist in Cherokee society.

The story of the Ani-Kutani sheds light on both the historical context of Sequoyah's introduction of the syllabary and why he may have taken the risk in reintroducing it to the Cherokee community at large. Historians remark that when Sequoyah introduced the syllabary to the Cherokee people they accused him of practicing witchcraft (Bender 2002, 29). This was not a primitive response to a new technology; Sequoyah's development of writing worried the Cherokee people because it evoked the Ani-Kutani, whose sole access to Cherokee ceremonial tradition through writing led to their abuse of power. Far from being irrational, the Cherokee had reason to fear the power of writing. Although literacy is usually portrayed as a democratizing force, scholars of writing are well aware that throughout history writing has been used as a tool of the consolidation of power and societal control. The treaty-making era of conflicts with Europeans and Americans might have strengthened the perception of those Cherokee who knew the story of the Ani-Kutani that writing was indeed witchcraft.

The story of the fall of the Ani-Kutani and the story of Sequoyah's reintroduction of the Cherokee syllabary are in fact parts of a larger story. The subject of that story is the relationship the Cherokee people have had with writing, and it continues to this day. In the context of the war with the Ani-Kutani, the Cherokee made a choice to abolish the use of writing as a means of recording thought; they asserted control over their means of communication.

It is telling that the Cherokee writing system surfaced only after three hundred years of contact with Euro-American forms of writing. This suggests that although the Cherokee were aware of writing, and were in fact literate in European languages, it was considered taboo to write the Cherokee language. Sequoyah's reintroduction of the syllabary to the Cherokee people as a form of communication is a deeply symbolic gesture in a Cherokee cultural context. A foundation of Cherokee thought is that the universe divides into complementary pairs: man/woman, sun/moon, and night/day, among many others. Imbalances develop when complementary pairs are separated or not relating properly with one another. Undoubtedly, there were practical reasons for having a Cherokee written language in the first decades of the nineteenth century, but from a Cherokee cultural perspective the deployment of the syllabary addressed a crucial imbalance.

The advent of a Cherokee form of writing established a symbolic balance between Euro-American forms of writing and Cherokee writing. With the fear of the Ani-Kutani as a backdrop, writing, Sequoyah's development suggests, is a tool that in a literate world must be mastered by the community as a whole. Through their use of writing Euro-Americans had become, symbolically, the successors of the Ani-Kutani. For the Cherokee to maintain control over their own cultural knowledge it was necessary to reestablish a form of their own writing. Sequoyah must have known the challenge that faced him when he brought Cherokee literacy to light once again. He had to convince the Cherokee people that writing did not corrupt. If used by all the Cherokee writing could help maintain cultural, if not political sovereignty. Tellingly, to this day Cherokee writing is used most often in spiritual matters, either in the form of the Christian Bible and hymns or in recording traditional medicine practices.

In key ways the history of writing in Native America mirrors the Cherokee conflict with the Ani-Kutani. From first contact European writings have been used as a form of control to colonize, proselytize, and subjugate Native America. The study of the oppressive uses of writing in the form of treaties and laws is a part of the intellectual foundation of Native American studies, and the critique of the argument that writing establishes authority while the oral tradition is ephemeral has been well established.[2] Recently scholars such as Robert Warrior, Maureen Konkle, Lucy Maddox, Sean Kicummah Teuton, and Lisa Brooks have shown that since at least the eighteenth century Native American writers have used Euro-American forms of writing to defend Indigenous lands, cultures, and nations. That trend continues today, with the battles over Indian Country playing out in the U.S. Congress, the United Nations, Native American and U.S. court systems, tribal newspapers, academic scholarship, and literary arts. Native American communities and those involved in the struggle for Indigenous political sovereignty, cultural autonomy, and social justice have established critical spaces by mastering the literacies of colonialism and modernity. We engage these discourses in the hopes that we may change them, for writing is here to stay.

American Indian literary studies has led the field of American Indian studies in drawing on the range of discourses that have been labeled "critical theory" to help examine Indigenous experiences with Euro-American colonialism and its ramifications on Indigenous life. Drawing on an interdisciplinary body of work, scholars have developed subdisciplines that address particular areas of political, scholarly, and theoretical interest. Decolonial studies, sovereignty studies, literary nationalism, tribal theory, red feminism, and environmental studies are proving to be fertile ground for the cultivation of Native American textual studies and will undoubtedly shape the future of American Indian critical studies.[3] American Indian literary studies is doing many things at once: pushing the boundaries of decolonial discourse, recovering intellectual traditions and texts, engaging critical theory, and, often most passionately, making a case for the values, cogency, and applicability of traditional Indigenous thought as a form of autochthonous critical theory. As the field of American Indian literary studies develops, however, there is a need to evaluate the critical vocabulary it has borrowed from Western discourse because that vocabulary impacts the way Native American literary studies is theorized and will develop in the future.

No two terms are more central to Native American literary studies than *orality* and *writing*. The idea that pre-contact Indigenous cultures were nonliterate peoples who passed on knowledge almost exclusively through oral storytelling traditions provides the standard cultural context for studying the contemporary literate texts Native American writers produce. Whether a critic advocates cosmopolitan, tribal theoretical, or literary nationalist approaches to the study of Native American literature, *oral tradition* remains the central expression of traditional Indigenous thought. The development of Native American written literature marks the appropriation of a Western form of communication (writing) which may be used as a tool to engage the colonial center. How American Indian literary studies defines *oral tradition* and *writing* matters deeply, for these terms carry an intellectual genealogy into their critical usage today. Their definitions delimit the current boundaries and future possibilities of Native American literary discourse.

Writing, Orality, and Figuring Native America

Historically, the study of Native America has been shaped by ideologically loaded binaries that privilege the West and denigrate the Indigenous Other. Beginning in the pre-Enlightenment era, when a culture's affiliation with Christianity determined whether it was ideologically inside or exotically Other, Native American cultures have continued to be a foil for Western cultural self-definitions (Li 2006, 4). The binary of Christian European–Indian heathen underwent a series of changes in the nineteenth century as social evolutionary typologies and their cultural hierarchies came to dominate European thought (4). The Indian was no longer exotically strange and different but was now "primitive," existing at an earlier point on an imagined evolutionary scale. The Indian was constructed as savage and irrational, in contrast to the civilized, rational Euro-American, and the perceived inferiority was used to justify colonialism and racial hierarchies.

Today the word *primitive* has been largely replaced in academic studies with more politically aware terms, such as *individual culture*, *traditional culture*, and *ethnic group*, but in the study of Native American societies the term *oral* as a descriptor of Indigenous cultures, societies, and peoples remains the status quo (Li 2006, viii). Whereas cultural relativism has flattened most other markers of primitivism, oral cultures remain defined in relation to that which they lack: the ability to write.

Native American societies never defined themselves as oral cultures. Yet definitions of oral and written discourses intimately linked to social evolutionary thought are entrenched and veiled within the study of Native America.[4] Michael D. Wilson states in *Writing Home: Indigenous Narratives of Resistance* that "authentic representation" in Native American literature is commonly marked by "correct cultural information, historical details, and oral traditions" (2008, 52). This "culturalist" approach to the study of Native American literature, which sets out to "account for the cultural beliefs and

termed "full" or "complete" writing is recorded speech in lasting, visual forms.[5]

The ability to write became perhaps the single most important marker of civilization.[6] Scholars claimed that recorded speech enabled language to flow across time and space, freeing human memory from its dependence on oral narratives to carry the weight of cultural knowledge. Writing encouraged complex, abstract, and conceptual thought; allowed us to study language and the world objectively; fostered the development of critical thought and skepticism; and shifted the emphasis of human perception from the aural to the visual.[7] Writing's sociopolitical function is of paramount importance as it "creates social coherence" and "regulates social control" through institutions (Coulmas 1989, 8, 11–14). All of these changes gave rise to the notion of the individual, the organization of government, and urbanization.

More recently scholars of orality and writing have resisted deterministic conclusions about the effects of writing on the human mind and civilization. Florian Coulmas argues that writing did not cause civilization but "has to be seen as a result as well as a condition of civilization, as a product shaped by civilization and a tool shaping it" (1989, 4). David R. Olson offers a more pointed critique, arguing that cultural historians and anthropologists have shown that oral cultures display "complex forms of discourse" and "complex modes of thought," severing the once necessary tie between literacy and cultural development (1994, 11–12). Writing is not necessarily a means of liberation or enslavement; current historical and cultural studies represent literacy as one among many factors that affect economic development, social control, and social roles (10–11). Regarding the privileging of the alphabet, it is now understood that all writing systems strike particular relationships and ratios between semantic and phonetic components and the specific ways they are understood within cultures. There are forms of representing and referencing experience that are not well served by writing as recorded speech. Musical notation, mathematics, and geographic maps all represent their subjects more efficiently and clearly than they would with writing (Boone 1994, 9). When writing as recorded speech is reconsidered outside of ethnocentric and social evolutionist definitions, it is only one among many forms of recording thought.

Historians of writing provide a clear genealogy of how writing has been defined, but definitions of orality are diffuse, taking different forms in classical studies, linguistics, anthropology, media studies, and literary criticism. Influential oral-literate theorists such as Eric Havelock, Harold Innis, Marshall McLuhan, Ian Watt, and Jack Goody have argued that human cultural development as explored by students of psychology, politics, and history may be understood through the relationship of orality and writing and their effects on perception and cognition. Their subsequent definitions of the oral arise antithetically in their investigations of the effects of literacy.

The study of orality as a form of communication has been approached in two primary ways. In one, written texts have been studied in order to uncover the "original elements of orality manifest in formulae and other features considered typical of the 'oral' state out of which the text emerges to be inscribed, or the text maintains within itself elements that persist as residual features of 'orality'" (Furniss 2004, 16). As a mode of communication orality may be studied in the "'written as spoken,' 'the graphic encompassing the written and evoking the oral,' 'the recorded spoken or sung,' [and] 'the spoken as then inscribed'" (1). These approaches provide the background for much of the engagement with orality in Native American literary studies. In the other camp, societies that have no knowledge of writing are termed "oral societies" and are studied with special reference to their "ways of recording the past, of socializing the new generations, and of articulating their values and their norms" (16). That which is oral is orally composed, transmitted, or performed (Jahandarie 1999, 284). Translators of oral compositions, ethnopoets, scholars of oral performance, and ethnographers working with Native American orally composed texts often value their work in reference to this definition of orality and their ability to document Native American cultural productions before it is "too late."

Like writing, orality has been defined in ways that reinforce notions of social evolution. Because the oral culture as a concept was constructed in the West, its definition is fluid and changes with the needs of Western culture. Oral cultures and the oral traditions they espouse may represent anything cultures of writing wish, from a degraded, nonrational way of life to a prelapsarian existence. These representations depend, of course, on how literate cultures are portrayed at the time and their relationship to what is considered progress. Graham Furniss explains that Western culture defined orality as "a 'condition' in which the pre-modern world of classical and medieval society found itself" but through time and the accumulation of knowledge was able to rise above (2004, 15–16). The state of orality was an earlier moment in European history, one that may be looked back upon fondly or derisively, but in any case from a more enlightened literate perspective (15–16). Oral cultures did not change, or, if they did, it was to their detriment. Unlike literate cultures, which thrive in transformation, the cognitive abilities of oral peoples are thought to exist in relative stasis.

According to oral-literate theory, primarily oral societies, those without writing as recorded speech, have different cognitive capacities and social organizations. The codification of oral societal characteristics is stated most succinctly (and controversially) by Walter S. Ong in *Orality and Literacy: The Technologizing of the Word* (1982). Ong argues that individuals in oral societies (which are small, communal, and depend on face-to-face interaction) think in particular, performative ways. He lists nine characteristics of the "oral mind" in primary oral cultures (those without any knowledge of writing): formulaic, redundant, conservative, agonistic, aggregative, close to the human lifeworld, situational, participatory, and homeostatic (36–57). For the oral person, knowledge exists primarily in formulaic, repeated stories: "Since in a primary oral culture conceptualized knowledge that is not repeated aloud soon vanishes, oral societies must invest great energy in saying over and over again what has been learned arduously over the ages" (41). The oral person thinks "additively," stringing together ideas and phrases using connectives such as "and"; the oral mind does not create subordinate clauses or concepts (37). Likewise the oral person is not analytical but thinks in an "aggregative" way, organizing important ideas into epithets that are memorized and incorporated into unchanging stories: "Without a writing system, breaking up thought— that is, analysis—is a high-risk procedure" (39). Lacking the capacity to analyze, the oral person situates all knowledge in the context of the known world and does not conceive the abstract (42, 49). Consequently stories are about the trials and tribulations of life, and their messages are to be understood in the context of action and the real world (42). The oral person learns through participation, not study, and all thought is homeostatic; knowledge or memories that have no present relevance are forgotten (46). The oral person is thus prehistorical (5). These traits that Ong identifies and defines offer perhaps the most well-known distillation of characteristics of oral thought, the foundation of oral cultures.

Oral-literate theory has been criticized for its reliance on inferential evidence and secondary sources, its reification of the effects of writing, and its psychological characterizations of the oral and literate "minds."[8] These critiques of standard definitions of orality and writing are beginning to shape a new discourse concerning the nature of human communication in which the functions of orality and literacy are understood in specific social contexts. In Native American literary studies, however, the oral-literate binary remains a point of reference and continues to affect approaches to Native American literary study.

The dominant way oral tradition has been analyzed in Native American literary studies is as a particular form of communication that in its unique usage allows for the articulation and performance of Indigenous consciousness and values. In studying oral tradition in this manner, Native American literary studies has drawn on the oral-literate binary, and thus has wedded itself to that discourse's definitions of oral and literate cultures and their characteristics. In *Other Destinies: Understanding the American Indian Novel* (1992), arguably the most referenced work of American Indian literary criticism, Louis Owens's analysis of oral tradition presents a standard approach. Owens draws on oral-literate theory to define Indigenous oral tradition and, by extension, the characteristics of the Native American novel. While he seeks to subvert the colonial "Vanishing American" stereotype of the Native American as a victim of Western progress, in the process he reinscribes an oral-literate theoretical position that differentiates non-Native and Native cultures through their relationship to orality and writing. In failing to challenge the standard definitions of orality and literacy that are a foundation of primitivist discourse, Owens's critique falls victim to what Victor Li calls "neo-primitivism," a "conceptual move through which the rejection of primitivism allows it to reappear in new, more acceptable forms" (2006, ix). Owens persuasively argues that "the Indian" is a discursive construction of the West, but he fails to recognize the oral-literate binary that underwrites the characterization of Native Americans as primitive.

Echoing Ong's notions of the "oral mind," Owens claims that oral tradition represents a communal, anonymous, prehistoric literature of origin for Native Americans that is determinative of a specific type of oral consciousness. For the Native American writer oral traditions are communal, whereas writing is an individualistic form of communication (1992, 10). When a Native writer writes he or she becomes imbricated in the individualized Western world. That person is no longer a mouthpiece of tribal tradition but a single creator of a story. Owens defines the differences between oral tradition and writing in temporal terms, harkening back to social evolutionary discourse: "Native American writing represents an attempt to recover identity and authenticity by invoking and

incorporating the world found within the oral tradition—
the reality of myth and ceremony—an authorless 'original'
literature" (11). Before writing, Owens argues, Native American signification was marked not just by communal modes
of expression but by a lack of historical consciousness: "With
written literacy, language becomes descriptive/historic and
begins to lose its unique power as creator of reality" (9). With
the advent of literacy, Native American consciousness shifts
from the "cyclical, ordered, ritual-centered, and paradigmatic world of traditional oral literatures" to the chaotic, secular
linearity evoked through writing: "For the Indian author, writing within the consciousness of the contextual background of
a nonliterate culture, every word written in English represents
a collaboration of sorts as well as a reorientation (conscious or
unconscious) from the paradigmatic world of oral tradition to
the syntagmatic reality of written language" (6). The changes
brought to the oral world through literacy are permanent, for
"try as he or she may, the Native American novelist can never
step back into the collective anonymity of the tribal storyteller. Ironically, for the novelist writing with a consciousness of
responsibility as a member of a living Native American culture, this irreversible metamorphosis from oral, communal
literature to the written commodity of published work may
be an essential objectification" (11). Owens's double bind is
clear: while Native writers attempt to recover oral traditions
through writing, they inevitably become more distanced from
the oral world they supposedly wish to preserve.

Owens's definition of orality as communal, paradigmatic,
and anonymous arises out of oral-literate theory, but instead
of devaluing these oral characteristics, as generations of historians of writing had, he privileges them. Whereas historians

of writing valued individualism, for example, Owens implicitly values the communal. His approach exemplifies the problems of failing to adequately critique the oral-literate binary and its formal definition of orality. Despite his revaluation of the characteristics of orality and writing, the oral-literate binary remains in place.

From its beginnings as a field, scholars of American Indian literature have studied the ways Native authors employ Indigenous oral traditions in their written texts. Drawing on ethnographic theories of performance and translation, and on the oral poetics of scholars such as Dell Hymes and Dennis Tedlock, critics of Native American literature have made sophisticated thematic readings of the oral dimensions of Indigenous texts a cornerstone of our field. Critics such as A. LaVonne Brown Ruoff, Andrew Wiget, Kenneth Lincoln, Larry Evers, Paula Gunn Allen, Brian Swann, Arnold Krupat, Kenneth M. Roemer, Greg Sarris, and Simon J. Ortiz, among many others, recognize that Native American written literature carries on Indigenous oral storytelling traditions. However, even though scholars such as Krupat, Vizenor, and Bernd C. Peyer have recognized the false dichotomy between orality and literacy, the oral-literate binary has continued within Native American literary practice.[9]

Recently, critics of Native American literature aware of how orality has been used in the colonialist enterprise have begun building a more sophisticated understanding of oral tradition and its importance to tribal culture as sources of critical epistemology and as models of critical methodology. To date, however, their work has not entirely separated itself from the definition of orality offered by oral-literate theory. In a hybrid approach oral traditions are figured as retaining some of the formal features characterized in oral-literate theory, while also having cognitive processes and capacities that oral-literate theory attributed only to literate cultures. Oral traditions remain anonymous, communal, mnemonic discourses that offer paradigmatic approaches to reality. However, they also may account for changing, complex, analytical thought commonly associated with literacy: "To serve tribal change, Indian storytelling must remain a dynamic, continuous site of theoretical investigation, evaluation, and revision" (S. K. Teuton 2008, 24). Oral tradition is described as a conversive, process-oriented discourse that derives its usefulness from maintaining a "changing but stable center of value" (Wilson 1997, 135). Referencing Simon J. Ortiz's discussion of Acqumeh oral tradition, Michael D. Wilson argues that oral tradition seeks "a state of well-being maintained not through the exclusion of outside elements, nor by remaining unchanged over time, but through an understanding of outside elements, especially if these elements pose a psychological threat to the continued existence of the people" (2008, 131). Oral tradition thus may offer a historical account of psychological change within a community, something Owens considers a development through literacy. It is this transformative power of language that Susan Berry Brill de Ramírez focuses on in her theory of "conversivity," a reading practice in which a "scholar becomes a listener-reader of literary works (like a listener participating in an oral storytelling event), and in turn becomes a storyteller-guide to assist others in becoming listener-readers of those literary works, not only in the classroom but also in one's written scholarship" (2006–7, 1).

Responding to a call for tribally specific critical approaches articulated most forcefully by Elizabeth Cook-Lynn, Craig

S. Womack and Penelope Myrtle Kelsey explore the political dimensions of oral traditions as a source of critical theory.[10] In *Red on Red: Native American Literary Separatism*, Womack studies Creek oral tradition in order to "formulate interpretive strategies" (1999, 76). He states, "We scholars haven't yet done enough to articulate how the oral tradition provides the principle for interpreting our national literatures—the genres; the unique approaches to character development, plot, theme, setting, and so on; the effect on the structuring of stories; the philosophies that come out of this tradition; the contexts it provides for understanding politics, religion, and society" (76). In *Tribal Theory in Native American Literature* Kelsey writes, "Language lies at the core of the study of all literatures, and Indigenous languages—whether visibly present or no—influence the composition and worldviews of all tribal texts" (2008, 1). Kelsey claims a tribal theoretical approach that is "based in part on key cultural concepts as they are embodied in the Dakota language because tribal theory necessitates involving Indigenous language's entwinement with worldview(s)" (11). It's exciting to read Kelsey's interpretation of Dakota pictography as a source of "affirming Dakota knowledges and narratives," but like Womack she does not thoroughly critique the oral-literate binary that creates the discursive boundaries of the study of oral traditions and written traditions.

These various engagements with Native American oral tradition extend the range of Native American literary discourse, but they do not resolve the issues raised by the legacy of oral-literate theory. A reassessment of what oral traditions are supposed to be and of how they are thought to function is needed if Native American literary studies is to expand the conversation initiated by Ortiz, Cook-Lynn, Womack, Kelsey, and other critics interested in articulating Indigenous critical theory. The tradition of orally transmitted knowledge is no longer thought to be unchanging oral forms and the interpretations of these forms. Instead the tradition includes ever changing orally maintained bodies of knowledge and the oral discourses through which these bodies of knowledge are expressed and developed. However, even as scholars demonstrate that orally maintained knowledge is dynamic and epistemologically sophisticated, they remain committed to the oral-literate binary insofar as they focus on oral tradition as if it existed in isolation from other means of communication. In fact, Native American cultural traditions have been created, recorded, and handed down through the ages in not just oral forms, but in myriad graphic and material forms, including wampum, beadwork, pottery, basketry, textiles, jewelry, paintings, rock art, and glyphs. Oral-literate theory is correct that if knowledge is maintained orally without any means of recording it in a lasting form, that oral knowledge will become conservative and homeostatic; historical thought would be out of reach. It is unclear how orally transmitted, unrecorded knowledge may function as a dynamic platform for historical and philosophical study without recourse to ways of referencing earlier thought that is not memorized. In theorizing how orally transmitted knowledge functions in Native American cultures, Native American literary studies has not yet identified which graphic forms of communication provide the counterpart to orality in an autochthonous context. But before investigating a more nuanced understanding of Native American textuality and signification it is first necessary to understand how the oral-literate binary has been so tenacious in Native American literary studies.

Graphocentrism in Native
American Literary Studies

Native American literary studies is shaped to a significant degree by the oral-literate binary, but as Jacques Derrida argues, the binary between orality and literacy is itself problematic, deeply traced with what he calls "logocentrism," a hegemonic privileging of speech over writing in the West. Through the construction of oral cultures Native Americans became objects of European logocentrism. Ironically, contemporary Native American literature's reification and nostalgia for Native oral traditions may be interpreted as a fulfillment of the West's logocentric desires. Native American writers and critics often fulfill the logocentric desires of the West by describing, referencing, and claiming the centrality of Native American oral traditions over literate traditions. However, these writers and critics have occupied this self-defensive critical position as a means of resisting the West's colonialist graphocentrism.

From a poststructuralist critical position the differences between specific forms of writing and their relation to oral modes of thought and being are largely built on specious premises. Writing as recorded speech is not a more efficient or clear system of communication because, in terms of signification, neither oral communication nor written communication has a claim to superior production of meaning.[11] Terry Eagleton writes, "Nothing is ever fully present in signs: it is an illusion for me to believe that I can ever be fully present to you in what I say or write, because to use signs at all entails that my meaning is always somehow dispersed, divided and never quite at one with oneself" (1983, 130). The problem is endemic to signification: "Since the meaning of a sign is a matter of what the sign is *not*, its meaning is always in some sense absent from it too" (128). As the work of Derrida shows, whether dealing with ideographs or alphabets "each sign in the chain of meaning is somehow scored over or traced through with all the others, to form a complex tissue which is never exhaustible; and to this extent no sign is ever 'pure' or 'fully meaningful.' At the same time as this is happening, [one] can detect in each sign, even if only unconsciously, traces of the other words which it has excluded in order to be itself" (128). The specific modes of communication are built on the same system of differential relationships within sign systems. Ultimately, no system of signification is "clearer" or more "efficient" than another because signs always may mean more.

Barbara Johnson elucidates Derrida's understanding of "the opposition between speech and writing": "Speech is seen as immediacy, presence, life, and identity, whereas writing is seen as deferment, absence, death, and difference. Speech is primary; writing secondary. Derrida calls this privileging of speech as self-present meaning 'logocentrism'" (1995, 43). By deconstructing logocentrism, as Jack Reynolds and Jonathan Roffe argue, "what Derrida aims to show is that there never was nor could there be such an order of pure intelligibility, no *logos* or meaning that would be an ideal presence, a pre-existing and occult (that is, *hidden*) spiritual realm beyond what is denounced as (worldly) writing" (2004, 7). As Johnson states, "Immediacy is an illusion." The sign, composed of the signified and the signifier, always contains a "gap of heterogeneity and distance . . . fundamental to the structure of language." Derrida's work reveals "that even when a text tries to privilege speech as immediacy, it cannot completely eliminate the fact that speech, like writing, is based on a *différance* (a Derridean neologism meaning both 'deferment' and 'difference') between signifier and signified inherent in the sign" (Johnson 1995, 43).

Derrida's critique of logocentrism is persuasive. When we shift our attention to Native America, however, a more powerful influence is exerted by the concept of graphocentrism. As my discussion of the history of writing argues, the technology of writing has historically been the West's central means of classifying cultures as either civilized or uncivilized. Though the study of Western logocentrism is important, as Barbara Johnson states, "An equal but more covert privileging of writing has also been operative." She continues, "The hidden but ineradicable importance of writing that Derrida uncovers in his readings of logocentric texts in fact reflects an unacknowledged, or 'repressed,' graphocentrism" (1995, 47). Thus in contrast to the privileging of the spoken word, graphocentrism suggests the privileging of the written word as a source of unassailable truth. As scholars such as Walter D. Mignolo, Roy Harvey Pearce, and Gordon Sayre have argued, European colonizers in the Americas authorized their actions by their self-claimed entitlement as bearers of the word of God in the form of a book, the Christian Holy Bible. From the time of first contact Native Americans have been thrust into the position of having to defend their modes of communication in comparison to the forms of European writing as recorded speech.

Forced into a reactionary position by graphocentric discourse, Native American writers and literary scholars have often staked out an epistemological space in which Native oral tradition takes a position counter to the authority of the written word. Both N. Scott Momaday and Paula Gunn Allen have spoken of language in ways reminiscent of oral-literate theory. Momaday writes, "In the oral tradition stories are told not merely to entertain or to instruct; they are told to be believed. Stories are not subject to the imposition of such questions as true or false, fact or fiction. Stories are realities lived and believed. They are true" (1997, 3). Similarly he claims that oral tradition is metaphysically powerful: "At the heart of the American Indian oral tradition is a deep and unconditional belief in the efficacy of language. Words are intrinsically powerful. They are magical. By means of words can one bring about physical change in the universe" (16). In a similar vein Paula Gunn Allen's essentialist claims regarding Indian identity and belief are inevitably rooted in a logocentric interpretation of oral tradition as a body of unquestionable tradition and moral authority, as when she states, "In contradistinction to other American poets and writers, American Indian women writers have as our first and most significant perceptual characteristic a solid, impregnable, and ineradicable orientation toward a spirit-informed view of the universe, which provides an internal structure to both our consciousness and our art" (1992, 165). Current scholarship on oral traditional discourse brings the contradictions to the surface. The historian Peter Nabokov offers a view of oral tradition as existing within discourses in which what is true is up for debate and revisable because "oral tradition's defining benefit and unending pleasure" is its "multiple versions" (2002, 47). The anthropologist Julie Cruikshank argues that "oral tradition is better understood as a social activity than as a reified text, that meanings do not inhere in a story but are created in the everyday situations in which they are told" (1998, xv). Other Native writers have been aware of these issues as well. At the same time as writers like Allen and Momaday wrote with the best intentions of the sacrality of oral tradition, writers such as Gerald Vizenor, Louise Erdrich, and Thomas King began to point to the fact that oral traditions are never stable, static, or sacred for their timelessness. What each of these positions points to is not a disagreement over Native American cultures and their relationship to tradition but a difference in understanding the functions and roles of Native American forms of signification.

One of the reasons Native American writers and literary scholars have embraced oral tradition is to preserve and support Native American cultural traditions that exist outside conventional notions of writing. When Native literary studies began to form as a discipline in the 1970s and 1980s poststructuralist criticism and Derridean notions were dominant. As Terry Eagleton writes, "The work of Derrida and others had cast grave doubt upon the classical notions of truth, reality, meaning and knowledge, all of which could be exposed as resting on a naively representational theory of language. If meaning, the signified, was a passing product of words or signifiers, always shifting and unstable, part-present and part-absent, how could there be any determinate truth or meaning at all?" (1983, 143). For writers and scholars whose notions of language had been shaped by the oral-literate binary, championing orally based epistemological, aesthetic, and spiritual concepts offered a politically viable critical position. Poststructuralism and deconstruction posed a significant threat not just to the coherence of their field of study but to their understanding of Native American cultures. If, according to contemporary notions of signification, meaning is undecidable, what is one to think of the mandates of oral tradition?

Cornered into taking two untenable positions in relation

to logocentrism and graphocentrism, Native American literary criticism has been unaware of a third, crucial discourse that works to disrupt the dominance of either the oral or written discourse. Neither oral nor written, the incredibly rich traditions of American Indian graphic modes of communication have been studied in art history but are nearly unmentioned in Native American literary studies. As with orality and literacy, Indigenous oral forms of signification had differential counterparts in the graphic traditions of Native America. Functioning in dynamic relation to one another, the oral and the graphic fill specific roles in relation to Native American knowledge as it is valued in the context of Native American community. This dynamic is what I call the *critical impulse*. Keeping the relationship between oral and graphic modes of communication in constant flux, the critical discourses that arise out of the critical impulse disrupt static forms of power and dominance that could threaten the survival of community.

Oral, Graphic, and Critical Impulses: The Textual Continuum in the Americas

Whereas orality and writing have been defined relationally and formally in the Western tradition, Native American communicative forms and contexts of signification are best understood by how they function socially. Native American forms of signification exist within an interpretive discourse dynamic that includes graphic and oral forms of signification that serve specific social functions in the context of recounting cultural knowledge. Rather than being vestiges of a preliterate era, these forms of graphic signification fulfill one function in a social framework that emphasizes a relationship between oral and graphic modes of communication.

In contrast to the oral-literate divide, I want to reframe Native American signification in relation to three fundamental cultural processes: the *oral impulse*, the *graphic impulse*, and the *critical impulse*. These impulses take shape in a textual continuum that recognizes both the differences and the connections between oral, sound-based forms of discourse (in the extreme case, vocables in songs or musical tones) and graphic, visual forms of discourse (for example, writing as recorded speech and binary codes). A critical approach that recognizes the interdependence of the oral, graphic, and critical impulses provides a vocabulary that affords American Indian literary scholarship an entry point into reimagining the place of Native signification in the genealogy of textuality in the Americas. I want to consider Native American forms of signification using Barthes's notion of a text, which is not a specific work, but, as Barbara Johnson defines it, "an open, infinite *process* that is both meaning-generating and meaning subverting" (1995, 40). As Gordon Brotherston argues, a text is "no more (or less) than a particular or framed instance of language." Within that frame a text "may actually frame and define itself, reflexively, whether it consists of words or some visual sign system" (1992, 45). What is particular about Native American forms of signification is the way they involve both oral and "graphic" elements.

Derrida's explorations of signification and the tension between presence and absence within referentiality offer a context in which to discuss the oral and graphic impulses. On a basic level Derrida argues that all signs exist in relation to presence and absence. The presence of signs or marks assures that the message of the sender will exist even in the ultimate absence (death) of the sender. The readable piece of "writing," as Derrida defines it, is one in which repetition and alterity necessarily coexist. Readability depends on both context ("No context permits saturation") and difference ("No meaning can be determined out of context" (Royle 2003, 68). A crucial outcome of Derrida's conception of writing is that there is no possibility of transcendent presence: context will never be saturated; and meaning will never be determined once and for all. Ian Adam explains that for Derrida "a principle of differentiation underlies and governs both speech and writing; he chooses to call that principle 'writing' at this point, but elsewhere it is to be termed 'archi-écriture,' 'trace,' 'difference' or 'nothing.' Derrida frequently blurs his use of 'writing' in this inclusive sense with the more usual use of 'writing' as something distinguishable from speech" (1996, 99–100). The relational nature of signs insists that they must be read against and within each other.

I want to extend this notion of context dependency as developed by Derrida to an understanding of Native American signification. The emphasis in oral-literate theory on writing as recorded speech has led to the perception that context-dependent forms of signification, including Native American forms of oral and graphic communication, are less culturally advanced. Oral and graphic forms, such as storytelling and pictograms, depend for their meaning on those who have knowledge of these signs. Although cultural knowledge may be recorded it remains partially dependent on the living memory of cultural members. Thus unless one has some cultural understanding of what a certain pictogram depicts, its meaning will be indeterminable. Rather than being a deficient mode of recording and creating knowledge, Native American forms of signification actively engage presence and absence through two interdependent and reciprocal modes of communication, the oral and the graphic. In doing this Native American signification attempts to avoid the pitfalls that both oral and graphic modes of communication are prone to in isolation, most notably the ephemeral nature of orality and the static nature of graphic forms.

While functioning within the same dynamic of presence and absence as do graphic forms of communication, oral discourses arise out of what I call an *oral impulse*. The oral impulse refers to the way texts invoke the cultural values that are expressed in oral discursive systems; it emphasizes a relational and experiential engagement with the world through sound-based forms of communication. This cultural desire exists all over the world, for as Graham Furniss notes, there is an "essential and inescapable social and individual need for the features of orality that are apparent in these forms of communication, quite apart from the obvious need for interpersonal oral communication whereby we run our own individual lives" (2004, 22). Oral modes of communication are not inherently more present than graphic forms, but they offer the potential for a more direct social engagement, if only because a speaker and a listener must be within earshot of one another. The oral impulse is the impulse communities and individuals feel as the need to create and maintain knowledge in relatively direct response to one another and to a rapidly changing world. This definition is essentially the opposite of how orality is understood in oral-literate theory (as redundant, conservative, homeostatic, etc.).

The *graphic impulse* expresses the cultural desire for the permanent recording of cultural knowledge in formats that will allow for recollection and study. Like oral discourses, graphic discourses can draw on a vast array of formats and styles. Walter D. Mignolo defines a graphic sign as "a mark on a solid surface made for the purpose of establishing a semiotic interaction. Consequently, a human interaction is a semiotic one if there is a community and a body of common knowledge according [to] which: (a) a person can produce a visible sign with the purpose of conveying a message (to somebody else or oneself); (b) a person perceives the visible sign and interprets it as a sign produced for the purpose of conveying a message; and (c) that person attributes a given meaning to the visible sign. Notice that in this theoretical definition of writing the links between speech and writing are not necessary" (1994, 229). In contrast to oral discourses, graphic discourses aspire to be expressed in lasting formats. Like oral discourses, graphic discourses inevitably change in time, but they do so more slowly and in response to the oral discourses with which they engage.

Together the oral impulse and the graphic impulse express contrasting desires for modes of cultural expression that reach alternately for presence and absence. Oral discourses are living forms of cultural knowledge, kept vibrant in the memory of members of a group; graphic discourses record tradition for posterity, to live beyond the lives of those who record them. Indigenous cultural traditions point to this concern for a dualistic approach to maintaining knowledge. Whether one is discussing cosmologies, gender, or social roles, Native American worldviews structure reality in what Anne Waters describes as "nonbinary, complementary dualist" constructs (2004, 98). Thus men and women, the sun and the moon, and life and death are not opposites but interdependent expressions of facets of reality, understood within a "syntax that puts together

such constructs without maintaining sharp and clear boundary distinctions (unlike a binary system)" (98). Deriving these
patterns from nature, Native American social and religious
life has constructed discourses of storytelling, writing, dance,
and song that mediate between these nonbinary, nondiscrete
dualist conceptions of reality. Combining oral and graphic
elements, these cultural forms disrupt the dominant power
in a discursive exchange, and in doing so reestablish a fluid
exchange of discursive power between oral and graphic modes
of communication. This mediating, balancing force in Native
American cultural expression arises out of critical discourses and is in turn energized by the *critical impulse.*

Oral discourses responsively engage the world; graphic
discourses record knowledge for posterity. At best they complement one another, but when either discourse infringes upon
the functions of the other the resulting imbalance can threat-
en the survival of the community. Without the counterbalancing effects of the graphic impulse to create a sense of cultural
and epistemological continuity, oral traditions will codify as
they attempt to do the discursive work of graphic discourses.
Where once an oral tradition represented a group's fluid intellectual engagement with the world, it now risks becoming
mystical dogma disconnected from the contemporary lived
experience of a community. This is the source of the frequently heard claim that traditional cultures are essentialist. Similarly, when cut off from the oral impulse the graphic impulse
may overreach its cultural roles and become abstract, theoretical in the narrow sense, freezing community knowledge
in objectifying, unchanging, authoritative forms. Cultural
knowledge remains healthy when both oral and graphic discourses are interacting through the critical impulse, neither

one dominating the other for long. The tension between the oral and the graphic is not only inevitable but necessary, as that tension within the textual continuum keeps the system supple and responsive to the changing needs of community, which ultimately controls both discourses through the critical impulse.

The critical impulse is always balancing but never creating a static balance. As within the trickster chronotopes of Rabbit, Monkey, Raven, Coyote, and Spider, the critical impulse is always undercutting, always making messes, always disrupting things when they seem to be functioning well enough. But it is precisely when things *seem* stable, *seem* natural, that they must be questioned by an infusion of knowledge from discourses that will undercut smug satisfaction. These are times when the elder corrects the anthropologist, when a Native student goes to law school, when members of the American Indian Movement take over the Bureau of Indian Affairs building in Washington, and when a traditionalist writes a book. The critical impulse arises out of a context of community consciousness, and it responds to the oral and graphic communicative needs of a community for survival. Aside from basic material needs, cultural survival depends on a community's vibrant, active engagement with the worldview community members continually construct. Cultural survival as I'm focusing on it here necessitates a culture's ability to create new knowledge in relation to experience, to maintain necessary knowledge for posterity, to share knowledge, and to critique knowledge.

The oral and the graphic are not opposites, but interpenetrating media that, brought into concert by the critical impulse, allow for a flow of ideas that may account for tradition as well as innovation, individuality as well as community, memory as well as record. What I call *balance* is the manifestation of reciprocity within this active system. In the context of signification balance is a discourse, and because we use it to think and adjudicate about our worlds it is critical. Without the critical impulse the oral and graphic impulses may become frozen and express static notions of cultural reality. When this happens, and one mode inevitably takes precedence over the other, epistemological problems arise: knowledge becomes privileged in oral or graphic formats, and the consequences of this steady state affects individuals, communities, and nations in myriad ways.

The critical impulse arises out of a community's need to survive through adaptation and ability to change. As in the Kantian view of criticism, the critical impulse exists in a social context and is "rational and reflexive, and a form of practical intervention in our conventional understanding of society—its values, ideas, and institutions" (Mohanty 1997, 3). In Native America the critical impulse is expressed as much by the form of cultural expression as by its cultural meaning. Oral and graphic discourses are always contesting one another, as they draw on different forms of authority and tradition. The purpose of critical discourses is to subvert the assumptions and authority of oral and graphic community discourses as they aspire to dominance, and it does this by critiquing dominant texts in new contexts and forms that counteract the static tendencies of which both graphic and oral discourses are prone. They appear in every format: an authoritative oral story may be counteracted with another oral story or with a graphic text; a graphic text may be undercut by another graphic text or with an oral story. Regardless of how it manifests, the critical impulse disrupts textual authority by critiquing dominant texts in new contexts and forms that counteract the static tendencies to which both graphic and oral discourses are prone. When fluid stability is achieved the critical impulse is integrated within those textual events. Critical discourses are fluid and ever changing; that is the nature of their power and function. They are the life force of cultural production and survivance.

In Native American forms of signification the oral, graphic, and critical impulses are interdependent and reciprocal. The critical impulse is the most vulnerable and fragile impulse because it requires a dialectical understanding of the oral and graphic impulses. The critical impulse strikes balances between oral and graphic modes, in the process expressing particular cultural values with regard to the maintenance of knowledge.

Three Examples of the Critical Impulse

The following examples offer explanations of how oral and graphic modes of expression related to one another in the context of community in three different Native American cultures: pre-Columbian Mesoamerica and the Aztec Empire in particular; the Diné, or Navajo; and the Haudenosaunee, also known as the Iroquois Confederacy. This geographically, temporally, and culturally diverse sampling of Indigenous cultural uses of oral and graphic modes of communication suggests a pattern of Native American signification that continues to this day.

Functioning in all levels of society and in cultural institutions, including formal education, the textual continuum as it existed in pre-Columbian Mesoamerican cultures offers a telling example of how both the oral and the graphic worked together to privilege and value a particular mode of Indigenous expression and knowledge preservation. Both oral and graphic modes of communication played a significant role in the preservation of Mesoamerican thought, but the graphocentrism of Mesoamerican signification arose as an attempt to assure the presence of the cycles of the past by controlling the interpretation of language. Understood from the theory of oral, graphic, and critical impulses I am proposing, the textual continuum of the Triple Alliance (comprising the city-states of Tenochtitlan, Texcoco, and Tlacopan), otherwise known as the Aztec Empire (1428–1521), was dangerously out of balance because of its privileging of graphic forms of recording knowledge. Although there were oral discourses, linguistic authority was rooted in graphic representations, including books and the calendar, and the result was that knowledge became codified and rooted in socially hierarchical frameworks that eventually played a significant role in the empire's downfall. The Triple Alliance's privileging of graphically recorded knowledge offers one example of what may occur when the textual continuum is not balanced by fluid oral and graphic modes of creating, recording, and critiquing cultural thought. Whereas Triple Alliance writing was context-dependent in the sense that its usage depended on the interpretations of priests in order for it to be understood, how those writings functioned was largely codified.

It is important to reference Mesoamerican forms of the textual continuum because it is in Mesoamerica where scholars of writing find what they consider the most sophisticated forms of pre-contact American Indian writing. Rather than using only pictograms or other forms of mnemonic representations, the Aztec, Mixtec, Zapotec, and Maya recorded speech in "*heterogeneous systems*, partly pictographic, partly logographic, and partly syllabic (or phonetic)" (Marcus 1992, 28). Writing was used as a means of control and power through the dissemination of propaganda (14). Imperial scribes would write of the deeds of their rulers, relating them to central cultural myths and constructing fabulous histories around their ascension to power, even changing birthdates to properly correspond with auspicious calendrical cycles and dates (14). From the earliest inscriptions on stone steles, altars, flights of steps, and monuments, Mesoamerican graphic texts exalt and attempt to legitimize rulers with reference to victorious battles, the sacrifice of prisoners, the dating of political events, and the naming of nobles for specific calendar days (42). Marcus contends that writing in Mesoamerica was an offshoot of political power struggles in these socially stratified societies, "*a tool and a by-product of this competition for prestige and leadership positions*" (15).

If in practice the heterogeneous modes of Mesoamerican writing that Marcus and others identify played a role in Mesoamerican cultural and political stratification and hierarchy, the ways knowledge was actually preserved and shared reflect more complexity and equilibrium in terms of the oral and the graphic. In virtually every Mesoamerican Indigenous culture the existence of tension between what have been identified as dualities or opposites provides a crucial framework for their worldviews. The eminent scholar of Mesoamerican cultures Miguel León-Portilla has stated, "One very important trait of the Mesoamerican pantheon is that most, if not all, of its members exist and act in pairs, reflecting the ultimate nature of the supreme dual god" (León-Portilla and Shorris 2001, 16).

This way of seeing existence within dualities extends to Meso-american uses of formal language, in which León-Portilla and other scholars see a necessary division between oral and graphic modes of expression. In the Triple Alliance *calmecac*, schools in which children of nobles were taught, "astrology, star lore, divination and the calendars, hieroglyphic writing, and 'life's history' *(nemiliz tlacuilolli)*" comprised the curriculum; this knowledge was relayed both graphically and orally (Marcus 1992, 50–51). Rather than being vested in graphic representations, León-Portilla argues, oral tradition was "the main vehicle for expressing human thought and feelings" (León-Portilla and Shorris 2001, 9). In priestly schools students "learned by heart the ancient songs, the old stories, the prayers, and the most celebrated discourses" (25). Knowledge was thus preserved orally and graphically.

Rather than supplanting the spoken word as a means of recording thought, graphic forms of communication worked in concert with oral recitation and interpretation, expressing the critical impulse. The Western notion of writing as recorded speech offers a confusing standard with which to classify Mesoamerican writing systems, for as Elizabeth Boone states, in pre-Columbian "indigenous America, visible speech was not often the goal" (1994, 3). Mesoamerican societies relied on oral and graphic methods of knowledge transmission working together. Hieroglyphic texts and graphic images exist together in single documents, both serving specific functions: "Generally there are texts on one hand (usually in text blocks, with their own reading order and structure), and there are pictures on the other. They complement each other, they have slightly different meanings, and they are closely tied to each other in providing the full meaning of the sculptural or painted effort, but they are nonetheless two parts acting in harmony. And they tend to occupy separate sections of the surface" (20). Mesoamerican writings were designedly open-ended, providing what Boone terms "accountability": "Because they are permanent, or relatively so, they functioned for their societies to document and to establish ideas. As records, they are memory that can be inspected by others. The hieroglyphic text and the pictorial-iconic presentation could be read or interpreted by many people other than their creator" (22). Thus in order to circumvent differences in language and script, Mesoamerican writing systems incorporated an open-ended form of interpretation within their very signifying structure.

When knowledge was transmitted it was thus not within the purview of the scribes, such as the Aztec *amatlacuilo*, "a name for the individual whose social role it was to paint on the *amatl*," but for the priests for whom the knowledge existed both in its graphic format and orally. Scribes were not priests, because wisdom did not exist in books. Instead, graphic works were designedly suggestive: "Those who had the wisdom of the word were those who could 'look' at the sky or at the painted books and interpret them, to tell stories based on their discerning of the signs. The oral narrative of the wise men seems to have had a social function as well as a rank superior to the *tlacuilo*, who was placed by [the Franciscan priest] Sahagún among those who were skilled craftsmen" (Mignolo 1994, 252). Knowledge did not exist in graphic form, but was accessed through a combination of both graphic and oral forms. Those who had "the wisdom of the word, (*tlamatinime* in Nahuatl; *amauta* in Aymara; *qo ru naoh* in Maya-Cachiquel), translated as 'orators' or 'philosophers' by Spanish chroniclers," were the keepers of knowledge in

Mesoamerica; they knew their worlds in both oral and graphic formats and privileged neither (239).

In Mesoamerica there was undoubtedly a reciprocal relationship between oral and graphic modes of communication, but there also was an evolving dependency and privileging of the graphic. The critical impulse's ability to balance the oral and the graphic was weakened. At stake was the control of human destiny; it was believed that by counting time human beings could discern universal patterns that repeat themselves. Working within the guidelines of universal principles such as duty and reciprocity, Mesoamericans believed that human beings could enlist the help of the gods in preventing chaos and death and ensuring order and prosperity. Mesoamerican calendars evolved before forms of graphic writing: "It seems almost certain that the use of the 260-day calendar pre-dated the first appearance of writing" (Marcus 1992, 33). In fact Mesoamerican writing developed out of the signs for specific calendar days.

Graphic forms of Mesoamerican record keeping were inextricably linked to ideas concerning social, political, and divine control. As such, the records of those in power inevitably linked them to the appropriate mythic events in cyclical history and validated and authorized their control. Though tragic, it is not surprising that the victors in Mesoamerican wars burned the records of the vanquished, as "during the reign of Itzcoatl, the Aztecs themselves had destroyed all the old books in order to rewrite history in their own fashion" (Todorov 1982, 60). In Mesoamerica graphic forms of knowledge and record keeping came to dominate and in fact dictate tradition as it was expressed orally. As Todorov argues, "The language privileged by the Aztecs is ritual speech—i.e.,

speech regulated in its own forms and its functions, memorized and hence always quoted" (79). In a worldview structured
by recurring cycles there is little room for novelty or innovation; "the interpretation of the event occurs less in terms of
its concrete, individual, and unique content than of the prees-
tablished order of universal harmony, which is to be reestab-
lished" (69). Faced with the reality of the Spanish, Moctezuma
Xocoyotzin, the tlatoani, or speaker for the Triple Alliance, is
virtually paralyzed by his reliance on sacred Aztec prophecy (Carrasco 1982, 204). If, according to the cycles of history,
the Spanish are incarnations of the avenging Toltecs (Quetzalcoatl in particular), of whom the Mexicas have purposely
claimed an undeserved descent, then they have no recourse and
are doomed (150). Even worse, perhaps, Moctezuma is faced
with the possibility that an "entirely new event can occur, and
that what the ancestors have not already known might come
to pass" (Todorov 1982, 86).[12] The conquest required impro-
visation in language and ceremonial action, something that
the highly codified world of the Triple Alliance, with its privileging of graphic modes of discourse, did not readily enable.

Undoubtedly Mesoamerican signification was dependent
on the reciprocal relationship between oral discourse and
graphic discourses, including hieroglyphic writing and other
forms of graphic representation. These societies valued oral
discourse as a means of recalling and reciting cultural traditions, but scholarship points to the true cultural authority residing ultimately within the traditions as recounted in
graphic form. Thus although the words of the tlamatine were
valued, they were valued insofar as his interpretations of contemporary events, signs, and omens could be related to the
past as recorded in graphic formats. With the weakening of

the critical impulse, oral discourse did not create knowledge but only served as a way of relating past and present.

Like Mesoamerican societies, traditional Diné thought and spirituality values cyclical time, reciprocity, and duality. However, as expressed in the context of the use of sandpainting in chantway healing ceremonies, Diné spirituality privileges wholeness, wherein all creation is integral, in contrast to the hierarchies that dominate Mesoamerican cultures. The relationship between oral and graphic discourses in chants models the form of wholeness and reciprocity that is key to Diné belief and is a form of critical discourse in a spiritual context. Understood as a whole, chants are healing ceremonies that balance the individual in the world by reestablishing hóžó, "translated as beautiful, harmonious, blessed, pleasant, satisfying, for it summarizes the idea of the controlled integration of all forces, both good and evil, natural and supernatural, into a harmonious world" (Parezo 1983, 12).

Diné cosmology, like the cosmologies of Mesoamerica, emphasizes the circularity of time as represented by the change of seasons and astronomical cycles. In a highly complex web of mythology, ritual, and ceremonies the Diné express their traditional understanding of the way the universe works: "Navajos believe that the universe is an orderly, all-inclusive unity of interrelated elements and that a principle of reciprocity governs man's relations with these elements. . . . This universe contains both good and evil, which are complementary yet embodied in each other in a complicated duality" (Parezo 1983, 11). Unlike Mesoamerican cultures, however, Diné spirituality is not governed by an organized priesthood: "There is no organized system of religious services, no fixed ceremonial calendar, and no institutionalized priesthood"

(11). Instead hataałí, "singers" who know particular "chants, prayers, and the myths which justif[y] these practices," create sandpaintings during ceremonies as a means of nullifying the evil that creates sickness (11). As Parezo explains, "Evil is the absence of control which depends upon knowledge; good is that which has been brought under control. Evil can be brought under control by investing it with holiness. Holiness is distinct from both good and evil and refers to some power which has been manipulated" (12). In curing ceremonies, sandpainting, or iikááh, the "place where the gods come and go," is the means by which power is manipulated through the exact representation of supernaturals, "thereby becoming the temporary resting place of holiness" (1). Through ritual actions that incorporate the patient into myth, he or she may be brought back to hózhó (12).

Whereas Mesoamerican forms of recording thought and speech are generally recognized as writing, sandpaintings are never designated by scholars as such. Instead they are described as presenting "exact pictorial representation[s] of supernaturals" and "stylized designs . . . full of sacred symbols" (Parezo 1983, 1). Sandpaintings are not, however, deficient means of graphically recording Diné traditions. They are designedly context-dependent and are parts of ceremonies that depend equally as much on oral components (singing and chanting) as on graphic elements for healing to take place. Unlike Mesoamerican writings, which seek to know the world through divination, sandpaintings are used as a means of communing with the supernaturals in order to reestablish hózhó. Although sandpaintings function as records of myth, their history suggests a wariness of the static potential of graphic representation if it is not actively engaged with oral forms of discourse.

Myths tell that sandpainting depictions were originally permanently represented on "buckskin, unwounded deer
skin, black or white clouds, sky, or spiderwebs" and were
"unrolled for the prototype ceremony held in the myth for the
protagonist after which they were rolled up and carried home
by the deities" (Parezo 1983, 11). These representations were
formed by sewing (naskhá). They were delicate and sacred,
and because the gods thought that in the hands of the Earth
People the "'sewings' might be stolen, soiled, damaged, lost,
or quarreled over," human beings were given sandpaintings
instead (11). As Parezo explains, the gods and the stories are
clear about a particular taboo: "Mythological rationales and
supernatural proscriptions mandated keeping sandpaintings
impermanent. To disobey would bring disaster, blindness,
illness, or death to the individual and drought to the tribe"
(11). Tellingly, by supernatural mandate sandpaintings, the
most sacred graphic representations of mythic narratives, are
to appear only in impermanent form and only for the dura-
tion of a curing ceremony.

The formal relationship between sandpaintings and the
songs of Diné healing ceremonies is in keeping with the critical
impulses of myth that these ceremonies continue in present
contexts. Trudy Griffin-Pierce claims, "The Navajos' emphasis on motion is the foundation of their view of the world"
(1992, 24). Their worldview privileges process and movement
and expresses the belief that "no state of being is permanently fixed. Thus, beauty, balance, and orderliness are conditions that must be continuously recreated" (25). The static
potential of graphic representation is ameliorated by both
song, which is an "indispensable component of Navajo ritual," and the impermanence of sandpaintings. Griffin-Pierce

claims that the whole process of creating a song is itself a part of the process of healing; the initial request of a singer's services, the collecting of the necessary payment by donations from friends and relatives, the preparation of meals by family members, and the ceremony itself all work to reestablish hóžó in the patient, who witnesses again and again how in so many ways people care about his or her well-being. As Griffin-Pierce states, "The emphasis of the sandpainting is on process, the dynamic flow of action, and on its ability to summon power through the process of its creation and use" (55). Both oral and graphic elements come together in chantway ceremonies utilizing sandpaintings, and in turn the ceremony itself functions as a critical discourse. The balancing of the ceremony affects all who participate in the event, spreading hóžó among them. Thus with both sandpainting and song working in concert the mythic past and the mythic present are united.

Like the Diné and Mesoamerican societies, the Haudenosaunee use of wampum belts represents the interplay between oral, graphic, and critical discourses in American Indian systems of signification. Wampum, known chiefly in the form of strings of carved quahog shells woven together in belts, have for hundreds of years recorded events, treaties, and obligations between Native American nations and those with whom they have treated, from the Atlantic to the American Southeast. The origins of the use of wampum date to the beginnings of the Haudenosaunee Confederacy. Commonly understood as simply mnemonic devices, wampum actually served as graphic forms of recording oral agreements. A message documented in a wampum belt lived in both the voice of the messenger and the materiality of the wampum. With oral and graphic discourses stabilized by their coexistence, Haudenosaunee diplomacy was able to flourish by this means of establishing trustworthy communications.

The origin of the use of carved quahog shells as a means of communication is told in the origin story of the Haudenosaunee Confederacy. The fatherless Huron known as the Peacemaker "formed the Iroquois Confederacy, endowed it with symbols, and supported it with ritual sanctions. Central to its plot are feuding factions which, one by one, grasp the message that is carried by a fatherless boy, the typical Iroquois culture hero" (Fenton 1985, 15). While the Peacemaker came to the Haudenosaunee and spread his message of peace through unity, it was his speaker Hiawatha's development of the wampum that offered a material representation of the word. The intractable and disbelieving Onondaga leader, Tadodaho, kills Hiawatha's wife and daughters. As Hiawatha wanders in his mourning, he meditates on his desire for consolation and an externalization of his grief: "This would I do if I found anyone burdened with grief as I am. I would take these shell strings in my hand and console them. The strings would become words and lift away the darkness with which they are covered. Holding these in my hand, my words would be true" (Wallace 1946, 52). In Paul Wallace's version of this story, words become beads and externalize emotions so that they may be considered and dealt with not individually but collectively. The shell strings would both absorb the grief in order to release it and guarantee the truth of the shared words and their expressed emotions.

The use of wampum became instrumental to Haudenosaunee conceptions of condolence, and this understanding of sharing and dispelling grief through the exchange of wampum became the foundation of Haudenosaunee diplomacy, which was modeled after the Condolence Council ritual (Fenton 1985, 6). Under the rules of diplomacy, opposing groups need to be condoled for their losses and the wrongs they have suffered before they can think clearly and make decisions with a good mind. Grief clouds judgment, and so it must be dispelled through its recognition and by condoling with others before the healing of damaged relations may take place. Through the sharing of words, wampum, and grief, the critical impulse expresses itself.

As with other Native American cultures, Haudenosaunee conceptions of the universe include a fundamental recognition of duality and reciprocity, and this is represented in the use and function of wampum (Fenton 1985, 12). Kinship and relationship are understood through the principle of reciprocity, with men and women as well as other family members working within specific roles and duties. These duties and obligations are extended from the literal family to the symbolic family. Thus the reciprocity between older and younger brothers is represented in organizational forms of the Confederacy. For example, in the Confederacy Council certain nations are referred to as older brothers and others as younger brothers. The interdependence, or kinship, of oral and graphic discourse in the form of spoken messages and recorded messages in Haudenosaunee diplomacy is another way their worldview is expressed.

Rather than being simply mnemonic devices, wampum function more accurately as living records that work in concert with messengers who know and may verbalize their authorized messages. The wampum chronicler Tehanetorens explains, "Wampum strings served as credentials or as a certificate of authority" (1972, 3). Official tribal relations were always guaranteed by the exchange of wampum, whether in strings or belts. When a wampum belt was commissioned by the chiefs, a council speaker "perform[ed] a speech act which roughly translates as 'reading the message into the wampum' (tēHatiwēnó:ta 'they will put the word into it')" (Foster 1985, 104–5). Thus, as with Diné sandpaintings, the form of the wampum does not play a secondary role to the content of its message. By reading the message into the wampum the words of the chiefs are bound in material form. The messengers who read the wampum "are seen as relatively passive bearers of the wampum, which nevertheless is described as being a 'heavy burden' which they bear on their backs" (104–5).

In contrast to Diné sandpaintings, whose safe usage is assured by their impermanence, the viability of Haudenosaunee wampum belts is determined by the ability of wampum keepers to remember and read with accuracy the details of their message. Writing of the wampum keeper of the Onondaga Council House, William Fenton states, "This 'reading' of the wampum belt was possible so long as the memory of the particular verbal stream could be recalled and taught by association with the character and design of the particular belt" (1985, 18). Haudenosaunee diplomacy demands that chiefs not only "recall the terms of the ancient agreements: one must be prepared to actually renew these agreements which, as far as the chiefs were concerned, were still in effect and never formally abrogated by the Canadian or American governments" (Foster 1985, 101). Thus although wampum belts seem to record diplomatic agreements in static, graphic form, the sharing and reading of wampum are designed to continually polish the covenant chain through critical discussions and diplomatic relations. From the perspective of cultures dependent on alphabetic literacy, the Haudenosaunee dependency on wampum may appear overreliant on a fragile form of oral memory. Indeed as Fenton points out, when the verbal streams attached with specific wampum were disrupted, for example when wampum were removed from their cultural contexts and kept in museums, "reading" the wampum "became less probable and in time virtually impossible" (1985, 18). How-ever, when functioning within the Haudenosaunee community wampum and their verbal streams exemplify the interdependency and mutual support of graphic and oral modes of recording and constructing knowledge. The use of wampum belts offers an example of oral and graphic discourses working in unison through the critical impulse as they are both lasting documents and dependent on memory. The drawback to the use of wampum belts as living documents is also the source of their virtue: the form demands face-to-face, oral discursive interactions in order to be activated and to continue. But as wampum function to bring together political factions and maintain relationships, the form works ideally within its functional context.

These examples provide insights into the ways oral and graphic discourses can exist on the textual continuum and how they may be put into conversation by critical discourses. As these examples illustrate, there are myriad consequences to the ways oral and graphic discourses are expressed and balanced in Native culture. One conclusion that may be drawn from these examples is that the vibrancy of cultural knowledge is ultimately dependent on the energy of critical discourses, which develop out of the tensions between complementary oral and graphic discourses. These discourses continue to have power in the present. In *Mestiz@ Scripts, Digital Migrations, and the Territories of Writing*, Damián Baca explores the legacy of Mesoamerican picture writing, arguing that the painting of "pictographic murals" during the Chicano civil rights movement in the 1960s drew on "Mesoamerican aesthetic structures for critiquing recent colonizing events" (2008, 74). Taiaiake Alfred invokes the ideas of the Haudenosaunee Condolence ritual in "advocating [for] a self-conscious traditionalism, an intellectual, social, and political movement that will reinvigorate those values, principles, and other cultural elements that are best suited to the larger contemporary political and economic reality" (1999, xviii). In *Ceremony* (1977) Leslie Marmon Silko makes a Diné sing the event that reveals a key pattern in Tayo's healing; in Eric Gansworth's novel *Smoke Dancing* (2004) beadwork becomes a graphic critical discourse that is a contemporary extension of Haudenosaunee wampum.

In the following chapters I examine how the writing of N. Scott Momaday, Gerald Vizenor, Ray A. Young Bear, and Robert J. Conley all theorize balancing, critical concepts that intervene in specific ways and cultural contexts on the textual continuum. Each addresses the privileging of writing and reasserts the oral, graphic, and critical impulse dynamic. The critical impulse, I argue, most succinctly manifests itself in theorizing culturally specific concepts that may serve as guidelines within and against which more oral, graphic, and critical discourse may be created.

When I think back on Sequoyah now and his reintroduction of the syllabary among the Cherokee people, I recognize his true genius. It was not that he was an incredible linguist. More important, he recognized that for writing to function safely in a community, to not be considered witchcraft, it must be accessible to all as a welcome counterpart to our oral communication. By recontextualizing Cherokee writing as belonging collectively to the Cherokee Nation, Sequoyah opened a space in which Cherokee cultural critical discourse could be reinvigorated. In the following chapters we will examine how contemporary American Indian writers are attempting to do something similar in their writing.

2

N. Scott Momaday's
The Way to Rainy Mountain

Vision, Textuality, and History

> The great adventure of the Kiowas was a going forth into the
> heart of the continent. . . . In the course of that long migra-
> tion they had come of age as a people. They had conceived
> a good idea of themselves; they had dared to imagine and
> determine who they were. | N. Scott Momaday, *The Way to
> Rainy Mountain*

Offering both a critical methodology and an articulation of
key critical concepts in ways that resolve the apparent binary of
oral and literate elements, N. Scott Momaday's *The Way to Rainy
Mountain* provides a model for interpreting American Indian
literature. The narrative describes a transformative intellectual journey in which a tribe reconceives itself as a people by
establishing relationships with a new homeland. Alienated
from his ancestors' way of knowing their world, the modern

narrator juxtaposes personal, family, and tribal history as a means of constructing a Kiowa identity. Imaginatively retracing the critical conceptual journey of his ancestors, he enlivens the oral, graphic, and critical impulses in his relationship to Kiowa life. In offering the narrator's conceptual predicament as emblematic of modern American Indian existence, *Rainy Mountain* shows how oral, graphic, and critical impulses may be brought back into more dynamic balances that serve the larger needs of Native American communities.

Published in 1969, *The Way to Rainy Mountain* is Momaday's most philosophically and structurally complex text, a work whose centrality to Native literary discourse is well recognized. Part oral tradition, part history, part personal reminiscence, *Rainy Mountain* is most often described as a memoir. But with its unnamed narrator and fragmented style, the text is less concerned with telling the story of a single person's conceptual journey than it is with presenting a type of map or template for reclaiming worldviews. Not autobiographical in any simple sense, the text is a work of ideas exploring through its narratives and structure the relationships between oral, graphic, and critical impulses. *Rainy Mountain* offers its readers a "way" of reconciling the apparent contradictions of modern Native life. Time and again the text intervenes in static cultural traditions, undercutting both Western and Native expectations regarding the function of and relationships between land, stories, and history. Rather than reifying either Western literate or Native oral traditions, *Rainy Mountain* instead aims at placing these traditions in conversation by invigorating the critical impulse. The text accomplishes this by undercutting the dominance of the graphic impulse in the narrator's epistemological perspective and reclaiming the social function of oral tradition. Privileging neither the oral nor the graphic, Rainy Mountain models how both forms may mutually support one another. When the oral and graphic are in conversation with one another the critical impulse flourishes.

The narrator's literal and metaphorical journey to Rainy Mountain, the heart of Kiowa country in what is now Oklahoma, provides a critical template for the reader to follow in reestablishing this dynamic balance between the oral, graphic, and critical impulses. Although he is a Kiowa by descent, the narrator recognizes that he does not understand the world through a Kiowa worldview as expressed by his relatives and ancestors. His preconceptions, which have been gleaned from Western notions of not only Kiowa but Native American culture and history, betray his initial privileging of a Western epistemological framework. Informed by both the oral-literate binary and colonialist conceptions of Native cultures and American history, the narrator begins his journey to Rainy Mountain as a way of trying to understand the past glories of a dead culture.

The misconceptions that structure the narrator's initial understanding of his Kiowa heritage concern relationships to the Kiowa homelands, the definition of history, and oral tradition. His early experiences in the Kiowa landscape evoke emptiness, loneliness, and disconnection (Momaday 1969, 6). He sees the oral tradition as "fragmentary: mythology, legend, lore, and hearsay," vestiges of an oral system of recording thought that at its peak was of dubious veracity (4). Kiowa history, for him, has a beginning, middle, and end, at which time there remain "many things to remember, to dwell upon and talk about" (3). The narrator has cognitive tools with which to interpret Kiowa culture and history, but those tools arise out of a Western epistemology and colonialist perspective that views the Kiowa as a people of the past. Only the fragments of their oral tradition and an empty landscape remain.

In a powerful act of the imagination, through the course of tracing his ancestors' "long migration" from the Yellowstone region to the Great Plains the narrator slowly recognizes the crucial conceptual differences between his and his ancestors' worldviews. By juxtaposing his thoughts, perceptions, experiences, memories, and stories with those of members of his tribe, he revises his way of knowing the world and establishes new relationships with the Kiowa homeland. He comes to understand and respect the social and epistemological functions of orality. He recognizes that the Kiowa continue and that he is a part of that story. The very subject of his meditations transforms him. Exploring the Kiowa worldview from perspectives that challenge his initial premises, he stumbles upon the critical discourses, both oral and graphic, that grant Kiowa culture its agency. The narrator taps into the same critical impulse and finds that his attempt to understand a Kiowa worldview is in fact part of the ongoing critical process of constructing a Kiowa culture.

In the epigraph to this chapter the narrator claims that migration was its own reward because in that self-determined movement the Kiowas had "come of age as a people"; that is, they matured philosophically and spiritually (4). As a recursive physical and intellectual journey, the migration describes the development of a way of being in the world. The Kiowa "conceived" their culture as an "idea"; through action, especially the creation of new relationships with a new landscape and its ecology, this idea attained extension in the world (4).

As the narrator comes to recognize, the "idea" is inseparable from its life in language: "In one sense, then, the way to Rainy Mountain is preeminently the history of an idea, man's idea of himself, and it has old and essential being in language" (4). The Way to Rainy Mountain is a rearticulation of this idea in a modern context, and as such embraces contemporary forms of signification.

Critics have described how the work's self-conscious, modernist structure signals its ambition to place multiple traditions into conversation, as the narrative embraces competing epistemologies that influence the narrator's understanding of his experience. Examining the book's three-part structure, William Oandasan claims, "The division titles suggest the three main episodes of the Kiowa story, and each of the twenty-four sections consists of three parts, which correspond to the three journeys, or times: the mythic, the historic, and the biographic" (1988, 62). Matthias Schubnell notes that sources in Rainy Mountain include stories from tribal elders and works by "anthropologists, folklorists, and translators of Kiowa oral tradition" (1988, 29). Schubnell observes that these stylistically distinct voices originate in contrasting worldviews that, consequently, express contrasting accounts of the Kiowa. Viewing this relationship in dialectical terms, Oandasan focuses on a core set of issues: "traditional Kiowa culture versus Kiowa society today; his [Momaday's] collective, Kiowa identity versus an individual, modern identity; and 'traditional' versus 'creative' mythology" (1988, 62). Similarly Schubnell claims, "The development of Rainy Mountain from a collection of Kiowa tales to the blending of these stories with anthropological material and personal reminiscences reflects a growing crystallization of Momaday's Kiowa identity" (1988, 30). In describing the process of identity creation, Oandasan's and Schubnell's analyses are useful readings of how the structure of *Rainy Mountain* reveals the intellectual processes that the narrator embraces in order to reconceive himself. However, these tend to read identity as a thing to be achieved rather than a process.

Momaday calls the three "voices" of the twenty-four sections of *Rainy Mountain* "the mythical, the historical, and the immediate" (1997, 107). Grounded in the oral, the *mythical* is a tribal voice that recounts stories and historical events as seen through Kiowa perspectives. The *historical*, associated primarily with the graphic, carries the authoritative tone of academic scholarship that, as Joan Henley states, "does not speak *for* the group; it speaks *of* the group" (1988, 51). The *immediate* voice of the text, associated with the critical impulse, consists of the narrator's personal stories, memories, thoughts, and imaginative creations and has been the focal point of scholarly work concerning *Rainy Mountain*'s treatment of identity. A site for analysis, contemplation, and imagination, the immediate voice attempts to make sense of both the mythical and historical voices by reflecting on their meanings.

In fact, Momaday presents identity as something that needs to be created, not simply found. As a text of juxtapositions of mythical, historical, and immediate voices, of the past and the present, of oral and graphic literatures, and of history and imagination, *Rainy Mountain* asks its readers to embrace the very critical impulse that the narrator accesses. Kimberly Blaeser claims that the active reader of *Rainy Mountain* "not only participates in literary co-creation but he also expands his personal horizons, learns to think in new ways, achieves deeper self-knowledge and imagines or creates himself" (1989, 43). Participation in *Rainy Mountain* means engaging the interpretive processes of the text by embracing the critical methodology of reading that the text both articulates and performs. By placing the oral and graphic, the oral stories and written histories, into conversation the reader can reflect on the tensions and concepts that inform the "idea" of the Kiowa worldview.

The reader is central to the aims of *Rainy Mountain* because it is through the reader that the text finds its extension in social reality. The narrative is fraught with tensions and contradictions that speak to the individual and social existence of American Indians in the early years of the Red Power era and raises profound questions: What is the source of a culture's unique perspective? Can a worldview survive colonialism? Can a cultural descendant who is disconnected from his tribal traditions somehow reclaim those traditions without disclaiming his modern existence? Can a relationship with one's homelands be reclaimed? *Rainy Mountain* responds to questions such as these by offering its readers a critical methodology for interpreting modern American Indian experience and by reconceptualizing key ideas that have a profound impact on the way orality, relationships with one's homeland, and history are understood. Ultimately the narrator identifies three essential facts about Kiowa experience. The journey to Rainy Mountain evokes "a landscape that is incomparable, a time that is gone forever, and the human spirit, which endures" (Momaday 1969, 4). Time passes, and yet the human spirit remains, forged in our continued relationships with unique homelands. The implications of these facts and the way they relate in language is the subject of *Rainy Mountain*.

The narrative shifts the discourse of cultural construction

from one that understands tradition as a static model of what occurred in the past to one that emphasizes the evolving relationships between human beings, the languages in which they explore their experience, and the places in which they live. The concepts of vision, textuality, and history theorized in *The Way to Rainy Mountain* act as interventions in the dominant cultural discourses that have shaped the narrator's initial misconceptions regarding Kiowa culture. Rather than turning away from the present, the text offers concepts that embrace the modern tensions in Native American life and literature between oral and graphic impulses, between academic discourses and Native community discourses, and between Western scholarship and Native epistemologies. As expressions of the critical impulse, vision, textuality, and history are dynamic processes that may be engaged in order to undercut the dominance of static definitions of literature, culture, and the past. The critical impulse is itself embedded in the traditions of the Kiowa, who, Momaday writes, "called themselves *Kwuda*, 'coming out'" (16). As the "coming out" people, the people who define themselves as emergent, the Kiowa model the inherently tension-filled processes of imagination and self-determination the narrator theorizes. By imagining who they would become, the Kiowa created a picture of who they could be, but the creation of that reality necessitated not just imagining but also acting upon the imagined picture.

Vision

In *The Way to Rainy Mountain* the concept of *vision* entails movement from alienation to knowledge, from lack of connection to a relationship with place, from a lack of cultural identity to a deeply felt cultural identity. More than an extension of physical sight, vision is a process of mediation that includes both physical sight and intellectual and emotional insight. Throughout the text metaphors of sight conceptualize the way the Kiowa and, eventually, the narrator understand themselves. When the Kiowa come down from the mountains and onto the plains the newfound ability to see into the "distance" answers a fundamental need. Expressing their living relationship with the places that would become their homelands, the ability to "see far" is the physical expression of a worldview. The intellectual counterpart of this worldview theorizes insight as an ever deepening exploration and understanding of life through the mind's eye. When the capacity for sight and insight is honed and kept vibrant, the members of a culture may attain a sense of vision that encourages actions that contribute to health and survival. In *The Way to Rainy Mountain* this type of vision lies near the core of the culturally specific Kiowa idea of imagination that is first expressed in language and is intertwined with the relationship between a people and a land.

The introduction to *Rainy Mountain* explores how vision is nurtured by charting the narrator's process of developing a Kiowa way of seeing. As the text makes clear, vision is not pregiven. As we see and think, we are interpreting the world. This process of reflection and self-reflection is characterized by its mutability; it represents an ever expanding dialectic between sight and insight, place and human beings. The more we see, the more we think; the more carefully we think, the more deeply we see. Although an individual may initially base his or her acquisition of vision on the sight and insight gained from the physical experience of a place, this process cannot be abstracted from culturally specific uses of language, memory, thought, and emotion. As the narrator finds out, vision is necessarily a communal concept, one that depends on the concept of relationship and finds its most complete expression in the shared vision of a people.

In *Rainy Mountain* the narrator's quest focuses initially on learning to *see* from a Kiowa perspective the lands that have shaped Kiowa identity. In the opening paragraph of the introduction the narrator describes the land surrounding Rainy Mountain, geographically placing it and then naming it: "The hardest weather in the world is there. Winter brings blizzards, hot tornadic winds arise in the spring, and in summer, the prairie is an anvil's edge" (5). Despite his attention to changes in the land, the narrator's vision of Rainy Mountain at first lacks a sense of interrelationship that the storytelling tradition so deeply values. The narrator claims, "Loneliness is an aspect of the land" and "All things in the plain are isolate; there is no confusion of objects in the eye, but *one* hill or *one* tree or *one* man" (5). Analyzed from the perspective of physical sight, the narrator's perceptions are clear; objects do stand out more clearly on the plains. But from the Kiowa cultural perspective, the narrator's understanding of Rainy Mountain is misinformed. His reading of the land as lonely, isolating, and divided into singular objects shows his limited understanding of both relationship and place. Though he uses the dialectic of sight and insight to create a partial vision of Rainy Mountain, he does not yet have the cultural tools—such as stories, histories, and even his own reevaluated experiences—to understand his ancestors' relationships to that land.

The narrator's misapprehension of place increases when in the next line he states, "To look upon that landscape in the early morning, with the sun at your back, is to lose the sense of proportion. Your imagination comes to life, and this, you think, is where Creation was begun" (5). Once again, the narrator's physical sight is clear; his interpretation is not so clear. Though a loss of proportion could be read as a way of seeing all things in creation equally, in relation to a tribal worldview predicated on balance it marks a sickening loss of dimension, a disruption of proper relationships. Gradually the narrator's perceptions move from sight to insight. By actively reading the land he engages in a process of creating a vision of Rainy Mountain; thus his imagination does "come to life." But vision gained through individual experience alone is not powerful enough to create the culturally informed understanding of place the narrator seeks. He might "think" Creation began at Rainy Mountain, but we later learn that the Kiowa creation story is older than their relationship with that place. Because the narrator does not yet fully understand the cultural processes from a Kiowa perspective, his interpretation of Rainy Mountain is his alone. Thus it is fitting that at this stage in his development he stands with his back to the sun, looking away from the source of light that is the Kiowa god.

Developing vision is important to the narrator's cultural growth, but the ability to imagine what one cannot physically see is equally crucial. Momaday argues that the imagination can stand in as a surrogate for sensation as a whole, including physical sight, and he gives several examples of this process. Of the narrator's grandmother, Aho, Momaday writes, "The immense landscape of the continental interior lay like memory in her blood. She could tell of the Crows, whom she had never seen, and of the Black Hills, where she had never been" (7). Aho's way of seeing is deeply informed by her immersion in Kiowa oral tradition, which sees no contradiction between valuing both experiences of the body and experiences of the mind. For Aho, stories are as vivid as physical reality; her imaginative construction of reality is not bound by space, time, or sensation. The "memory" that lives in her "blood" suggests that she understands herself as continuous with the past by means of body, mind, "blood," and "memory." The blood and the memories have been passed down to her in a chain of stories that have transformed her body and mind. Because the narrator lacks this understanding of the oral tradition, his concept of reality is limited. His imagination is not yet expansive enough to immediately accept the reality of his mind as seamless with the reality of the physical world. Still, he builds on the thoughts he has gained through physical sight and states, "I wanted to see in reality what she had seen more perfectly in the mind's eye, and traveled fifteen hundred miles to begin my pilgrimage" (7). The difference between his sight and Aho's imaginative vision signals cultural, epistemological, and perceptual differences between him and his grandmother. Recognizing these differences, the narrator sets out on a literal and figural pilgrimage to try to understand Aho's culturally constructed Kiowa vision.

In the Yellowstone country of Kiowa origin the narrator attempts to engage the epistemological processes his ancestors used to construct and understand their world. He begins by exploring his emotional responses to the land: "Yellowstone, it seemed to me, was the top of the world, a region of deep lakes and dark timber, canyons and waterfalls. But, beautiful as it is, one might have felt the sense of confinement there" (7). The narrator's ability to speculatively imagine what his ancestors "might have felt" on their journey from the Rockies to the Plains shows his evolving trust in the epistemic status of his emotional responses. As his vision grows he becomes more confident in his speculations, claiming, "There is a perfect freedom in the mountains, but it belongs to the eagle and the elk, the badger and the bear" (7). He creates a nascent theory of "freedom" as a creature's suitability to its environment, which has a direct impact on the creature's ability to become what it desires to become. Empowered with this knowledge, which began as intuition, a feeling, a hunch, the narrator is able to make a full-fledged epistemological claim about his people: "The Kiowas reckoned their stature by the distance they could see, and they were bent and blind in the wilderness" (7). His cultural understanding has been transformed by his experience of the Rockies and his theorizing the meaning of those experiences. The dialectic between sight and insight transforms his epistemology. He can now offer a more culturally integrated Kiowa theory of place. The experience of a place and the epistemology of a people are coextensive; physical distance and metaphysical freedom are dependent on each other for definition. By theorizing his emotions in relation to the land, he imaginatively constructs a theory of how the Kiowa "reckoned" themselves as a people.

As he continues to trace the journey of his ancestors, the narrator intuits the motivational force behind the Kiowa migration: the feelings of wonder and delight. Descending from the mountains, he thinks, "The earth unfolds and the limit of the land recedes. Clusters of trees, and animals grazing far in the distance, cause the vision to reach away and wonder to build upon the mind" (7). As with Aristotle's concept of beauty and Kant's concept of moral duty, the Kiowan concept of the "good life" begins with wonder. The physical ability to see far into a limitless landscape is linked metaphorically to intellectual openness and curiosity, imagination motivated by wonder. As the narrator's vision grows, so too does his capacity to imagine not only what his people might have felt looking upon the Plains, but *how* they felt it.

As with vision, wonder is a culturally dependent concept that grows with and builds one's knowledge of how to see and interpret the world. Recounting the Kiowa journey from the mountains to the foothills, the narrator says, "There the Kiowas paused on their way; they had come to a place where they must change their lives" (7). As with his own previously inadequate theory of place, the narrator claims that the Kiowa were at first metaphysically unequipped to understand the land they saw: "They must wean their blood from the northern winter and hold the mountains a while longer in their view" (8). Their conception of themselves was rooted in an epistemology born of their relationship with the mountains. But by acquiring the sun-worshipping Tai-me religion from the Crow, they also acquired the intellectual and emotional means to understand the Plains, for "precisely there does [the sun] have the certain character of a god" (7). The process of building relationships in a foreign land and transforming it into a homeland requires arduous intellectual and physical work.

Experiencing an unfamiliar place can also be dangerous and frightening. As the narrator's initial experiences at Rainy Mountain show, in the absence of a culturally grounded understanding of a place, the natural features of a landscape may seem lonely, isolating, and proportionless. With a more developed sense of vision, the narrator comes to understand the Kiowa cultural imperative of confronting the unfamiliar with story, thereby integrating it into an existing web of relations. Seeing Devil's Tower the narrator thinks, "Two centuries ago, because they could not do otherwise, the Kiowas made a legend at the base of the rock" (8). This story tells of seven sisters who are chased by their brother, who has turned into a bear. They climb a tree to escape their brother, and the great tree carries them into the sky, where they become the Big Dipper. The seven sisters, the bear, the rock tree, and the stars all play necessary roles in a cosmology that reaches from earth to sky and is defined by interconnectedness. Experiencing a new land compelled the Kiowa to reconsider their world, but that reconsideration maintains a sense of fundamental relationships: "From that moment, and so long as the legend lives, the Kiowas have kinsmen in the night sky. Whatever they were in the mountains, they could be no more" (8). Telling a story in response to a new place creates an interrelationship between the land and the Kiowas; their cultural identity is changed through relating to the land on which they live. In a reciprocal relationship their perception of the land is also forever changed.

Once he develops his understanding of how Kiowa vision comprises many elements—thought and emotion, imaginative reality, story, and the concept of wonder—the narrator can interpret the most imaginative of Kiowa conceptualizations, their origin story. Momaday writes, "According to their origin myth, they entered the world through a hollow log. From one point of view, their migration was the fruit of an old prophecy, for indeed they emerged from a sunless world" (7). Moving from darkness into the light, from the mountains to the Plains, the Kiowa engage in the process of growth embedded within this story. By coming to understand the story, the narrator brings his concept of vision into accord with a Kiowa explanation of their origin. Like his ancestors before him, his journey to Rainy Mountain contains elements of both the contingent and the determined. Called out onto the Plains by their origin story that is at once a mandate and an invitation to wonder, the Kiowa define their epistemology as a process of growth.

Employing a socially constructed and culturally informed process of seeing and thinking, the narrator revises his understanding of the landscape. As the introduction draws to a close, the narrator's vision of Rainy Mountain has changed. Whereas before the narrator saw a proportionless, isolating, and lonely land, he now says of the houses on the plain, "They belong in the distance; it is their domain" (11). This recognition of belonging leads him to conflate his grandmother and her house, both of which were central to a Kiowa community of old: "Once there was a lot of sound in my grandmother's house, a lot of coming and going, feasting and talk" (11). The pleasure of recollecting the many visitors his grandmother and her house would host for feasts and conversation is suddenly broken by the reality of the present condition of the house: "Now there is a funeral silence in the rooms, the endless wake of some final word" (12). The narrator sees his grandmother's house, emptied of life and words, with new eyes: "When I returned to it in mourning, I saw for the first time in my life how small it was" (12). In sudden grief he falls back upon a lonely, individualistic vision, one dominated by the loss of relatives and community.

In this moment of doubt, when the narrator's new vision is being tested by sorrow, the chance alignment of a cricket on a handrail and the moon in the night sky provides a regenerative metaphor to replace his desolate vision of his grandmother's house. The cricket, small, inconsequential, and fleeting, is made whole and eternal in its superimposition on the moon. This icon, which is represented on the following page of the text by Al Momaday's illustration of a cricket in a circle, encapsulates a central process in The Way to Rainy Mountain: the transformation of that which is momentary, small, and inconsequential into something whole, meaningful, and eternal. The narrator muses about the cricket and the moon: "It had gone there, I thought, to live and die, for there, of all places, was its small definition made whole and eternal" (12). Life passes, but it remains "whole and eternal" in memory.

The narrator's tested, maturing vision now allows him to see objects on the Plains as ordered and having their place, rather than as contingent and disconnected. His vision signals a development of a Kiowa sense of imagination: "There, where it ought to be, at the end of a long and legendary way, was my grandmother's grave. Here and there on the dark stones were ancestral names" (12). His grandmother's grave, like everything else at Rainy Mountain, has its rightful place on the land, and his new knowledge of where things "ought to be" shows his developed understanding that the land and the people are one. As imagination develops, story shapes insight into a way of seeing into the distance, as the Kiowa intuited when they looked out onto the Plains. That sense of imagination is carried within a person; as the narrator says at the end of the introduction, "Looking back once, I saw the mountain and came away" (12). The narrator's new relationships with his Kiowa homeland do not simply reflect the recovery of an old Kiowa way of relating to place. He establishes his own relationships with the land by embracing the same critical impulse his ancestors accessed and which I define as vision. Vision represents the critical impulse in a person's relationship with place, and it is activated through the person's imaginative engagement with place. Recovering and nurturing these relationships in the context of language involves reconsideration of the concept of textuality.

Textuality

Creating relationships in the context of language requires, on a fundamental level, imagining connections with words. In *Rainy Mountain* these imaginative connections occur on the level of narrative through the relationship between three types of formal language expressed by the mythic, historical, and immediate voices. The critical impulse dynamic of vision finds a parallel in textuality, which consists of the fluid, interpenetrating, and reciprocally related mythic, historical, and immediate voices. To lay claim to a Kiowa cultural identity that reflects his own experience, the narrator establishes a dynamic balance between the oral and mythic voice and the graphic and historical voice, placing them in conversation and relating to them through the appropriately named immediate voice. The immediate voice embodies the critical impulse. Through his interpretation of the mythic and historical vignettes in the context of his own experience, the narrator prevents any one mode of expressing Kiowa life or history from dominating the other, thus keeping fluid the "idea" of the Kiowa.

Rather than defining oral and literate traditions with respect to their formal differences, Momaday understands language as a social phenomenon that may be understood in the context of its specific functions and in terms of the responsibilities that come with its use. When asked whether he saw his "work as continuing some tradition," Momaday responded clearly, "Yes. I think that my work proceeds from the American Indian oral tradition, and I think it sustains that tradition and carries it along. And vice versa. And my writing is also of a piece. I've written several books, but to me they are all parts of the same story. . . . My purpose is to carry on what was begun a long time ago; there's no end to it that I can see" (Schubnell 1997, 107). The formal differences between oral tradition and writing are secondary to "carry[ing] on what was begun a long time ago," which is a tradition of expression through language. In fact Momaday claims that the oral and the written are interdependent and exist in a reciprocal relationship, continuing that tradition in different forms in the present.

In light of his belief that orality and writing are coextensive it is not surprising that Momaday's notion of the role and responsibilities of the writer parallel the role of the storyteller. When asked, "[Does] the writer [have] a responsibility to the people of his society? To keep alive that sense of wonder in the power of words?" Momaday replied:

> I think so. I think so. He is a storyteller and there is nothing more important, I think, no function more important than that of story telling within a given society. It consists in language. I think of language as an element in which we exist. We all share in it; we have no existence apart from it. Therefore the story teller, the man whose function it is to deal primarily with language, has an enormous responsibility. It is his job to keep language alive to his fellow men; he must always demonstrate the

possibilities of language—and that's a big job; that's a heavy responsibility. But it is a necessary one. (Morgan 1997, 47)

A writer is a storyteller because both share the same responsibilities toward language and community. Momaday's claim that it is the storyteller's and the *writer's* responsibility to "keep language alive" and to "demonstrate the possibilities of language" underscores his belief that this can be accomplished regardless of the particular form in which language is expressed. His understanding of the functional equivalence of oral and written stories is a radical stance because it contradicts how the social dimensions of oral and literate traditions are conventionally understood.

Rather than engaging oral-literate theory directly, *Rainy Mountain* posits theories of language as reflected in Kiowa stories. These stories about stories offer a hermeneutic centered on relationship and express symbolically the social responsibilities that are inherent in Kiowa language use. Nowhere in the text is this better illustrated than in the story of the arrowmaker:

> If an arrow is well made, it will have tooth marks upon it. That is how you know. The Kiowas made fine arrows and straightened them in their teeth. Then they drew them to the bow to see if they were straight. Once there was a man and his wife. They were alone at night in their tipi. By the light of the fire the man was making arrows. After a while he caught sight of something. There was a small opening in the tipi where two hides were sewn together. Someone was there on the outside, looking in. The man went on with his work, but he said to his wife: "Someone

is standing outside. Do not be afraid. Let us talk easily, as of ordinary things." He took up an arrow and straightened it in his teeth; then, as it was right for him to do, he drew it to the bow and took aim, first in this direction and then in that. And all the while he was talking, as if to his wife. But this is how he spoke: "I know that you are there on the outside, for I can feel your eyes upon me. If you are a Kiowa, you will understand what I am saying, and you will speak your name." But there was no answer, and the man went on in the same way, pointing the arrow all around. At last his aim fell upon the place where his enemy stood, and he let go of the string. The arrow went straight to the enemy's heart. (46)

Deeply metaphorical, the story of the arrowmaker addresses many concerns: arrowmaking, protection, danger, enemies, and strategy. But as Momaday stated in a 1970 lecture at Princeton University, the story of the arrowmaker "is about language, after all, and it is therefore part and parcel of its own subject; virtually, there is no difference between the telling and that which is told" (1997, 108). For the arrowmaker, the most important function of language is its ability to define his relationship to his world.

When he finds himself threatened, the arrowmaker uses language to test whether or not the stranger looking in his home is a friend or an enemy. Despite his apparent disadvantage, he first reaches out with language as a way of making relationships. Momaday claims, "The point of the story lies, not so much in what the arrowmaker does, but in what he says—and indeed that he says it. The principal fact is that he speaks, and in so doing he places his very life in the balance"

(1997, 108). The arrowmaker raises the possibility of shared meaning by making a call to the person outside his tipi, his world. The lack of response signals disconnection and, in the context of his world, danger. As Momaday states, "Of the ominous unknown he asks only the utterance of a name, only the most nominal sign that he is understood, that his words are returned to him on the sheer edge of meaning" (109). The arrowmaker takes a risk in holding back for a moment, not immediately killing the person who watches his family, in order to make the offer of a linguistic relationship. Momaday says of the arrowmaker, "He ventures to speak because he must; language is the repository of his whole knowledge and experience, and it represents the only chance he has for survival" (109). The arrowmaker's survival depends on shared meaning; his social world is constructed through language. Momaday argues that the story turns on "the very idea that language involves the elements of risk and responsibility; and in this it seeks to confirm itself. In a word, it seems to say, everything is a risk. That may be true, and it may also be true that the whole of literature rests upon that truth" (109). The two ways of confronting the risk and responsibility of language are represented by the arrowmaker and the stranger. The arrowmaker defines a relationship as a form of dialogue in a shared language. He risks himself and his family when he respects his social responsibility by first asking the stranger's name. In contrast the stranger is a cipher; all we know is that the unknown person did not speak and thus in the story is named "enemy." The irony of the arrowmaker's story is that we do not know if the person the arrowmaker perceived as an enemy was in fact a true enemy. We know virtually nothing of the stranger, and that is precisely the point. The only thing we do know is that the "enemy" was unwilling to run the risk of relationship and accept the responsibilities of language.

As creatures of language, humans are all arrowmakers, for arrowmaking and "wordmaking" are conflated in the text, and both are essential to survival. Like arrows, words extend the reach of the human in both practical and abstract terms. The art of creating arrows and the art of giving voice to thought through language share a similar process; both require "time and patience" to construct a potential weapon for use as a means of survival and protection. The immediate voice of section 13 in *The Way to Rainy Mountain* explores the consequences of this power by imaginatively constructing a picture of an old man, Cheney, whom the narrator's father knew as a boy: "Every morning, my father tells me, Cheney would paint his wrinkled face, go out, and pray aloud to the rising sun. In my mind I can see that man as if he were there now. I like to watch him as he makes his prayer. I know where he stands and where his voice goes on the rolling grasses and where the sun comes up on the land" (Momaday 1969, 47). Like the narrator, who uses his words to imagine reality, Cheney's words find extension in prayer, and they continue in the narrator's imagination as the living oral impulse. There is a connection between Cheney's prayers moving over "rolling grasses" and his existence as an arrowmaker; both facets can engage and change reality. Cheney's use of prayer, like the narrator's use of language, begins in his mind in the form of imagined connections; prayer creates relationship only when it is expressed in language, let loose upon the world and finding a response. In the mythic voice section, the narrator tells us, "If an arrow is well made, it will have tooth marks upon it" (46). Momaday writes in the historical voice of the same section, "The old men were the best arrowmakers, for they could bring time and patience to their craft. The young men—the fighters and hunters—were willing to pay a high price for arrows that were well made" (47). Like words, arrows are straightened in the mouth by "chewing" them in discussion. When the maker draws his bow, figuratively filling his lungs with breath, he imbues the arrow or word with power. There is a tension in the fact that the arrow or word is poised to fly and yet remains still, its straightness, or truth, being tested. When released, the arrowmaker's words unleash the tension and power in a way that requires a response or kills discussion. The narrator begins his journey like the silent observer, and the structure of *Rainy Mountain* intervenes to teach the reader the responsible way of risking language through interpretation.

While the story of the arrowmaker is about the consequences of not risking the linguistic relationships social existence demands, other self-reflective stories in *Rainy Mountain* actively teach how language functions properly in the construction of relationships between human beings and the universe. Central to all these stories is that it is the animals and supernaturals that teach humans how to properly create relationships with language. When enemies are near a hunter it is a dog that warns him and proposes a deal: "The dog said: 'You know, I have puppies. They are young and weak and they have nothing to eat. If you will take care of my puppies, I will show you how to get away'" (20). Similarly, the hero twins, sons of a Kiowa woman and the Sun, are taught by Grandmother Spider how to survive by manipulating language. The precocious twins test their limits by playing in the cave of a giant. They have been instructed by Grandmother Spider to say the phrase "thain-mom," which means "above my eyes," if ever they should be caught in the cave. When repeated, the phrase renders ineffective the smoke the giant uses to blind his prey. The boys are caught and repeat the phrase as their grandmother instructed them, and the giant's smoke remains above their eyes, allowing them to escape harm. The giant is able to physically manipulate the world through the use of smoke, but the boys use words, which prove more powerful. In the midst of the storm spirit, the mythic voice of section 14 tells us, "[The Kiowa] speak to it, saying 'Pass over me.' They are not afraid of *Man-ka-ih*, for it understands their language" (48). The Kiowa were taught the power of language by others, showing performatively that existence and survival, like language, are contingent on relationships—those between humans and other creatures included. The historical voice in section 8 says, "A word has power in and of itself. It comes from nothing into sound and meaning; it gives origin to all things. By means of words can a man deal with the world on equal terms. And the word is sacred" (33). Even as the narrative signifies in self-reflective mythical stories the origins of a Kiowa understanding of the risks, responsibilities, and power of language, the narrator has yet to balance the influences and authority of the multiple oral and graphic forms with which he accesses his own and Kiowa experience.

The narrator's modern experience includes relating to Kiowa culture and history through multiple forms of discourse: oral tradition, writings, personal memories, and stories. The problem is that these forms of discourse do not carry the same authority as each does in its relationship to reality as perceived by the narrator. Though he has a rich reservoir of personal memories, stories, and oral tradition from which

to draw as he constructs a Kiowa identity, the narrator's initial experiential authority yields to written works of history, anthropology, and folklore. The three voices—mythical,
historical, and immediate—that structure the twenty-four
sections of *Rainy Mountain* begin the work disconnected and
disjointed. Both the mythical and historical voices reflect on
the Kiowa in the past tense. The mythical voice seems mystical, presenting parts of traditional stories and observations
without any context that would explain their social meaning;
the historical voice recounts the dead Kiowa past, recounting
facts, dates, and events. They are speaking past one another
and are not in conversation. Slowly, by reflecting on the mythical and historical narratives and his own thoughts, memories, and stories, the narrator begins to energize both these
discourses. In the process he learns that his knowledge has a
necessary place on the textual continuum and is on par with
Kiowa oral tradition and Western scholarship.

To establish a balance between the mythic, historical,
and immediate voices of the text *Rainy Mountain* disrupts the
dominant historical voice and undercuts its graphic authority. This begins in section 7 of "The Setting Out," when the
narrator's immediate, narrative voice usurps the position of
the historical voice and tells of his grandfather, Mammedaty:
"*Mammedaty owned horses. And he could remember that it was essentially good to own horses, that it was hard to be without horses. There
was a day: Mammedaty got down from a horse for the last time. Of
all the tribes of the Plains, the Kiowas owned the greatest number of
horses per person*" (31). With these words the narrator takes own-
ership of his memory as a valid form of history. His recounting of his grandfather in memory continues and parallels his
grandfather's own way of knowing: "*He could remember that*

it was essentially good to own horses." Like his grandfather, he engages the Kiowa world using knowledge accessed through remembered oral tradition. This personal remembrance of Mammedaty could not initially be accessed through the historical voice because it does not exist in the historical record until recounted by the narrator. Performatively, the narrative suggests that the measured objectivity of conventional academic history, so often described as cold and unfeeling by Native commentators, may be transformed by the establishment of relationships with the past. In *Rainy Mountain* the narrator's remembrances of his grandparents, Mammedaty and Aho, provide the means of making Kiowa history and his personal experiences interpenetrate one another.

In a similar fashion the mythical voice is also transformed by recollections of Mammedaty. Momaday writes in section 21 of "The Closing In," "Mammedaty was the grandson of Guipahgo, and he was well-known on that account" (72). The story recounting Mammedaty's strange sighting of a little boy who disappeared in the prairie grass exists as tribal myth, but it is the narrator's immediate voice telling of how Mammedaty acquired "possession of a powerful medicine" that adds empirical depth to the mythic account. In the same section the immediate voice offers a factual description of Mammedaty in the only picture of him, but ends the description by bringing it back to its meaning in relationships: *"A family characteristic: the veins stand out in his hands, and his hands are small and rather long"* (73). Once again, the narrator's knowledge provides the deeper context for understanding the meaning of both the historical and now the mythic. Tellingly, the last two sections of the narrative model this same pattern wherein the immediate voice speaks in the mythical and historical vignettes, showing performatively how all three voices may interpenetrate one another and function reciprocally, offering different perspectives on experience while at the same time existing in a dynamic equilibrium.

The Kiowa cultural identity the narrator recovers is accessed through the critical impulse that places these different forms of expression—mythic, historical, and personal—into conversation. Because the narrator begins his conceptual journey beholden to a graphocentric understanding of the Kiowa and of oral knowledge, the particular way the critical impulse compensates for this imbalance between the oral and the graphic is through the narrator's development of a critical agency that finds its grounding in oral tradition. As the expression of living tradition, stories told by the mythic voice are social in nature; oral knowledge is responsive and always present. The inclusive, social nature of the oral impulse invites the narrator to reestablish his relatedness to the Kiowa through reinterpreting, remembering, and recognizing the epistemological value in the stories of his tribe's, his family's, and his own past.

Although the narrator's development of critical agency occurs in a very personal manner, one that depends on his imagination to piece together the connections between himself, Kiowa oral tradition, and Kiowa history, his recovered identity as a Kiowa is socially situated and could not occur in social isolation. Louis Owens claims that for Momaday "identity is acquired through an act of self-imagination" (1992, 93), but it is clearer to say that self-imagination is a necessary step in the development of identity. Individuals may imagine who they are and even express this imagined self in language, yet in order for the imagined self to refer to the world it must also be acknowledged by others. After Momaday states in "The Man Made of Words" that "an Indian is an idea a given man has of himself" he goes on to say, "And that idea, in order to be realized completely, has to be expressed" (1975, 97). Identity exists in a recursive relationship between the social community and the individual subject. Asking himself what it means to be a Kiowa, Momaday says:

> It means that he has an experience in a way that enables him to think of himself in a way that other people cannot think of themselves; his experience is unique. It involves a history, a history of their migration from the Yellowstone to the Washita. Each time a Kiowa ponders his Kiowan-ess, he invents that whole history—and it is his invention, it is whatever he makes of it in his own mind. It is not written down, and he can't go to a book and find out what happened to the Kiowas in the Black Hills. All he can do is imagine. But it is his invention, finally. (Schubnell 1997, 127)

From this perspective Kiowa identity is an "invention" in the sense that all identity is an invention. In saying a Kiowa is a person with a particular heritage and experiences, Momaday points to something outside the individual as a source of identity. As *Rainy Mountain* shows, stories are neither created nor interpreted in a cultural vacuum, and one cannot create a cultural identity without somehow engaging stories other than one's own. For the reader of *Rainy Mountain* the narrator's conceptual journey provides a model of how to engage the oral, graphic, and critical impulses on the textual continuum. Although the narrative is squarely contextualized within Kiowa oral tradition, history, and the narrator's experiences as a Kiowa, its model of textuality is applicable in other cultural contexts. With its multivoice structure that requires readers to participate in the conceptual journey in order to understand the text, *Rainy Mountain* models one critical methodology that can traverse the divide between oral and graphic discourse. The structure of *Rainy Mountain* makes interpretation a social event. Without the reader's participation in juxtaposing the three voices of the narrative and actively seeking the connections between them, the text will remain fragmented, disjointed, and discursively out of balance. Just as the critical impulse arises out of the particular communicative needs of a community as reflected in the balance between the oral and the graphic impulses, so too does the interpretation of a text. With this radical critical methodological shift, Momaday's reader is implicated in the critical impulse and its social responsibilities. Momaday's view of literature, however, implies that this critical position is necessary if one takes seriously the implications of language.

The text reaches out to the reader in one final, telling way through the illustrations that accompany the narrative. Al Momaday's ten spare, black ink illustrations each occupy a two-page layout. On the first page a few key words from the previous section are repeated, and on the opposite page a drawing references the words. There are drawings of the rock tree, the bear, and the seven sister stars, the cricket encircled by the moon, the tarantula, the water beast, the sky horse, the steel-horned buffalo, the buffalo hunter, the greased buffalo skulls, the horse with an arrow in its neck, an iconic bird, and stars falling from the sky. Beyond their stark, iconic beauty, of particular interest in terms of the critical impulse is that these illustrations are each drawn with reference to images depicted by the immediate, mythical, and historical voices. By depicting images from each of these voices, the text undercuts any privileging of one voice over another in the inspiration of graphic art. The historical voice may inspire just as well as the mythical voice. Symbolically, then, the illustrations provide an artistic parallel to the narrator's immediate voice, commenting on the narrative as a whole through the representation of central natural images.

On a structural and thematic level *Rainy Mountain* demonstrates how a reader committed to a graphocentric view of language may reconceptualize the interpretation of words as a social process in which the individual voice plays a crucial role. As the experience of the narrator shows, the textual engagement of literate people with the modern world owes much to interactions with both graphic texts and oral texts; neither form may be discarded if we are to remain true to our experiences of signification. The challenge that is presented to the narrator and, by extension, the reader is to place the oral and the graphic in conversation with one another by developing the critical impulse from which interpretation arises. When isolated from the graphic voice, the oral and mythic voice ossifies and becomes a static vestige of an obsolete way of knowing the world. Similarly, in isolation from the oral and mythic voice the historical and graphic voice assumes an authority that deigns to explain cultural experience through dates, facts, and explanations of the past. The reader's and listener's interpretation is the only means by which the oral and the graphic may be juxtaposed in a dynamic, critical balance. Interpretation enables the reader and listener to open an "immediate" space in which an individual's voice and experience may find validation as part of the story of tribal experience.

The survival of living culture depends on this development of language, for as Robert Warrior writes, "Language, . . . for Momaday, is much more than words. Language is something out of which humans make their lives, something in which they stand as they fashion their future, and a refuge from the vagaries of the petty politics of the everyday that they inhabit in the modern world" (2005, 172).

History

If, as Warrior argues, language is something with which humans "fashion their future," it is also a tool we may use to refashion the cultural concepts that have shaped our perception of the past. As a living anachronism, the narrator of *Rainy Mountain* understands that the romanticized Kiowa of his colonized imagination are lost to history. To claim a future in which he has an existence as a Kiowa, he must develop a historiographic critique of Western colonial Kiowa history. In delicate shifts in perception he reclaims a Kiowa way of interpreting the past and a living history of which he is a member. In doing so he reestablishes balance between the oral and graphic impulses as they negotiate relationships with the past.

The critical impulse emerges in the intellectual flux the narrator experiences when reflecting on Kiowa oral history, his own accounts of the past, and Western historical accounts of the Kiowa past. The prologue offers a conceptual model in narrative form and a critical key to reading the central narratives of *Rainy Mountain*. In it the narrator conceives Kiowa history in two opposing ways that are both reproduced seamlessly in his immediate voice. The first historical perspective understands the Kiowa through a rise-and-fall model of culture. The nadir of this mode of history, with its smug cultural chauvinism expressed most often in nostalgia for the "Vanishing American," offers a teleological conception of Kiowa history. Describing his own people's decimation as an act of nature, the narrator says, "The end, too, was a struggle, and it was lost. The young Plains culture of the Kiowas withered and died like grass that is burned in the prairie wind" (Momaday 1969, 3). He adopts the rhetoric of evolutionary progress which played a crucial role in supporting the racialist arguments that shaped nineteenth-century U.S. Indian policy. The Kiowa, as "grass," have no agency and are burned away by progress, figured as a "prairie wind" sweeping across the Plains. After reproducing this colonialist myth, the narrative quickly undercuts it.

An alternative way of figuring Kiowa history is an openended process of relating individual and cultural experiences through the imagination; in this way history has a living relationship with the past. When he recognizes that the Kiowa "dared to imagine and determine who they were" and that "man's idea of himself . . . has old and essential being in language," the narrator is expressing the idea that the Kiowa not only had critical agency through their use of language, but that they may continue to have it (4). History did not act upon them; they created their own history. The narrator says of the "whole journey" that is the subject of *The Way to Rainy Mountain*, "Finally, then, the journey recalled is among other things the revelation of one way in which these traditions are conceived, developed, and interfused in the human mind" (4). Anchoring this revised sense of history in the Kiowa concept of the reciprocal relationship between language and imagination, the narrator offers a radical leveling of the ways humans may experience the past: "The imaginative experience and the historical express equally the traditions of man's reality" (4). While this provocative statement is worked through in a performative manner in the central narrative of *Rainy Mountain*, the final paragraph of the prologue offers the reader the initial premises that are necessary to begin to reconceptualize history.

The narrator claims that the journey of the Kiowa "is an evocation of three things in particular: a landscape that is incomparable, a time that is gone forever, and the human spirit, which endures" (4). Culture is forged in the relationships between these "three things," and those relationships may be understood in dramatically different ways. As my discussion of the concept of vision illustrates, the land may be viewed as empty and meaningless or filled with stories and meaningful. The human spirit may endure in isolation or in enlivening relationships, as the acquisition of textuality suggests. The emotions that the narrator identifies as central to the "human spirit" are "wonder and delight," which he references in Ko-sahn's experience of the Sun Dance, an event that is irrevocably of the past: "It was all for Tai-me, you know, and it was a long time ago" (4). Ko-sahn's words signal to both the narrator and the reader that the events of the past cannot be reproduced in the present. Yet what may be recovered is the sense of wonder and delight that shaped the Kiowa as a people. Those emotions, unlike specific ethnographic characteristics, the narrator discovers, are accessible. In coming to terms with what the passage of time means for himself and the Kiowa, the narrator must slowly work through the implications of how that passage is understood in different ways.

In "The Setting Out," "The Going On," and "The Closing

In" portions of *Rainy Mountain* the historical voice is marked by a clear Western historical method. It is decidedly objective and dispassionate in recounting the facts and figures of Kiowa life as it was lived in the nineteenth century: *"In the winter of 1872–73, a fine heraldic tipi was accidentally destroyed by fire"* (45). When it branches off into ethnographic and anthropological studies of the Kiowa, it does so from a distance: *"Tradition has it that the founder of the Ka-itsenko had a dream in which he saw a band of warriors, outfitted after the fashion of the society, being led by a dog"* (21). But even as this voice masquerades as a documentary record of Kiowa life, as a discourse it aspires to dominance and cannot help but exclude and limit other ways of interpreting Kiowa existence, which are exemplified by the mythic voice and the immediate voice. At the same time, the historical voice is also washed over by colonial ideology, which is manifested most clearly in the narrator's initial assumption that Kiowa history has ended; the only sections that speak of events in the twentieth century are those in which the immediate voice has supplanted the historical voice.

The narrator's articulation of a coherent Kiowa history that can account for the historical, mythic, and immediate voices depends on his ability to confront the colonialism that underwrites the dominance of the historical voice. In the prologue the narrator wishes to gloss the era of Kiowa colonization, dismissing their "lost" colonial "struggle": "But these are idle recollections, the mean and ordinary agonies of human history. The interim was a time of great adventure and nobility and fulfillment" (3). Instead of even acknowledging what happened to the Kiowa in their conflicts with the United States the narrator opts to reminisce about the glorious "golden age" of the Kiowa on the pre-contact Plains. At this point in the narrative he is happy to exchange a living history (which belongs to the United States) for a dead, romanticized past. Slowly the foundations of colonial history weaken as the narrator articulates conceptual differences between the Kiowa and their colonizers. Although he is as yet unwilling to state such things clearly, he implies that for the United States warfare was about killing others for gain, whereas "warfare for the Kiowas was preeminently a matter of disposition rather than of survival, and they never understood the grim, unrelenting advance of the U.S. Cavalry" (6). Warfare as a "disposition" implies a privileging of values over ends; it suggests a way of being rather than a drive to conquer. But as the narrator inches toward an understanding of colonialism as an act of aggression, not an act of nature, he repeatedly falls back on the terms of history that colonialism allows.

Once again the narrator waxes nostalgic for the Kiowa past, but when the subject of his reverie is his own grandmother's life his notion of history leads to baffling inconsistencies. Speaking of his grandmother, he says, "Her name was Aho, and she belonged to the last culture to evolve in North America" (6). Does the narrator claim the Kiowa culture that Aho belonged to is in the past, or that it has stopped evolving? His ambivalence about whether history has ended or continues for the Kiowa reflects his ambivalence about the present existence of the Kiowa. If the Kiowa stopped evolving a hundred years ago, where does that leave the narrator? In a similar vein he is quick to make a connection between the near extinction of the buffalo and his fatalistic vision of Kiowa culture and people: "When the wild herds were destroyed, so too was the will of the Kiowa people; there was nothing to sustain them in spirit" (3). In the past tense and passive voice, the phrase "were destroyed" implies that the Kiowa suffered the same fate as the buffalo. At the same time the narrator fails to mention which people it was that virtually exterminated the buffalo. The truth that he must recognize is that he is part of the history of his relatives and that both the Kiowa and the buffalo survived. The irony that he begins to recognize is that for all its desire to appear objective and factual, the historical voice cannot account for forms of history that exist outside of its ideological purview. His fatalistic, romantic vision of the Kiowa past becomes irreconcilable with the facts of his present existence.

Reflecting on his grandmother's experiences of colonialism—knowledge of which exists only in his family—finally enables the narrator to claim that Kiowa history is more than the documentary records suggest. He considers Aho in the context of her ways of knowing the world. She experienced the Sun Dance as a young girl, but the virtual extermination of the buffalo in effect ended the tribe's ability to perform the ritual correctly. When live buffalo were no longer available the people tried to have the Sun Dance with just a buffalo hide. Even then "a company of soldiers rode out from Fort Sill under orders to disperse the tribe" (10). The narrator continues, "Forbidden without cause the essential act of their faith, having seen the wild herds slaughtered and left to rot upon the ground, the Kiowas backed away forever from the medicine tree. That was July 20, 1890, at the great bend of the Washita. My grandmother was there. Without bitterness, and for as long as she lived, she bore a vision of deicide" (10). In stark contrast to his earlier desire to gloss over colonial history and embrace romantic depictions of the Kiowa, the narrator now unites Kiowa history and colonial history. Not only does he make vivid the extermination of the buffalo, but he identifies a specific date on which the United States forbade the Kiowa to practice their religion. This watershed moment of conceptual revision is founded on the narrator's ability to relate to the past through his own family: "My grandmother was there." Pushing both himself and the reader to a deeper understanding of Kiowa beliefs, he offers an almost incomprehensible claim concerning Aho: "Without bitterness, and for as long as she lived, she bore a vision of deicide." As if in recognition of both a "time that is gone forever" and "the human spirit, which endures," the narrator calls attention to the incredible amount of courage and hope it would take to not only bear deicide, but do so without bitterness. What the narrator comes to understand is that Aho used the terms of that very religion to explain its demise. Her "vision" of the death of the Kiowa god explained its end in Kiowa terms. Understood in such a way, Aho retains her agency and does not grant the colonizers the final word in controlling her conceptualization of her world. She resists colonization by explaining it in Kiowa terms.

Rainy Mountain suggests that a people's history begins in their imaginative constructions of their past. History is narrative, and Kiowa history exists first in the imagination's piecing together of events and ideas through storytelling. In interpreting Aho's experiences of colonialism the narrator articulates a Kiowa form of history that may be both factual and reflective of Kiowa cultural experience. This form of history is lived, for it continues to have meaning in a relational context of Kiowa experience and is not in the service of a discourse whose facts concerning an objective past mask a colonial agenda. Accessing the oral impulse in the form of Kiowa oral tradition provides the narrator a means of compensating for and balancing the dominant effects of the graphic impulse, which in this case takes the form of Western colonial history. The narrator's sense of himself as a Kiowa grows along with his intellectual agency; validating his knowledge as Kiowa knowledge, he reinterprets his personal experiences as a part of Kiowa history. He has reconceived himself as a Kiowa and can now speak as a Kiowa through his memories, without recourse to authentication from Western historical texts. History in the Western sense has been transformed into *Kiowa history*, and that sense of history is rooted in a necessary balance between the historical, the mythic, and the immediate voices.

Conclusion

In the epilogue *Rainy Mountain* revisits the stereotypical "Vanishing American" trope with which the text began, but with a revised understanding of the Kiowa that reveals the genocidal absurdity of the image. The representation of this image exists as a sort of test of the reader's newly acquired critical acumen. The narrator frames his intellectual test in a discussion of a meteor shower the Kiowa experienced on November 13, 1833: "It is among the earliest entries in the Kiowa calendars, and it marks the beginning as it were of the historical period in the tribal mind" (85). It was as if, the narrator suggests, history began for the Kiowa, and it was a finite history. He continues, "The falling stars seemed to image the sudden and violent disintegration on an old order" (85). Like the prologue, the epilogue compels the reader to see through the narrator's fatalism to understand the deep sense of cultural continuity and freedom that the Kiowa never surrendered.

After reading the narrative and exploring its transformed concepts, a critical reader is now equipped to see how static definitions, whether of culture or of history, are inconsistent with Kiowa thought. In reproducing this fatalistic vision of culture in the epilogue the text makes us aware of how much we have grown in our perception of Kiowa culture and the critical impulse that enables it to form itself. Thus we are critical of the narrator when he makes statements such as the following: "But indeed the golden age of the Kiowas had been short-lived, ninety or a hundred years, say, from about 1740. The culture would persist for a while in decline, until about 1875, but then it would be gone, and there would be very little material evidence that it had ever been" (85–86). Our capacity to see beyond cultural hegemony has grown to such an extent that we recognize the narrator's understanding of Kiowa culture is incorrect.

It is in this same spirit of the critical impulse that we may interpret the poem "Rainy Mountain Cemetery," which concludes the work, as carrying on the generative processes the text invokes as a whole. Beginning with the line "Most is your name the name of this dark stone," the poem invites us to conflate the death of Aho with the implied loss of Kiowa vitality, figured in the static recording of a name (89). But contrary to its initial appearance, the poem is not morbid, only cognizant of the need to focus on life's processes rather than on the inevitable loss of relationships that are a part of all life.

> Deranged in death, the mind to be inheres
> Forever in the nominal unknown,
> The wake of nothing audible he hears
> Who listens here and now to hear your name. (89)

Like the narrator's own evolving "mind to be," the mind that grasps on to the "nominal unknown" of that which has passed will hear the "wake of nothing audible" at the grave site. Thus the spirit of Aho and her living memory do not exist at the grave, but only the stone, engraved with her name. In the second stanza Momaday invokes the place of Rainy Mountain as that which captures Aho's spirit: "The early sun, red as a hunter's moon, / Runs in the plain. The mountain burns and shines" (89). The sun, the Plains, and the mountains continue, and silence is natural, the "long approach of noon" rather than an absence (89). With the concluding line Momaday signals that it is we humans that impose a sense of finality with the transformation we call death, signified by an unspoken, written name on a grave marker: "And death this cold, black density of stone" (89).

Not only can we use our own minds and perceptions as readers to become better interpreters of the use of language in anticolonial works such as *Rainy Mountain*, but we have become actual anticolonial readers. Seeing through the narrator's implicitly colonialist and fatalistic interpretations, we place ourselves in a subject position predicated on Kiowa concepts. When we resist literary interpretations that depend on concepts of culture that are not amenable to the cultures to which they are applied, we fight for cultural self-determination. As philosophical concepts are the models with which a culture grasps its own freedom, the need for conceptual self-determination is fundamental to not only cultural sovereignty, but political sovereignty as well.

If we critical readers learn something from the narrator's struggle to balance the oral, graphic, and critical impulses of the textual continuum, it may be that, like the narrator, we must implicate ourselves in all the forms of signification and experience we encounter if we hope to sustain the conceptual health of our communities. Only by placing these often contradictory forms into conversation may we develop terms like *vision* and *textuality* and revise concepts like *history*.

By emphasizing the "way" of Kiowa culture as a critical process and rooting that process in cultivated relationships between people, land, the past, and the present, Momaday re-imagines culture as something we endlessly re-create through interpretation, not simply a system of beliefs from the past that we struggle to uphold. The "way" flows through *Rainy Mountain* in many forms: its meandering, episodic style; its recursive movement between the immediate, the historical, and the tribal voices; the reader's voice; its back-and-forth movement between the physical world and the mental world; its negotiation of the relationship between past, present, and future; and its vision of the literal and figural movement of the Kiowa people on their path to the physical and metaphorical Rainy Mountain. A place and an idea, a written story, an oral story, and an interpretation of stories, Rainy Mountain exists in the mind and the body and is accessed through a communally shared method of interpretation, a "way" not only of reading texts and contexts but of reading the world.

3

Trickster Leads the Way

A Reading of Gerald Vizenor's
Bearheart: The Heirship Chronicles

We have occupied this building in the name of the tribes and
the trail of broken treaties, she says, and the government will
answer all of our demands or else we have come here to die
together for freedom. She smiles, proud to hold freedom in
terminal creeds.

Their freedom is your suicide. | Gerald Vizenor, *Bearheart:*
The Heirship Chronicles

The Anishinaabe writer Gerald Vizenor begins his groundbreaking 1978 trickster novel *Darkness in Saint Louis Bearheart*
at the heart of a colonial struggle, during the 1972 takeover
of the Bureau of Indian Affairs building in Washington DC.
In the epigraph above, a dialogue between Songidee Migwan, an American Indian Movement activist, and Saint Louis
Bearheart highlights one irony in the Native American political struggle against the United States. Willingly becoming

a martyr, the AIM activist Songidee would die for a concept of freedom controlled and defined by her relationship to a colonial power. The last stop on the Trail of Broken Treaties, the occupation of the BIA was an event in which Indian people literally and symbolically confronted a technology that had been used to manipulate them from the time of first contact with Europeans: the written word. In *Like a Hurricane: The Indian Movement from Alcatraz to Wounded Knee* Paul Chaat Smith and Robert Allen Warrior discuss the violence the occupiers released upon the BIA building: "The ferocity of the vandalism could not be explained only by the fear of imminent attack. The looting and trashing was so widespread, so deliberate, that it pointed to a hatred on the part of many Indians for the documents because they were documents; records that must be destroyed because of what they and the building that housed them represented" (1996, 162). Both the real-life events that occurred during the BIA takeover in 1972 and the opening pages of Vizenor's novel demonstrate that the treatment of tribal documents is central to our understanding of American Indian culture, politics, and survival. For hundreds of years written discourse—treaties, court rulings, contracts—have been used by Europeans and Americans to whittle away tribal national land holdings and rights. *Bearheart* asserts that this implicit dominance of the graphic impulse has slowly insinuated itself into Native worldviews. When Bearheart states *"The heirship stories are hidden in a metal cabinet with other tribal documents,"* he is claiming that both the liberative and the constraining words have been locked away together. Through his story in the form of a novel-within-a-novel titled "The Heirship Chronicles: Proude Cedarfair and the Cultural Word Wars" he hopes to liberate those who believe in the "terminal creeds" that government documents represent (Vizenor 1990, vii). *Bearheart* functions as a critical intervention in the history of the graphic domination of Native existence, the political bureaucracy and word deceptions of which the BIA building is a symbol. Trickster stories enliven the critical impulse in *Bearheart*, subverting common assumptions regarding Native colonial resistance. When stories and government documents reside in the same space, the novel asserts, there is an imbalance on the textual continuum. *Bearheart* actively seeks to reestablish balance between the oral and graphic impulses.

In his "Letter to the Reader," which precedes the narrative, Vizenor foregrounds *Bearheart* as a story with real-world, political impact. Published at the end of the Red Power era, the novel should be contextualized within this politically charged period and its uncertain outcomes. The "Letter to the Reader" sets the stage for *Bearheart* to be understood as a novel of ideas and introduces neologisms such as "terminal creeds," "word wars," "visions," and "trickeries to heal," all of which are central to the arguments Vizenor poses. The "Letter to the Reader" immediately implicates the reader in the ensuing conversation between Saint Louis Bearheart, "an old man who works in the Heirship Office of the Bureau of Indian Affairs" who has spent ten years writing "The Heirship Chronicles: Proude Cedarfair and the Cultural Word Wars," and the female activist Songidee, who with other members of AIM occupy the BIA building (Velie 1993, 156). The differences in the ways the two experience the world through language and imagination provide a nascent model of Vizenor's conception of "trickster discourse," a method of reimagining the world through liberative language and stories.

The complex point Vizenor makes in the "Letter to the Reader" is that political engagement on behalf of American Indian causes must not supersede or contradict living life informed by the concepts of Native worldviews. These concepts are understood in the context of the critical impulse. Vizenor foregrounds this point by detailing how Bearheart acquired his liberative vision while being abused at a federal boarding school. Focused on teaching Native children trades, the boarding school system was bound tightly to a colonialist definition of American Indians as uncivilized, conquered peoples. Bearheart is given the "heirship chronicles" in a vision and responds, *"Not since the darkness at the federal boarding school and the writing of this book, the heirship chronicles on the wicked road to the fourth world, has the blood and deep voice of the bear moved in me with such power"* (Vizenor 1990, vii). Beaten for resisting assimilation, Bearheart gains his bear spirit and vision in a method that offers an ironic twist on the isolation and darkness required in a traditional vision quest: *"We were pushed and punched, cornered in a narrow closet by the superintendent. We were the heirs he would never tame, and his promotions were measured by our assimilations, our tribal death"* (ix). Taming came not just in the form of corporal punishment, but in forcing Native children to reject tribal belief systems, in which oral tradition is central. Locked in a closet and cut off from home, he and his fellow prisoners subvert colonialism by invoking imagination and spiritual vision: *"We dreamed free from our chains"* (viii). Of course, the boarding school teachers were unable to perceive the oral traditional worldviews secretly embraced by Bearheart and his fellow survivors: *"We survived as crows and bears because we were never known as humans. Those cruel teachers never heard our avian voices, they never roamed with us at the treelines"* (viii). Bearheart's story offers a form of political resistance that is activated by embracing a similar form of the oral impulse.

Bearheart survived the boarding school by imagining himself out of time and place, retreating to his own "interior landscapes," yet he implies that the AIM political activists have succumbed to Western notions of "freedom in terminal creeds," liberation in static beliefs. The activists are wedded to words that owe their definition and power to colonial graphic discourses and have nothing to do with traditional worldviews: *"The aimless children paint hard words on the federal windows in their material wars, and the words are dead, tribal imagination and our trickeries to heal are in ruins"* (ix). Instead of discovering their own means of attaining metaphysical freedom by using their imaginations, Bearheart claims that the AIM activists are "mouth warriors," those who "would be a word bear, [their] religion a word pile" (ix–xii). He prods Songidee to defend her concept of "revolution" in a Native conceptual context:

> We speak for the people, she insists.
>
> Then we must be the enemies of ourselves in the darkness, rushed to hold our praise, our vision in the fourth world. Did the people lock us in this room? (x)

Whereas Songidee considers politics central to her understanding of herself as a Native person, Bearheart refuses to be defined by a conflict with the U.S. government grounded in debates over the written word. Whereas Songidee defines freedom in material terms, according to treaty rights and land claims, Bearheart is concerned with psychic and spiritual freedom accessed through the oral impulse. Bearheart argues that if Native people actually start to believe that their rights and beliefs are necessarily defined in colonial relations through writing, then they have, metaphorically, locked themselves up in the BIA building. In the boarding schools it was the ability to imagine themselves into animals that enabled the children to survive. If we believe that freedom can be attained by a real battle with the federal government, Vizenor implies, we succumb to the colonizer's will. When Bearheart tells Songidee "*Their freedom is your suicide,*" he is stating clearly that martyrdom is not an aspect of psychic trickster survival.

Vizenor's Bearheart offers an alternative politics and invites Songidee and us, the readers, to reimagine tribal reality by interpreting his story and embracing the critical impulse it seeks to enliven. In this novel, a written work of fiction, the oral impulse intervenes in a graphic form: "One word at a time, the heirship documents and bears on the road to the fourth world. Proude Cedarfair, the old shaman, our bearheart on the winter solstice. We are there now, in our own documents" (xiii). In the cryptic fashion typifying Bearheart's mode of decentering the conventions of written language, he personifies the critical impulse in the form of a bear. He claims, "Bears see memories, not our bodies tuned to concepts" (xiii). Whereas concepts describe abstract principles, memories evoke lived experience. Bears embrace experience; humans define it in retrospect. By the end of the "Letter to the Reader" Songidee has been seduced by the raw, generative, healing animal energy of Bearheart. Fittingly it is the joining together of their twin desires for American Indian survival (expressed in twin oral and graphic modes) that conceives the story and brings it into motion: "*She rises, opens the cabinet in the closet, opens the bound manuscript, and reads out loud sections in the heirship documents*" (xiv).

Vizenor's ability to draw on multiple worldviews, epistemologies, and philosophies for his fiction has gained him widespread recognition as one of the most innovative and brilliant American Indian writers. Alan Velie describes *Bearheart* as a "post-modern novel" and places Vizenor in the company of "Jorge Borges, Alain Robbe-Grillet, and Italo Calvino" as well as Kurt Vonnegut, Robert Coover, Donald Barthelme, and Ishmael Reed (1993, 161). According to Kimberly Blaeser in *Gerald Vizenor: Writing in the Oral Tradition*, Vizenor's writing is shaped by "the reader-response theories of such scholars as Wolfgang Iser and Umberto Eco, the explorations of the oral tradition by Walter J. Ong, the language theories of Mikhail Bakhtin and Jacques Derrida, and cultural studies theories such as that of Jean Baudrillard" (1996, 10). This mixing of Western and American Indian sources is intentional. Vizenor hopes to reinvent the way we use and think about language by bringing oral and graphic discourses into contact with one another, in turn enlivening the critical impulse.

Vizenor's work has been particularly influential in American Indian literary studies. Robert Warrior writes that Vizenor's "agonistic invitation to enter the arena of independent thought, self-criticism, and credal uncertainty make his work the most theoretically sophisticated and informed to date" (1995, xviii). Louis Owens claims that as a "trickster, contrary, muckraking political journalist and activist, poet, essayist, novelist, and teacher, Vizenor confronts readers with shape-shifting definitions, inhabiting the wild realm of play within language and seeking, trickster-fashion, to trick and shock us into self-recognition and knowledge" (1998a, 247). Vizenor's usefulness as a writer and critic rests on his unrelenting dedication to subverting the static definitions that limit the possibility of transforming Native lives, among them "Indian" identity, history, oral tradition, literature, criticism, and tribal culture. Using his understanding of Native texts as mediating between the needs of Native and non-Native audiences, James Ruppert claims that Vizenor's "technique is to embed contradictions in the heart of his constructions" (1995, 93). He argues that for Vizenor "contradiction is the essence of oral tradition in its emphasis on variation; its play between text and interpretation, its imaginative freedom, its subversion of absolute definitions of reality, and its ability to guide without demanding" (94). Similarly, Elizabeth Blair states, "When its contraries and contradictions are acknowledged, language is freed to become the stuff of play. In the trickster text, words heal by refusing to take themselves seriously" (1995, 88). Owens sums up the position of Vizenor's supporters: "His poetry, fiction, drama, and critical theory foreground the serious playfulness of the Native trickster, reminding us at all times that indigenous Americans are born out of a timeless tradition of stories that create and re-create the world with each utterance. Vizenor's writing might thus aptly be termed truly re-creational, as the world, in tribal trickster fashion, is born anew or re-created with each word, phrase, and story" (1997, 2). Vizenor's comic approach to literature has serious goals. While he has "consistently argued against nostalgia" as an anchor of Native culture, Elizabeth Blair observes, "he may be suggesting that the appropriate way to retain the values of the past in the midst of the present is through stories like *Bearheart*, which imagine tradition in a modern context" (1995, 79). Ruppert agrees, claiming that Vizenor's aim in *Bearheart* is to offer the reader a "tribal experience of myth, not as an abstract body of stories but as an epistemological structuring of all experience" (1995, 93). Vizenor's blending of oral tradition and postmodern theory has made his work central to American Indian literary studies.

As in American Indian literary studies, politics and history are central in Bearheart. However, the book has been touted as a trickster novel committed to subversion as a principle. Citing Vizenor's use of Derrida and Foucault in his critical work, Blair claims in reference to Bearheart, "In Vizenor's view, one looks for neither meaning nor truth in the postmodern novel" (1995, 75–76). The postmodern novel is a tool of the iconoclastic reader. Echoing this view of Vizenor's work, Alan Velie claims that Bearheart is truly about "play": "As for philosophical and aesthetic depth, Bearheart is as devoid of it as are the works of Barthelme, Reed, and Elkin" (1993, 162). These critical definitions of Bearheart gloss the politics that the text explores by privileging its postmodern aesthetics.

The confusion in understanding the political conversation presented in Bearheart revolves around Vizenor's writing style. Blaeser describes Vizenor's works as "open texts," which "include intentional gaps, paginal and typographical layout, implication through juxtaposition, concreteness and dramatization without generalization (signifiers without signified), a rhetoric of process (writing as if the ideas are only that moment being formed, self-contradiction, tentative statements, stated or implied questions, transgression of literary conventions, self-conscious prose or metafictive techniques, and abandonment of the guise of author/creator" (1996, 35). These techniques Vizenor admittedly borrows from postmodern fiction, but Blaeser proposes that "Vizenor's effort is to write in the oral tradition, to invite or require an imaginative response similar to that required in the oral exchange"

(29–30). She argues that Vizenor's writing "has much in common with the professed philosophies of the reader-response theorists and displays many of the stylistic devices they have noted" (37). If Blaeser is correct, then Vizenor's presentation of different forms of political resistance in the stories of the Proude Cedarfairs is inviting reader response, political debate. Blaeser says Vizenor's "primary goal" in his writing "seems to center on presenting or creating a space of survival" (39). The first "space of survival" is created through dialogue between text and reader; when this conversation is short-circuited by ascribing to *Bearheart* not simply postmodern writing conventions but postmodern politics, this "space of survival" dissolves into simply a space of postmodern play.

In *Bearheart*, his first novel, Vizenor introduces trickster theory and the neologisms that characterize his work. *Bearheart* was originally published in 1978 as *Darkness in Saint Louis Bearheart*. Blaeser observes that *Darkness* "introduced many of the themes, methods, and metaphors that Vizenor would develop in his later works: the spiritual pilgrimage; the political confrontation carried out with wit, not weapons; the challenge of romantic Indian stereotypes; the deliberate transgression of 'polite' sexual limits; the theories on the power, as well as on the misuse, of words; and the use of tribal myths, images of transformation, and dream vision experiences" (1996, 4). In 1990 *Darkness in Saint Louis Bearheart* was republished with a newly added "Letter to the Reader," which encourages the reader to understand the body of the text in different ways. These differences point to Vizenor's evolving understanding of language, politics, and the role of the reader in interpretation.

The "Letter to the Reader" was originally an opening

section titled "Darkness in Saint Louis Bearheart" in the 1978 edition. Whereas the 1990 edition highlights aesthetic issues, the original foregrounds the novel as a political statement. The original version explains what the heirship documents are: "the names of the tribal people who would own the land if the tribal people who have died had owned the land" (Vizenor 1978a, xii). *Darkness* explicitly challenges Songidee's definition of freedom, offering in its stead "freedom from the word." Bearheart tells her, "You have come to a prison, to the cultural center of evil to find your freedom. There is no freedom here in colonial governments. Not even word freedoms" (xv). Excising these political pronouncements, the revised edition purposely omits explanations and overt political pronouncements that would limit a reader's interpretation of the text. Still, the political dialogue that opens *Darkness* remains in *Bearheart*. Twelve years after the text's original publication, Vizenor's stance toward trickster discourse, with its liberative championing of the indeterminacy of language, has become more pronounced. The revised edition resists authorial explanation, opting for a more open text. This embrace of the critical impulse suggests that free interpretation is a necessary aspect of Native political struggle.

Saint Louis Bearheart's story, which makes up the body of *Bearheart*, is itself titled "The Heirship Chronicles: Proude Cedarfair and the Cultural Word Wars." This novel-within-a-novel, Louis Owens states, "is a trickster narrative, a post-apocalyptic allegory of mixedblood pilgrim clowns afoot in a world gone predictably mad": "As the pilgrims move westward toward the vision window at Pueblo Bonito, a place of passage into the fourth world, their journey takes on ironic overtones in a parody not merely of the familiar allegorical pilgrims found in *Canterbury Tales* but more pointedly of the westering pattern of American 'discovery and settlement'" (1998a, 248–49). The unacknowledged leader of the pilgrims is Fourth Proude Cedarfair, "the last in line of the Cedarfairs who refused to leave their ancestral home in northern Minnesota to go to the Red Cedar Reservation, the fictional name of the White Earth Reservation where Vizenor's forebears lived" (Velie 1993, 157). Forced from his home to protect the cedar trees from a vengeful tribal chief and greedy federal agents attracted by his resistance, Proude and his wife, Rosina, set off from Minnesota for New Mexico. They are joined along the way by a surreal cast of mixed-blood and white characters, the "circus pilgrims," whose actions in turn trick the reader into deeper self-awareness.

Every one of the circus pilgrims incarnates some aspect of the traditional Anishinaabe trickster, called Manabozho, Naanabozho, and other names. Like Manabozho the circus pilgrims trick both others and themselves. Proude and Rosina first meet Benito Saint Plumero, or "Bigfoot," whose "oversized" nose, feet, and "glorious uncircumcised" penis, which he has named "president jackson," "should belong to a man ten times his altitude" (Vizenor 1990, 38). Mirroring the overreaching and highly sexual characteristics of the trickster, Bigfoot joins Proude and Rosina on their pilgrimage. Other mixed-blood tricksters join the group, each adding their own brand of trickster subversion: Zebulon Matchi Makwa, "a talking writer and drunken urban shaman"(49); Scintilla Shruggles, "a new model pioneer woman" (67); Belladonna Darwin-Winter Catcher, a mixed-blood daughter of a white journalist and a Lakota holy man; Bishop Omax Parasimo, a renegade priest; Inawa Biwide, Bishop Parasimo's sixteen-year-old assistant; Lillith Mae Farrier, "the child hater and mistress of two boxers," who had taught on the White Earth Reservation (78); "Sun Bear Sun, the three hundred pound seven foot son of the utopian tribal organizer, Sun Bear" (78); Little Big Mouse, "a small whitewoman with fresh water blue eyes," who is carried by Sun Bear Sun in "foot holsters attached to his waist" (78); Justice Pardone Cozener, "one of the new tribal bigbellies," an "illiterate law school graduate" who was one of "those overpaid tribal officials who fattened themselves overeating on expense accounts from conference to conference" (78); Doctor Wilde Coxwain, Justice Pardone Cozener's lover and the tribal historian, who "directed tribal studies programs at several universities before the government stopped funding the education of radicals and idealistic separatists" (78); and Pio Wissakodewinini, "the parawoman mixedblood mammoth clown," whose sentence for rape was that he have a sex change and who subsequently sought a "special tribal herb" to bring back the "woman dreams and voices" that had been lost when his prescriptions for female hormones could no longer be filled. Add to the raucous mix a shaman dog named Pure Gumption and a trickster dog named Private Jones, and one may see why James Ruppert writes, "*Bearheart* does not exactly place us in a mythic world; rather it places us between myth and reality" (1995, 96). Instead of defining just what exactly is a shaman dog and a "parawoman," Vizenor lets readers come to their own conclusions. *Bearheart* makes certain that readers do not privilege socially acceptable Western concepts of reality, and initiates this reenvisioning of what is considered real by portraying a Western world "which has exhausted its petroleum, its soul" (Owens 1998a, 249).

Bearheart offers an apocalyptic, visionary perspective on

what happens when the structures that uphold mainstream American culture crumble: "Electrical power generating plants closed down. Cities were gasless and dark. Economic power had become the religion of the nation; when it failed people turned to their own violence and bizarre terminal creeds for comfort and meaning. New families were made from aberrations" (Vizenor 1990, 23). Vizenor envisions a landscape no longer occupied by machines running on fossil fuels, but by roving bands of genetic mutants, superstitious vigilante mobs walking along the interstates: "Mile after mile in the hot sun there were more cripples and bizarre creatures walking and sitting in the road" (145). Vizenor argues that reality itself is maintained by a stable politics, economics, and cultural machine (149). Without an economy and a media promoting a consumer reality, Americans are left to envision their own, unique realities: "Dressed in strange clothing of phantoms and angels and dreams the cripples walked little and seldom spoke" (145). He portrays people literally falling apart, as in the case of the "hlastic haces," whose faces have rotted off from skin cancer (149). Having surrendered the responsibility of creating their own realities, Euro-Americans lack experiential knowledge of ethics, morality, and values. In their stead the Americans in *Bearheart* reconstruct American culture as a disturbing palimpsest of values and ethics drawn from memories of popular cultural images and referents. In a last-ditch effort to re-create the American, Vizenor portrays Euro-Americans westering across the dead landscapes of Middle America.

Vizenor offers examples of how America's ethics have gone to ruin. In the chapter titled "Last Attraction," a reference to Larry McMurtry's 1966 novel and Peter Bogdanovich's film

The Last Picture Show (1971), the pilgrims stop in Big Walker, a city "named in honor of the founder, Thomas Barlow Walker, a true antisalooner and capitalist treekiller who in good conscience raped the cedar and red pine on virgin woodland reservations" (53). Although the town is in ruins, the movie theater "which had served the fantasies of the hard drinking whitetown for three generations was unharmed" (53). The theater shows a western: "The last attraction was a film about ceremonial violence and death, starring a cast of evil whitefamilies convicted for the ritualistic murder of tribal people" (53). Vizenor portends the allure of reality television in America, explaining that the movie itself was a reenactment of a real event: "The members of the evil families were released on parole to the film producers through an arrangement with correctional authorities. It was a new effort to raise funds for treatment when the public and conservative legislatures became more punitive about corrections. The public did not mind the cost of admission to a motion picture about ritual violence, supporting the power of entertainment, but would not approve an increase in taxes for treatment of violent people and their victims" (53). Vizenor presents a genealogy of how destructive ethical and moral systems get passed on in American culture, and how these beliefs become a part of government and mainstream society. Greed is preserved through stringent economic policy, violence is upheld as noble, and profits are made off both the incarcerated and those who are victims of violence. The entertainment industry sensationalizes violence, and those who commit violence become an essential part of society. The pilgrims abandon their car as a horde of "whitepeople" literally tear the vehicle to pieces, beating one another to get close to that symbol of American progress: "Whitepeople were fighting with each other for control of the wheel" (56).

With such pointed critiques *Bearheart* assumes a strong political position. In fact Owens describes *Bearheart* as a moral work: "Unarguably the most radical and startling of American Indian novels, *Darkness in Saint Louis Bearheart* is paradoxically also among the most traditional of novels by Indian authors, a narrative deeply in the trickster tradition, insisting upon values of community versus individuality, upon syncretic and dynamic values versus the cultural suicide inherent in stasis, upon the most delicate of harmonies between humanity and the world we inhabit, and upon our ultimate responsibility for that world" (1992, 230). But how can a trickster novel "insist upon" anything? How can a trickster novel, which is wedded to contradiction and subversion, posit a political position? Owens attempts to find in Vizenor's novel a stable footing on which to make his point, claiming that the "trickster shows by negative example the necessity for humanity to control and order our world" (235). He continues, excising "order" as a category from the society in which it is created, "Through language, stories that assert orders rather than order upon the chaos of experience, a coherent, adaptive, and syncretic human identity is possible without the 'terminal' state of stasis" (235). However, Owens's argument that trickster stories may "assert orders rather than order" does not truly solve the problem of definition this concept inherently presents; whether existing as one or a million, an "order" creates boundaries.

In abstracting the trickster's existence and his methods of trickery from the Native communities that the trickster supports, scholars have neglected to emphasize that the goal of trickery, as an expression of the critical impulse, is the survivance of the group. Owens claims that Vizenor's neologism "terminal creeds" and his use of trickster discourse highlight the apparent impasse between the trickster's role as a subverter and his role as a defender of tribal values. Trickster discourse is "never nihilistic," Owens insists: "It is the utopian impulse that guides Vizenor's mythic parodies, a quest for liberation from the entropic forces that attempt to deny full realization of human possibilities" (1992, 227). Vizenor finds his model of "utopian potential in American Indian mythologies; and in trickster—who overturns all laws, governments, social conventions—Vizenor finds his imaginative weapon" (227). Wedded to subversion, trickster discourse is supposed to liberate psychic energies that will ultimately nurture communal values. Owens speaks to this apparent contradiction in *Bearheart*:

> *Bearheart* seems to embody dialectically opposed conceptions of chance, or random event. On one hand, a deconstruction of "terminal creeds," in trickster fashion, represents an insistence upon the infinite proliferation of possibility, including the polysemous text. This is the kind of celebration so common to postmodern literature and theory, an insistence that "coherent representation and action are either repressive or illusionary," and a reveling in what we might call chance. On the other hand, a mere capitulation to chance, or random event, would deny the emphasis upon our ultimate responsibility for ordering and sustaining the world we inhabit that is central to Native American ecosystemic cultures. (234)

Owens's "key to reconciling, or at least containing, this apparent dialectic" is no answer at all, but simply a reiteration of the trickster's desire to constantly contradict and subvert language: "Trickster ceaselessly dismantles those imaginative constructions that limit human possibility and freedom, allowing signifier and signified to participate in a process of 'continually breaking apart and re-attaching in new combinations'" (235). In other words, the trickster offers nothing but critique. It is inconsistent to at once claim, with Barbara Babcock, that "through his trickery, that is, his negations and violations of custom, he [the trickster] condemns himself to contingency and unpredictability," and at the same time claim this chaos is generative and nurturing (1985, 162). However, when trickster discourse is conceptualized as an expression of the critical impulse, this contradiction resolves itself. Trickster subversion serves a larger purpose in balancing oral and graphic discourses.

James Ruppert claims that the broader effects of trickster discourse are reached through the transformation of the reader as he or she interprets the text. Ruppert argues that *Bearheart* is not committed to total subversion. Although Vizenor's goal is to subvert through trickery, this aesthetic position is "not, however, an attempt to avoid claims to absolute truth or uncontested meaning" (1995, 94). Though subversion is an essential facet of the trickster's being, it may not be so for the reader who witnesses his actions. In *Bearheart* the critical reader inevitably creates meaning. Ruppert theorizes Vizenor's concept of meaning making as "mythic verism": "To follow Vizenor's mythic restructuring is to explore the discourse as contradiction, as a concordance of voices, and to abandon verisimilitude and facts for a new narrative realism that is more than a reflection of what we think to be natural" (99). In what can be described as Vizenor's conception of epistemology, Ruppert claims that a "mythic perception" is set in opposition to "terminal creeds," which "cannot be overcome with confrontation by other more accurate representation, but rather with discourse, with conversation, with countering privileged representations with other representations, some of which might also claim absolute truth" (99). Both the readers of Vizenor's texts and his characters, according to Ruppert, "must remain 'between.' They must waver and continue to transform" (99). In this transformative space the reader directly engages the critical impulse of the text.

Bearheart invites the reader to play a central role in the interpretive process the novel requires. Owens writes, "As conversation and discourse, the novel shifts meaning production away from terminal creeds of an author, with their one-dimensional allegories and privileged representations, and onto a reader who has many perspectives" (1992, 103). Blaeser claims that Vizenor's attempt to decenter his texts is a hallmark of his writings: "Over and over again, in every quarter of his work, Vizenor calls for these simple interrelated essentials of writing and life: liberation, imagination, play, and discourse. His writing seeks to function as both the presentation of an idea and as an invitation to discover where that idea might lead, an invitation to engage in a dialogue" (1996, 4). Blaeser and Owens are correct about Vizenor's goal of engaging the critical impulses of his readers, and for this reason it is all the more ironic that much of the political symbolism crucial to an understanding of Bearheart, one of the most well-known works of Native fiction, has rarely been discussed. The political history of the four generations of Proude Cedarfairs and the trickster strategies they use to retain control of their cedar nation provide models of political resistance. Bearheart makes a political claim for trickster subversion and defines the ethical limits of subversion on the textual continuum within a political and historical context.

History and Politics in *Bearheart*

Considering the political "Letter to the Reader," it is fascinating to note that scholars have not analyzed the opening chapters of "The Heirship Chronicles: Proude Cedarfair and the Cultural Word Wars" for their investigation of history and politics. The first six chapters are instrumental in contextualizing the structure of *Bearheart* as a whole, offering a political history of the Cedarfairs and their struggle to preserve their homeland "cedar nation," as well as a nascent definition of the political values and methodologies of trickster discourse. Vizenor's text imaginatively places the Cedarfairs' trickster politics in a history of American Indian political relationships that is all too familiar, with threats by outside forces who are concerned just as much with attacking one's worldview as taking one's land. In portraying a history of struggle and in modeling how trickery is used as a weapon against colonialism, Vizenor's text shows how trickster discursive strategies may help defend generative, life-sustaining values by acting as a technique to expose ideologies and beliefs that are anathema to tribal change and survival.

In "Morning Prelude," the first chapter of Saint Louis Bearheart's manuscript, the reader is introduced to Fourth Proude Cedarfair, Vizenor's model of a person who lives within a tribal trickster consciousness. Vizenor introduces Proude with a thick tribal metaphor: "Proude Cedarfair is a ceremonial bear" (1990, 5). Proude does not simply mimic or act like a "ceremonial bear," but *is* one, while at the same time being a human. According to Nora Barry, Vizenor's associating both Saint Louis Bearheart and Proude Cedarfair with the bear makes a direct link between his characters and the sacred and important figure of the bear in the Midewiwin initiation rituals of the Ojibwa (1993, 18). A. LaVonne Brown Ruoff claims that Vizenor's conception of animals, in particular the bear, comes from an understanding that they have their own language, society, and life that mirror those of humans (1993, 44). Proude is an inherently liminal character, occupying the categories of bear and man at the same time, and thus should be recognized as a shape-shifting trickster.

"Morning Prelude" offers a portrait of life in the "cedarfair circus," Proude's woodland home, before the way of life he and his ancestors have cultivated is violently upset by the outside world. Proude "determines his thoughts from morning dreams and moves through the trees in whispers" (Vizenor 1990, 5). His break from normative Western concepts of reality does not stop with blurring the boundaries between the dream world and the waking world. His conception of the four worlds, Ruoff claims, is based on a combination of "the emergence and migration myths of Southwestern tribes with the flood myths of the Algonkin-speaking tribes" (1993, 44), but undoubtedly draws on Vizenor's own unique conceptions as well.

In mythic fashion "Morning Prelude" gives a synopsis of the journey to come, beginning with an explanation of the changes that have come to the four mythic worlds that define Proude Cedarfair's cosmology:

> The earth turtles emerge from the great flood of the first world. In the second world the earth is alive in the

magical voices and ceremonial words of birds and the healing energies of plants. The white otter is the carrier of animal dreams in the new hearts of humans. The third world turns evil with contempt for living and fear of death. Solemn figures are slashed open on the faces of tribal dream drums. In the fourth world evil spirits are outwitted in the secret languages of animals and birds. Bears and crows choose the new singers. The crows crow in their blackness. Ha ha ha haaaa the bears call from the sunrise. (Vizenor 1990, 5)

Like Aho in *The Way to Rainy Mountain*, Proude refuses to accept the Western concept of progress. His conceptualization of the decline of the "third world," the one we humans live on, is explained by his own mythology. He does not point the blame for the third world's turn to evil at a race, an economic system, or a politics, but at a stance toward both life and death. Proude's existence as a "ceremonial bear" shows he is between worlds, neither completely outside of the ills of the third world nor yet completely in the fourth world, and as such is a worthy model of trickster existence. "Morning Prelude" explains Proude's quest in images that defy chronology; he "dreams in sudden moods and soars through stone windows on the solstice sunrise" (5). It is as if Proude's journey has already been completed and he has already passed through the solstice window at Pueblo Bonito, New Mexico, traveling into the fourth world. These dreams foreshadow his journey and eventual passage into the fourth world.

Vizenor's depiction of Proude does more than challenge normative Western conceptions of reality; it foregrounds the strengths of one worldview just as it will be challenged by yet another worldview. Having dreamed of traveling through the solstice window, "the last old man of the cedar nation stops at the tender center of the *migis* sandridge which parts the sensuous mouth of the *misisibi* from the lake like a mythic smile" (5–6). Proude's conception of his world is rooted in both a place—the headwaters of the sacred Mississippi—and his and his forefathers' history with that place: "He chants ha ha ha haaaa then walks into the silent water as his fathers have done for more than a thousand new tribal moons from the same sacred place" (6). As a trickster Proude encounters the world with the laughter of bears, but his liminality as a trickster does not prevent him from having a place of origin.

Bearheart begins by historicizing the relationship between the Cedarfairs and their "cedar nation," their home among the "sacred cedar trees." The first line in the next chapter, "Cedar Celebrants," is "Four Proude Cedarfairs have celebrated the sacred cedar trees" (7). The next five chapters present a history of the struggle between each Proude Cedarfair and those who would separate the Cedarfair family from their home. Although Fourth Proude Cedarfair may travel freely in space and time, Vizenor's depiction of the history of the Cedarfairs is deeply chronological, and for good reason. In showing how each Proude Cedarfair combated colonialism using trickery, Vizenor offers a political agency to his characters supported by a history of struggle.

The Cedarfairs have always placed themselves apart from all forms of colonial society, whether it was with their fellow Anishinaabe or with non-Native people, and clearly align themselves with the trickster's liminal social position. Vizenor writes of First Proude, "The first refused [the missionaries'] religion and would not remove himself from the fair cedar wood to the grim reservation" (7). From this first description of the Cedarfairs Vizenor's text weaves together trickster subversion and radical politics. By subverting the colonialist institutions of Christianity and federal reservations by his willful nonparticipation in them, refusing to leave the "sacred cedar trees," First Proude uses trickery to sustain his freedom. *Bearheart* creates a history of political subversion, with each of the four generations of Proude Cedarfairs facing new threats: "Three Proude Cedarfairs have defended their sovereign circle from national and state and tribal governments, from missionaries, treekillers and evil tribal leaders. Seven sons have died defending the sacred nation. One son in each generation has survived to protect the dominion of natural cedar" (7). The "sacred nation" the Cedarfairs have sustained is a trickster nation, one that exists outside both the U.S. national and state governments as well as tribal governments, which Vizenor characterizes as coercive. And yet their willingness to die in protecting the cedar nation shows that the way of living they protect is as valuable as life itself.

The political resistance of First Proude and Second Proude is morally and ethically grounded. First Proude's trickery upholds freedom and the rights of the cedar trees; Second Proude's militant resistance upholds the same values using an alternative and, ultimately, self-defeating method of resistance. *Bearheart* clearly is presenting a genealogy of Native political resistance, one that is complicated by its presentation of the benefits and detriments of each strategy.

Vizenor explains that the Cedarfairs defend the cedar trees because they are spiritually united. In offering this explanation he removes questions of treaty and property rights, with their objectification of land as a thing rather than a living ecosystem, and makes the struggle for the cedars a struggle for the Cedarfairs' existence. Vizenor states that for First Proude, "cedar became his source of personal power. He dreamed trees and leaned in the wind with the cedar" (7). The Cedarfairs and the cedar become one being, and they claim sovereignty over their "circle" of trees as they claim their own freedom: "'We are the cedar,' he [First Proude] told his sons. 'We cannot leave ourselves. . . . We are the breath and voice of the woodland'" (7). It is clear that First Proude Cedarfair justifies his defense of the "sacred nation" as a defense of self and family.

First Proude Cedarfair combats the "federal officials" who come to cut down the cedars and send the Cedarfairs to the reservation by utilizing his transformative trickster power. He explains to the officials why they cannot take the cedars: "This is our sovereign nation. These trees are the families of the earth here. . . . You will not mark them for death. . . . You will not cut them down" (8). When the officials ignore his words and attempt to take him by force, Proude uses trickery to protect both himself and the cedars:

> "Seize that man," ordered the federal official. His hand trembled as he pointed and yelled. "Seize that goddamn black savage. . . ."
>
> Proude drew a deep breath and exhaled in a slow whistle. Then he raised his head high like an animal scenting his enemies on the wind, expanded his chest and growled with the great power of the bears. The sound was deep and wild. The federal official and the detachment turned and ran from the cedar circle.
>
> First Proude tumbled into the water laughing. The clown crows crowed and circled overhead. He plunged

his head beneath the water and growled again in his bear voice. The crows crowed and laughed. He squatted just over the river and farted into the surface water. The crows laughed. (8–9)

When Proude breathes deeply and exhales "in a slow whistle" he is invoking the trickster spirit of Manabozho, whose father is the wind and whose power is often associated with the blowing wind (Barry 1993, 18). Proude becomes a "ceremonial bear" and scares off the officials. But the key to this passage is that Proude laughs at both himself and the officials, subverting the apparent power the officials grant him in their fear. Farting into the sacred misisibi is Proude's way of undercutting his bear power, and whistling out of the opposite end of his body is his trickster reminder to not take himself too seriously. The crows, living barometers of life-renewing trickery, laugh appreciatively.

Significantly, the passage does not posit a complete epistemological break between Proude and the officials. A lone surveyor is not afraid of Proude, but laughs uncontrollably, "rolling back in the coarse shore grass," and says to Proude, "You must be a clown bear" (9). Proude answers with an affirming fart, and "the surveyor told him he wanted to share his courage and defend his sovereign cedar nation" (9). Trickery, this episode shows, does not divide people arbitrarily on the grounds of race, but on their worldview and their ability to see through the trick to the life-affirming values trickery defends. In telling the reader that the surveyor joined the Cedarfairs in the "cedar war," was captured, and "was shot nine times in the back, three in the head and impaled on a cedar stake facing the circus," Vizenor highlights the racial divides that have impaired intercultural solidarity. Those who defend tribal nations and worldviews are subject to violent retribution by dominant colonial forces (9).

Vizenor's clear characterization of Proude as justified in his defense of the cedar nation calls into question the definition of the trickster as amoral. Proude does preserve himself and the cedars by confusing and frightening the federal officials by crossing species boundaries and growling in a bear voice, but what he protects is defined as antinomian only by the societies that threaten it. The Cedarfairs live a harmonious life sustained by a mythic understanding of good and evil in balance. In this understanding, that which is good conforms to nature and is free and life-affirming; that which is evil unnaturally restrains life and is violent and destructive. Proude resists all those who would control him, and this subversion brings an attack:

> Tribal leaders on the new federal reservation surrounding the circus, coveted the power of the cedar and the man who spoke and acted from his heart. Proude told the leaders that he would recognize no government but his own, no nation but the cedar, and no families but his own blood. We are sovereign from all tribal and religious and national governments, he told the leaders, and we will listen to nothing more about the future. That settles that, said the old tribal leaders, but his words were misunderstood and his sovereign circus was misrepresented as a selfish possession. (10)

In a bitter irony that clearly reveals the danger of trickster discourse, Proude's assertion of freedom is refigured as selfishness by those who would control him. Vizenor writes, "The

warriors of evil, the religious oppressors, the leaders from tribal fears, envied places of peace and personal power. Proude
contradicted their blackhearted energies. He and other families exposed the evil of tribal governments and taught people
to control themselves and not to fear the political witching
of shamans from the evil underworld and *tchibai* island" (10).
Proude's way of life offers freedom from moral dogma, but
that freedom, even in critical definitions of the trickster, is
misinterpreted as wholly subversive by those who ally themselves with systems of power that maintain power by dominating others. The Cedarfairs' dedication to simply protecting
the autonomy of the cedar circus and one another undercuts
this relativistic understanding of the trickster.

Each Proude Cedarfair spends his life defending the cedar
circus, and *Bearheart* historicizes their conflicts with the United States and the tribal government that claims the circus.
The methods each Proude Cedarfair uses to defend the cedar
circus vary in style and effectiveness. Although an "evil tribal
fisherman" murders First Proude, "split[ting] his chest open
with an axe," his death is not figured as a failure. His blood
blends with the cedar water of the *misisibi* and "in his dreams
his lungs filled until his chest burst beneath the water of the
great salt seas" (11). Second Proude, "burdened with the image
of his brave father," becomes alcoholic and takes as his example of defense the strategies he learned in the First World
War (11–12). Meanwhile "men of evil and tribal fools were
propped up in reservation offices to authorize the exploita-
tion of native lands and natural resources. The cedar nation
and all the sovereign circuses surrounding the cedar wood
resisted all government controls, federal and tribal" (12). Second Proude quits drinking but does not follow the example of

the trickster; instead he attempts to fight evil with destructive violence by heading a militant band of circuses:

WARNING
Declaration of War
Against Evil
Oppressive and Putrescent Officials
Federal and Tribal Governments (13)

Vizenor writes, "Second Proude has won his war, he had fought in the word wars of the whiteman and for the sacred dominion in the cedar tree" (14). In his use of an alternative strategy, one that flies in the face of the trickster's nonaggressive subversions of power, Second Proude has been influenced by the First World War, another "word war" that had nothing to do with the cedar circus. While the "circus candidates were elected and controlled the reservation government for the next two decades," Second Proude's victory cannot stave off subsequent attacks on the sovereignty of the cedar nation. The ultimate futility of his method of resistance is clear. As an old man he walks to "Wounded Knee in South Dakota where the American Indian Movement had declared a new pantribal political nation" (14). Upon his arrival he is stopped by a "tribal government policeman," who shoots him "in the face and chest with a shotgun" as he sings "in the deep voice of bears" (14). Violent resistance, Vizenor argues, cannot fight colonial ideologies that have been adopted by tribal people themselves.

Slowly circling back to the method of survival through trickery that First Proude used, Third Proude Cedarfair becomes a "warrior diplomat" who learns from the errors of his father: "He abhorred violence more than evil and corruption" (14–15).

Instead he uses wit and trickery as political weapons: "'Evil men,' he once told his children, 'can be outwitted but never eliminated. . . . Listen to the sinister sounds from tchibai island. . . . The ghosts of evil men who have died through violence indict the living for their revenge'" (15). Third Proude breaks free from the oppositional politics of his father, which ended in death, and focuses on trying to live well. "'Peace has no revenge but trickeries,' he tells his daughters. 'Beliefs and traditions are not greater than the love of living'" (15). Third Proude "avoid[s] conflicts," lives a peaceful life, and dies a natural death.

But as Vizenor shows in his portrayal of Fourth Proude Cedarfair, conflict is sometimes unavoidable, and in those instances a nondestructive method of defense must be used, one that is nonviolent but also proactive. As Blaeser states, "That space of survival may be more imaginative than physical" (1996, 39). Fourth Proude Cedarfair models this method of imaginative survival. Like his father, "Fourth Proude saw his cedar nation existing in the minds and hearts of the living, he did not feel he needed to prove the endurance of sovereignties" (15). Like Saint Louis Bearheart, who admonishes Songidee about her reification of sovereignty granted by a colonial power, Fourth Proude Cedarfair understands the cedar nation as something lived through experience. He refuses to define the cedar nation with documents and "avoid[s] word wars and terminal creeds" (15). At the same time he is practical: "[He] convinced himself that through political and religious interdependence he could protect the sovereign nation as well as did his diplomatic father who abhorred human violence" (15). Fourth Proude strategically uses a public persona to defend the cedar nation, "honor[ing] those politicians

who respected the cedar nation and avoid[ing] direct con-
tacts with evil tribal leaders" while upholding the cedar circus's "image of independence" by invoking its independent
political status as "recognized by several governments" (15).
In an emblematic case of trickster irony, Fourth Proude, his
wife, Rosina, and the clown crows that ever shadow him are
compelled to leave the cedar circus not by federal forces, but
ultimately by the corruption of tribal officials.

Vizenor's model of how the sovereignty of an independent nation is lost involves a complex convergence of forces.
These forces culminate in a distancing between experience
and reality through the dominance of the graphic impulse and
its effects on language and institutions of power. In Vizenor's
postapocalyptic vision, federal forces once again rob Native
nations of natural resources. Federal agents come bearing a
written "executive order" which they claim justifies seizure of
the cedar circus for firewood. They read from their authority-
granting document, but Proude tells "them to stop speaking
like machines." "I will not listen to you speaking as an institution," he adds (25–26). He calls on tradition and experience
for his defense of the cedar nation: "Our families have lived
in this circus with these cedar trees for more than a hundred
years. . . . When you speak as individuals in the language of
your dreams I will listen, but I will not listen to that foolish
green paper talking to me" (26). When his invocation of tradition and experience does not persuade the agents, Proude
resorts to trickery. He brings the agents back into a relationship with their bodies and themselves as humans, a necessity for them to feel sympathy for the cedar circus. He forces
the agents to recognize that they are not simply instruments
of the government, but flesh and bone. He asks the female

federal agent, "Do you fuck with words?" (28). Even though she "turned deep red with embarrassment and rage," Proude's words conjure up lustful emotions, and the two federal agents give in to their sexual passion. After a night of sex in the cedar circus the female federal agent wakes to a new appreciation of the Cedarfairs' life in the circus: "She finished, in silent thought, her official report, never mentioning the existence of the cedar trees" (30). Proude's trickery compels the agent to spare the cedar nation from the federal government's energy needs.

Vizenor foregrounds the cedar nation's conflict with the tribal government that lays claim to it as, at heart, a crisis of worldview represented by their different relationships with words and experience. Though the "federal humanoids" no longer threaten the cedar nation, the vengeful tribal chief, Jordan Coward, is still a menace to its survival. Vizenor writes, "Tribal religions were becoming more ritualistic but without visions," implying that the participation in ritual carried more meaning than living a worldview. Instead of defending the tribe from the federal government, "Coward attached the cedar nation to meet the demands of the government" (23). Unable to control his destructive emotions, "Coward, possessed by evil revenge, dreamed of the cedar nation being cut into little sticks and burned in the federal offices of the bureau of public remorse" (23). The source of Coward's vengeance is never explained in terms other than his perception of the cedar nation as "shunn[ing] his evil energies" (25). As the trickster nation resists his power, Coward wishes to destroy that which he cannot control, a will to dominance that is anathema to the critical impulse.

Proude, Rosina, and the clown crows leave the circus to

protect the trees, but they maintain both their worldview and their connection to the cedar. Like the narrator in *The Way to Rainy Mountain*, who can leave that place and retain his way of perceiving the world, Proude carries the cedar trees with him in memory. Upon their decision to leave Rosina states, "I am prepared to leave this cedar circus and the distance between our memories" (31). Although their being exists in their relationship with the cedars, Proude and Rosina realize that the only way to defend both themselves and the cedars is to leave the circus. Even the federal agent realizes that Jordan Coward is "punishing the cedar for the values of men" (29). Proude knows that the trees are not threatening to Coward; Coward is threatened by the Cedarfairs' generative relationship with the cedar forest. He says, "[Coward] will not harm us. If we are gone he will have no use for these trees" (28). Because Coward's vengeance is attached to Proude, his fleeing the cedars saves the circus, but because Proude is leaving his place of "personal power," his home, his own existence is threatened.

By focusing on Proude's trickster ideas one may lose sight of Vizenor's attempt to place Proude and Rosina's story in a pan-Indian historical context. Proude and Rosina's experience of being "removed" from their tribal homelands was and is a very real historical experience for nearly all American Indian nations. By necessitating that Proude, Rosina, and the clown crows leave the circus, heading west toward the vision window at Pueblo Bonito, New Mexico, Vizenor enables *Bearheart*'s narrative to focus on trickster strategies of psychic and physical survival. Once this fact is recognized, the remainder of the narrative can be evaluated according to the usefulness of the anticolonial political strategies that *Bearheart* offers performatively. James Ruppert is correct in asserting that readers approach *Bearheart* with an "expectation of literary realism" and that it is Vizenor's goal to "establish a representation of mythic awareness dynamic enough to excite meaning and yet static enough for the audience to recognize novelistic conventions, even if such conventions are in the process of being subverted" (1995, 93). Vizenor's unique style comes from his belief that "any representation of the mythic falsifies it since its essence is fluid" (93). And yet his work must find a balance between contradiction or subversion and structure or static representation (93). Ruppert argues that *Bearheart* presents myth as epistemology: "For Vizenor, myth's essential role in Native survival is more than a set of laws or coded set of instructions. It is at the very heart of how to think, how to imagine: it is the essence of world view" (96). Mythic stories embody the critical impulse, and so the engagement with myth may also be the source of a strong political defense. Proude, Rosina, and the circus pilgrims must survive a world thrown hopelessly out of balance by life-draining technologies and controlling institutions. They find their source of power, disconnected from a relationship with a specific place, in the mythic traveler Manabozho.

Four generations of Proude Cedarfairs struggle with federal, state, and even tribal governments because of anger over the cedar nation's existence outside these discrete realms of power. The Cedarfairs themselves are not exempt from the alluring power of force and violence, as Second Proude's militancy shows, but in coming full circle back to the trickster politics of First Proude, Fourth Proude Cedarfair shows that trickster methods of defense offer the best hope for survival in a dangerous world. Even at the cost of his beloved cedar circus, Fourth Proude continues to live by moving on, which is perhaps the trickster's strongest characteristic (Babcock 1985, 162). Vizenor's text justifies the Cedarfairs' defense of their cedar nation by invoking the values of liberation and freedom. Above all else the call to be free, to be able to create relationships with other humans and nonhumans, and to sustain evolving relationships with places defines the goal of trickster politics and is an expression of the critical impulse.

Terminal Creeds and Vizenor's Ethical Gamble

If trickster subversion is to protect Native communities as it protects Proude, Rosina, and the circus pilgrims, it needs to be figured clearly in understandable terms. Critics claim that Vizenor's neologism "terminal creeds" is the linchpin to his theory of trickster subversion. As this term is first explored in *Bearheart* and has become central in many of Vizenor's other texts, it warrants a careful analysis. When Fourth Proude Cedarfair gambles with the mythical Anishinaabe Evil Gambler, depicted as Sir Cecil Staples, he does not defeat Sir Cecil by embracing a relativistic worldview that sees all values as destructive terminal creeds. Instead he offers a generative, life-sustaining, and adaptable trickster ethics rooted in communal experience. Proude beats the Evil Gambler at his game of chance by embracing the personal agency that the critical impulse both nurtures and demands.

Third Proude's assertion that "beliefs and traditions are not greater than the love of living" may be the overall message of *Bearheart* (15), but there is a difficulty in his claim: Just how should one live? Critics of *Bearheart* have explored Vizenor's neologism "terminal creeds" in an attempt to explain the ethical conundrum the novel presents. Owens argues, "'Terminal creeds' in *Bearheart* are beliefs which seek to fix, to impose static definitions upon the world. . . . Such attempts to fix meaning according to what Vizenor terms 'static standards' are destructive, suicidal, even when the definitions appear to arise out of revered tradition" (1992, 231). Using this concept, critics have argued that the novel levels all moral and ethical claims: "The liberation of language and consciousness is Vizenor/trickster's aim" (226). As Owens suggests, words themselves can become static, leading Vizenor to embrace an "open," "postmodern" style. However, in steadfastly arguing that *Bearheart* is completely subversive of normative ethical claims and, at the same time, "never nihilistic," critics such as Owens contradict themselves (227). Can trickster subversion justifiably subvert the value of freedom itself? What values does *Bearheart*'s trickster discourse propose in order to avoid nihilism? Contrary to what critics have argued, absolute subversion and absolute freedom and anarchy are not valued within the ethical system Vizenor's text theorizes. *Bearheart* lays out a clear ethical theory that finds its ideal expression in a concept of freedom that values life. Absolute forms of subversion and freedom are ultimately destructive of life. Fourth Proude's contest with Sir Cecil Staples shows that absolute freedom itself may become a terminal creed, and that as an expression of the critical impulse trickster discourse is dependent on constantly theorizing our ethical place in the world.

Although the four chapters of *Bearheart* that present Fourth Proude's outwitting of the Evil Gambler are, as Nora Barry claims, "narratively and philosophically at the center of Vizenor's text" (1993, 16), Owens has derived his interpretation of terminal creeds from a later chapter, titled "Terminal Creeds at Orion." In that chapter the circus pilgrims are given shelter and food by a group of postapocalyptic settlers who call themselves "hunters" and "breeders" and survive by questioning terminal creeds: "Depersonalize the word in the world of terminal believers and we can all share the good side of humor in our own places.... Terminal believers must be changed or driven from our dreams.... Until then we will continue our mission against terminal creeds wherever and whenever we find them" (Vizenor 1990, 193). The philosophy of the hunters and breeders is akin to Vizenor's trickster conception of language as indeterminate: "The perfect hunter turns on himself.... He lives on the edge of his own meaning and humor.... The humor is in the contradictions of the hunter being close and distant at the same time, being the hunter and hunted at the same time, being the questioner and the questioned and the answer. The believer and the disbeliever at the same moment of mental awareness" (193). The hunters and breeders supposedly support no value but critique. However, they violently enforce their law against terminal creeds. When they catch Belladonna Darwin-Winter Catcher espousing terminal creeds concerning her Native identity, they murder her by feeding her a poisoned cookie.

Teasing out logical discrepancies, the hunters and breeders identify Belladonna's mistake in thinking her values are "exclusive" to her "mixedblood race" (194). When asked to define her difference from a white man, Belladonna states, "I am different than a whiteman because of my values and my blood is different.... I would not be white" (194). Owens sees Belladonna as a believer in static concepts and argues that she is "the most obvious victim of [believing in] terminal creeds," "defin[ing] herself as 'Indian' to the exclusion of her mixedblood ancestry and, more fatally, to the exclusion of change" (1992, 232). If the hunters and breeders had simply shocked Belladonna into a self-awareness of the contradictions that inform her identity, they would be partaking in the trickster tradition. Instead they justify her murder for her belief in terminal creeds: "Speaking as a romantic invention indeed, a reductionist definition of being that would deny possibilities of the life-giving change and adaptation at the center of traditional tribal identity, Belladonna is further caught up in contradictions and dead ends" (233). It is true that in many Native origin myths "men and women share responsibility for the creation and care of the world," and by "defin[ing] herself and all Indians according to predetermined, authority-laded values, Belladonna has forsaken such responsibility" (234). Still, Belladonna draws on her experiences as an "Indian" to define "Indianness," an impossible task to which the hunters and breeders have clearly set her up to fail. In their relativistic worldview any general definition of identity that goes beyond personal experience is automatically a failure, as there are bound to be exclusions in such a definition. An argument for the justification of her death might claim that as a believer in terminal creeds Belladonna was already psychically, if not physically, dead. But this justification rings hollow.

This discourse concerning terminal creeds is complicated by the fact that the hunters and breeders who condemn Belladonna are themselves guilty of believing in terminal creeds. They insist on a worldview exclusive of terminal creeds, which are figured as truth claims. Though they pose as extreme epistemological relativists, they reject any claims to value as a means of defending their own terminal beliefs. They go beyond condemning Belladonna and actually accuse all tribes of whining about suffering colonialism: "The histories of tribal cultures have been terminal creeds and narcissistic revisionism. . . . If the tribes had more humor and less false pride then the families would not have collapsed under so little pressure from the whiteman. . . . Show me a solid culture that disintegrates under the plow and the saw" (Vizenor 1990, 198). The hunters and breeders show their own terminal creeds, figuring colonialism as "progress" and invoking manifest destiny as the "plow and saw." They do not acknowledge the use of colonial violence.

The concept of terminal creeds must be understood in relation to the tribal values it serves to defend. James H. Cox argues, "Terminal creeds are those beliefs that terminate plots, foreclose on human possibility, and serve the will to dominate by imposing inflexible and exclusionary definitions on people and cultures" (2006, 109). Still, the extreme relativism of the hunters and breeders should not be the model for understanding terminal creeds. In fact, their unthinking lethal belief in their static definition of terminal creeds expresses the antithesis of Vizenor's concept. Whereas they empower terminal creeds as a method of iconoclastic critique of knowledge, they do so only to eschew any challenge to their static definitions of history, culture, and their own beliefs. In the chapters of *Bearheart* in which Fourth Proude Cedarfair gambles with the Evil Gambler, terminal creeds are juxtaposed with nurturing beliefs and experiences. Although it is important for Proude to identify the Evil Gambler's terminal creeds, this identification alone cannot defeat the gambler. The challenging of terminal creeds is a necessary tool of culture creation and revitalization, but it is not its own end. Proude boldly asserts his own nurturing beliefs in order to defeat the Gambler's conception of evil.

Bearheart's exploration of the tribal metaphor of gambling proposes a complicated cross-cultural philosophical conflict. As a representation of the mythic Evil Gambler and of the ills of the modern world, Sir Cecil refers to multiple realities. Likewise, Proude's act of gambling with Sir Cecil comments on his engagement with Anishinaabe myth and the collapse of the postindustrial world. Gambling in *Bearheart* "provides a means to theorize about the role traditional belief systems might play in resisting, if not defeating, the demands of a colonial occupation" (Pasquaretta 1996, 21). Gambling's central concept is "chance," and the way the circus pilgrims, Proude, and Sir Cecil understand chance determines the way they engage the world and whether or not they will survive the Evil Gambler's game.

Like the hunters and breeders, it would at first appear that Sir Cecil Staples, Vizenor's version of the Anishinaabe Evil Gambler, is a figure whose goal is to subvert all institutions and values. Paul Pasquaretta observes that Sir Cecil represents Nita Ataged, a *wiindigo* spirit who is a "destroyer," whereas Proude represents Manabozho, the trickster and creator of Anishinaabe myth (1996, 23). A postapocalyptic confidence man, Sir Cecil advertises his business on a large sign at the edge of the town of What Cheer, Iowa:

SIR CECIL STAPLES

The Monarch of Unleaded Gasoline

and

The Mixedblood Horde of Mercenaries

Presenting

LIVING OR DYING FOR GASOLINE

Gamble for Five Gallons

NEW TRAPS AND OLD TORTURES
Follow the Rows of Abandoned Cars to the Altar Trailers
OPEN FOR BUSINESS (Vizenor 1990, 103)

Blending the modern with the mythic, Vizenor figures gambling as a business in which, in a tautology, one lives or dies for gasoline. However, Sir Cecil has attracted "hundreds" of gamblers who have wagered their lives and lost not simply because they need gasoline in a world that has run out of it, but because they desire the freedom that gasoline represents. Vizenor portrays Sir Cecil as being shaped by the freedom of gasoline, having literally been raised on the interstates, living in his kidnapping mother's eighteen-wheeler. His destructive freedom was cultivated by his mother:

> She said we should feel no guilt, ignore the expectations of others and practice to perfection whatever you choose to do in the world. She believed that people should do things that gave them pleasure. As it turned out killing gave me a whole lot of pleasure then. . . . My business has been to bring people to their death. Like an artist I practiced the various means of suffocating people. Later I was attracted to traps and poisons . . . secrets and surprises on the road to death. (126)

However, Sir Cecil is no longer as enamored of killing: "Death does not thrill me as it once did" (126). The problem, he points out in a humorous section of social commentary, is "that thin plastic film known as social control hanging over the savage urge to kill was dissolved when the government failed and the economic world collapsed" (126). When killing each other became the norm, everyday people infringed upon Sir Cecil's turf: "Death was too simple then. No struggle between good and evil when the good power has failed. . . . What does it mean to know evil power when love and the power to do good has died in the hands of indifferent bureaucrats?" (127). With the world hopelessly out of balance, the Evil Gambler has fallen on boring times; this is why he is excited by the arrival of the circus pilgrims.

Vizenor makes clear that Sir Cecil Staples as the Evil Gambler and Proude Cedarfair as Manabozho are gambling for not only their own fates, but the fate of tribal peoples. The circus pilgrims are confronted by Sir Cecil's version of Cerberus, a group of "three mixedbloods, dressed in diverse combinations of tribal vestments and martial uniforms, bangles and ideological power patches and armbands" (103). Having "furrows of ignorance and intolerance stretched across their unwashed foreheads," the violent mercenaries are disarmed by the circus pilgrims. The mercenaries explain that they have suffered injustices, which have shaped them into killers, necrophiliacs, and respecters of evil. The mercenaries are clearly marked as being of the same mold as Songidee Migwan in the "Letter to the Reader." Their "promotional hierograms of cultural suicide" include uniforms of "beads and plastic bone and chicken feathers" (104). Violent and self-pitying, they have capitulated to the destroyer, the Evil Gambler. Wearing their "chicken feathers," they have conceived themselves as victims and have channeled their anger into killing and intimidating, destructive acts that Vizenor's tricksters abhor.

Sir Cecil Staples plays the ancient Anishinaabe dish game in which the winner and loser are determined by the way they conceive the concept of chance. Two players toss a dish containing four figures representing "the four ages of man," and the winner of each of four rounds is determined by how many of the figures are still standing when the dish is slammed down. The game is about life and death, the standing and the fallen, and the way human beings understand this dichotomy. The mixed-blood mercenaries view themselves as victims; they allow their histories of colonial oppression to turn their worldviews destructive, thereby granting epistemological power to their oppressors. In addition, the circus pilgrims show their frailty by even choosing to gamble for gas. They think chance is a benign concept, choosing Lillith Mae Farrier as their gambler by chance, even though Proude makes a crucial observation. "Nothing is chance," he says. "There is no chance in chance. . . . Chances are terminal creeds" (110–11). Proude figures chance as an "attempt to avoid the fear of death," adding, "We must fear the living to leave so much death to chance" (112). In arguing against the use of the concept of chance Proude argues against a fatalistic view of life in which one may consciously or unconsciously give up personal responsibility for what happens to oneself by capitulating to a destructive force outside oneself.

Bearheart argues that people lose their agency when they fail to be personally responsible for the way they live their lives. Lillith Mae Farrier loses the dish game with Sir Cecil because she gives up her sense of agency and believes in "luck and chance and being a good gambler" (116). Playing the dish game is a metaphor for living life, and Lillith Mae "did not know the rituals of spiritual balance and power" necessary to realize that there is no chance in life, no need to arbitrarily grant power to potentially destructive forces that exist outside oneself. Chance is not inherently good or bad; one may win or lose a game of chance. But believing in chance does take away agency from the gambler, and in doing so takes away our right to control our fate as best we can within the natural forces of the universe. Even the Evil Gambler is aware of how debilitating the concept of chance is; as he says, "Fools believe in luck" (118). If chance is a terminal creed, a static belief in a teleology whose final cause is outside oneself, how does one beat the Evil Gambler at his game? What is the alternative to chance?

Proude beats Sir Cecil at the dish game by denying a belief not only in chance, but in the Manichaean concept of good and evil in which Sir Cecil wishes to constrain him. In a brilliant intellectual exchange Proude shows that the malignancy the Evil Gambler represents is conquered not by violence and destruction, but by out-reasoning him or, as in the title of the chapter in which their exchange takes place, "outwitting the Evil Gambler." Wit is figured not simply as clever and entertaining language, but as intellectual acumen. James H. Cox notes, "To avoid capture by texts, the pilgrims must reject these terminal creeds and terminal storytelling traditions. . . . By continuously hinting at an imaginative space that cannot be translated into language, Vizenor reinforces the idea that texts in non-Native storytelling traditions cannot capture some fundamental aspects of the human and specifically Native world" (2006, 109). But while Cox maintains that Vizenor's *Bearheart* asks readers to embrace a "paralinguistic" world outside of language as a means of "seek[ing] their own liberation from those written words that place boundaries on human, cultural, and spiritual possibilities" (109), Proude's exchange with Sir Cecil shows that liberation must be fought for within the context of the interpretation of language. Sir Cecil tells the horrific story of his upbringing to Inawa Biwide as if it could justify his actions. Inawa Biwide responds with a myth about an "evil stranger" whose "lust for revenge and death" leads him to kill himself (Vizenor 1990, 129). Inawa Biwide's myth, arising out of the oral impulse, counters Sir Cecil's modern, graphic impulse rationalization of his actions in a much stronger way than any sociological argument could make. There is no rational, objective justification for violence and destruction, Inawa Biwide argues. The story of the evil stranger foregrounds the ethical debate that ensues between Proude and Sir Cecil and highlights Sir Cecil's false reasoning.

Proude outwits Sir Cecil by changing the very terms of their discussion. Sir Cecil believes he and Proude represent polar opposites. He recognizes that Proude has life-affirming power, telling him, "The pilgrims wanted gasoline which is a part of the game, but you want to balance the world between good and evil. . . . Your game is not a simple game of death. You would change minds and histories and reverse the unusual control of evil power" (130). Perhaps more clearly than anywhere else in *Bearheart* this passage suggests that a worldview is more important to survival than material possessions or technology. Sir Cecil correctly recognizes that Proude's goal is political, and that in confronting the "evil power" that Sir Cecil embodies Proude is modeling a method of political and spiritual resistance. In *Bearheart* the political and the spiritual are intertwined, as "histories" have been under "the unusual control of evil power."

Proude allows Sir Cecil to believe that their powers oppose one another as if in balance, and it is his subversion of this duality that allows him to beat the Evil Gambler. As they begin to play the dish game Sir Cecil takes a moment to reflect on what he sees as his and Proude's necessary cosmological roles: "At the end, the end of all games, when we both have the power to balance the world and raise the four directions, we will find a new game because we are after all bound to chance. . . . Evil will still be the winner because nothing changes when good and evil are tied in a strange balance" (131). As though seeing two sides of a coin, Sir Cecil sees good and evil as "tied in a strange balance," and this thought comforts him. After his first turn with the dish the "four figures were upright and rigid," standing in four directions as they should be, and his initial success compels him to further ruminate, asking Proude, "What holds our power together over these directions? What holds us together in this game mister proud? . . . What holds us to believe the rules of our own games?" (131). This view of good and evil as opposites proposes a worldview locked in a static balance reminiscent of the way the oral and graphic impulses have been polarized. Proude draws on the critical impulse and cuts through the binary oppositions through which Sir Cecil draws his power.

Embodying the trickster strategies of Manabozho, Proude lures Sir Cecil into a false sense of cosmological security, only to undercut his claims. He plays into Sir Cecil's cosmology by answering his question as he knows the Evil Gambler would like him to: "Places in opposition" (131). Sir Cecil tells Proude, "We are equals at this game of good and evil mister proud. Nothing is lost between equals" (132). At this point Proude reveals his agency in this game of intellectual gambling that the Evil Gambler wishes to rule with deterministic chance. Proude grounds his understanding of the critical impulse and balance on the textual continuum within an ethical, social dynamic:

"But we are not equals," Proude responded. "We are not bound in common experiences. . . . We do not share a common vision. Your values and language come from evil. Your power is adverse to living. Your culture is death."

"And so we are equal opposites."

"Death is not the opposite of living, but you are the opposite of living. . . . Your evil is malignant. The energies to live are never malignant." (132)

In this short exchange Proude both undermines Sir Cecil's argument and proposes a grounding for a trickster ethics. Rather than simply subverting Sir Cecil's opposition as a terminal creed, he subverts the conceptualizing of good and evil as opposites and proposes experience as the grounds for binding people together. Sir Cecil proposes an abstract understanding of forces in which good and evil are essentially asocial and disembodied, bereft of any experiential element necessary to their being felt by humans. In the place of this static conception of life, a true terminal creed, Proude draws on the communal critical impulse and asserts that a "common vision," "values and language" are what ultimately bind people together, not polarity.

Sir Cecil attempts to reestablish his position by claiming that he and Proude, the Evil Gambler and Manabozho, are "equal opposites," but Proude subverts his argument by claiming, "Death is not the opposite of living" (132). Sir Cecil would like to divide the universe into the living and the dead, but Proude rejects this division. Death is a necessary part of life, and by calling Sir Cecil "malignant" Proude sets him outside the forces of life, which include death. He undermines Sir Cecil's false reasoning and shows that his abstract conception of good and evil is a terminal creed that serves only to justi-fy his "malignant" power.

In a telling example of the way *Bearheart* links politics and terminal creeds, Sir Cecil falls back on a fatalistic descrip-tion of the U.S. government's coercive power over believers in terminal creeds as a way of undercutting his own intel-lectual defeat. He implies that although Proude may have won the dish game, people will not stop believing in good and evil, as exemplified by their political "faith": "What hap-pens between us when the game ends is what happened to the government when the political games were exposed . . . nothing! Nothing but the loss of faith among gambling fools. Nothing but chance. Fools and the games with their fanta-sies that living is more than death and evil is less than good-ness. . . . Winning is losing" (132). Sir Cecil claims that faith in any authority outside of oneself is a terminal creed, and that faith cannot be undermined; therefore to win is to lose. He argues that people resist owning their agency, preferring to have faith in an authority outside themselves. Even when the authority does not fulfill what it promises, the Evil Gam-bler argues, a people's dedication to the terminal creed of faith does not weaken.

Proude wins the dish game for humanity by revealing the terminal creed in Sir Cecil's worldview, showing that the concept of chance on which the power of the Evil Gambler depends is itself illusory, built on a nonexistent opposition between good and evil. In their final tosses of the dish Proude invokes the trickster Manabozho and makes a "teasing whistle on the wind," toppling the figures in Sir Cecil's dish. Proude tosses the dish "seven times in succession," and "each time the four figures were standing in the direction of their color and place in the good world," showing that Proude's method of playing the dish game, a representation of life, is not determined by chance. His final pronouncement summarizes his ethics: "Good is an ordeal, evil is not" (133). The act of achieving the good is a struggle, a test of endurance, and an intellectual challenge; it is difficult to strive for the good, but easy to be evil.

Proude's victory over Sir Cecil puts a finer point on the concept of terminal creeds as it is used in *Bearheart*. As a whole, the text supports the subversion of those beliefs that impose static definitions on the world, but that ethical stand does not prevent *Bearheart* from proposing an alternative ethics, one that is flexible, communal, and experiential. *Bearheart* shows how trickster discourse, an expression of the critical impulse, undercuts dominant discourses as a means of keeping oral and graphic forms of discourse in a dynamic balance. Before his game with Sir Cecil, Proude traveled "backward into the sun and flew with the crows back to the misisibi and migis sandridge," his ancestral home, and it is from his experiences with that place that he draws his trickster strength: "He soared underwater through the colors of the families in the universe ha ha ha haaaa with the whales and bears and sacred crows" (121). Proude has strength as a clown bear and uses it to outwit Sir Cecil by finding the terminal creeds on which his philosophy is based.

Conclusion

Bearheart places a high value on trickster ethics as a means to resist colonialism and the ravages of a postindustrial world become ecologically malignant. The development of the generations of Proude Cedarfairs in *Bearheart* proposes that knowing one's history and the politics involved in that history is a necessary step in resisting forces that impose terminal creeds and limit our freedom to express ourselves as individuals, communities, and nations. The Cedarfairs embody the critical impulse, counteracting an apocalyptic world by embracing and interpreting their visionary, oral, and historical experiences. *Bearheart* does not propose a relativist approach as the answer to colonialism, as that strategy would commit those who are colonized to the graphic terminal creeds created by institutions and governments. Instead the text encourages us to theorize how an alternative worldview, such as Fourth Proude Cedarfair's, may enable us to avoid the destructive political, intellectual, and ethical pitfalls that may lead us to destroy each other and the world. Accessing the critical impulse through trickster subversions and an engagement with the world, we can undermine those people and institutions that define freedom by their free ability to control others with words. In turn we may uncover new methods of balancing our own uses of language in relation to the creative forces of life.

4

Transforming "Eventuality"

The Aesthetics of a Tribal "Word-Collector"
in Ray A. Young Bear's Black Eagle Child
and Remnants of the First Earth

> In these few hours before the fiery orange sun ascends the
> wooded terrain, replacing the foggy shroud with clear daylight,
> it seems as if this place, my home, is momentarily surround-
> ed by the wide, sweeping waters of an invisible ocean called
> eventuality. | Ray A. Young Bear, *Remnants of the First Earth*

In the preface to *Remnants of the First Earth* the character Edgar
Bearchild creatively blends Black Eagle Child mythology with
his unique perceptions of his homeland to describe the way the
Black Eagle Child settlement looks before daybreak. Bearchild,
Ray A. Young Bear's fictionalized alter ego, is a citizen of Black
Eagle Child, itself modeled on Young Bear's Meskwaki Tribal
Settlement in central Iowa. Created from "remnants of a pre-
vious earth" taken from the "claws of the muskrat who dove
into the great body of water to retrieve mud," the current world,

according to Black Eagle Child myth, was built on an endless body of water (Young Bear 1992, 150). But in his depiction of fog over the central Iowa hills, Edgar's words offer more than a reference to how the world was created. In fact, he embellishes tradition by naming those waters both in the past and in their current, "invisible" incarnation: "eventuality."

In *Black Eagle Child: The Facepaint Narratives* (1992) and *Remnants of the First Earth* (1996) "eventuality" is a name Edgar gives a Black Eagle Child cosmological process in which time is cyclical, events reoccur, and worlds are created and destroyed in ever diminishing replications. As Edgar's grandmother, Ada Principal Bear, states, "We were here, after all, as a reflection of other events and past lives. We merely reenacted this constant battle of right and wrong, a promise kept and transgressions committed. We who are but Remnants of the First Earth" (1996, 111). "Eventuality" names a destiny of destruction that humanity may only partially engage through prophecy, predicting what will happen by noting what has already once occurred. Edgar describes the traditional purpose of the Black Eagle Child people: "This, according to my limited knowledge, was the original wish of Bear King, the Settlement's founder: to find a sanctuary where generation upon generation would flourish and maintain the customs that would forever identify them as Black Eagle Child" (x). Eventuality, however, undercuts this idyllic hope. In the past eventuality arose "in different forms; the early versions brought forth war, disease, famine, and undreamt-of atrocities" (1992, 32). It finds its contemporary incarnation, however, through what Edgar terms "forgetfulness," the loss of not only what has been remembered, but of the capacity to remember. Because of colonialism, modernity, and its main vehicle of epistemological change,

Western education, the Black Eagle Child people have nearly lost their capacity to hold cultural memory in their bodies. Edgar politicizes "forgetfulness" as an effect of colonialism, stating, "[Those who] so connivingly and viciously sought to make us forget ourselves by subjugating us, the Euro-Americans, would be the root cause [of the ultimate destruction of the Black Eagle Child people]" (xii).

The most effective tool for creating cultural forgetfulness is writing, that seductive means of displacing memory from the body onto an external form. At the same time, writing is most often used as a means of preserving cultural knowledge threatened by forgetfulness. The paradox is that by privileging writing in the preservation of cultural memory, the process of destroying the capacity to maintain memory in the body is further diminished. The oral, graphic, and critical impulses are out of balance, and one method by which the dominance of the graphic impulse may be subverted is by employing forms of writing that draw on the oral impulse of community engagement in order to reinvigorate the critical impulse.

As a culturally traditional Black Eagle Child citizen who has been taught by his grandmother his people's Principal Religion, Edgar initially embraces eventuality as a means of living according to Black Eagle Child cultural precepts. In the course of his development as an artist who takes inspiration not just from Black Eagle Child tradition but from American popular culture as well, Edgar realizes that eventuality must be transformed, as it leaves no room for human agency and creative responses to cultural change. As a means of preserving tradition, tradition has been codified, but in the process it has nearly been killed. Rebelling against the static notions of cultural tradition that he has been taught, Edgar uses self-reflective creative writing to embark on a "Journey of Words," which leads him to create a Black Eagle Child literary aesthetic that can accommodate both tradition and change. To reestablish cultural memory he does not attempt to reinvigorate oral tradition, but instead seeks to make writing speak to the needs of the Black Eagle Child community. Edgar's "Journey of Words" uncovers both the roots of his artistic apprehensions and the critical impulse that may allow his writing to respond to the needs of his community. Writing enables him to analyze how and to what end his interpretive apparatuses have been shaped. In this lonely quest ventured over many years, writing itself is a subject of Edgar's investigation, a form of language that temporarily distances him from his community but which in turn affords him the critical distance needed for self-understanding.

Both *Black Eagle Child: The Facepaint Narratives* and *Remnants of the First Earth* combine elements of biography (as the Library of Congress classifies *Black Eagle Child*) and fiction (as it classifies *Remnants of the First Earth*). Existing somewhere on the border between fiction and reality, the texts embody a conceptual tension whose structure mirrors Edgar Bearchild's own epistemological dilemma. Both books interweave similar traditional stories, tribal history, and fictional accounts told through the eyes of Edgar Bearchild and other characters. The only notable stylistic difference between the two texts is that *Black Eagle Child* is written in prose verse, each page divided into unbroken columns, its typographical control and rhythm revealing a poet's deep regard for language. *Black Eagle Child* and *Remnants of the First Earth* are best understood using LeAnne Howe's concept of the genre of "tribalography":

"Native stories by Native authors, no matter what form they take—novel, poem, drama, memoir, film, or history—seem to pull together all the elements of the storyteller's tribe, meaning people, the land, multiple characters, and all their manifestations and revelations, and connect these in past, present, and future milieus" (2008, 330). As a tribalography, both texts may be read together, each focusing on Edgar Bearchild's growth as an artist but from different perspectives shaped by his relationships with key friends and mentors.

Young Bear's tribalography continues in his poetry, for which he is best known. His three volumes of poetry, *Winter of the Salamander* (1980), *The Invisible Musician* (1990), and *The Rock Island Hiking Club* (2001) have contributed to the critical image of his writing as brilliant but obtuse. His work has earned the praise of numerous Native writers, including Sherman Alexie, who states, "I'm not exaggerating when I tell you that Ray Young Bear is the best poet in Indian Country and in the top 46 in the whole dang world" (Young Bear 2001, back cover). Although he began publishing in the late 1960s and was included in Geary Hobson's groundbreaking collection, *The Remembered Earth* (1979), Young Bear's writings are not well known outside literary circles. A crucial reason for this is that, unlike his contemporaries Joy Harjo, Simon Ortiz, and Leslie Silko, after 1980 Young Bear quite suddenly dropped out of the literary scene. In *Black Eagle Child: The Facepaint Narratives* and *Remnants of the First Earth* Young Bear signals his return in two prose works. Elizabeth Cook-Lynn praises *Black Eagle Child*: "For the first time, we encounter an articulate, bilingual, tribal Phaedrus wrestling with his imperfect life vis-à-vis his own value system without the intervention of a Christian monitor or omniscient literary interpreter, and it is an inspiring event" (1996, 17). Robert Dale Parker praises *Black Eagle Child* for "integrating cultural exposition with poetic narrative, at times almost like a novel," claiming, "In all his books Young Bear pursues something like a Euro-American surrealism while also writing more thoroughly from within a Native culture than any other Native American literary writer that I know of" (2003, 101–2). The complex mix of American popular culture, Meskwaki oral traditions, and allusions to canonical Western literature make Young Bear, as Parker claims, "a writer who remains almost unwritten about, daunting to read and teach, and much of whose poetry is out of print" (103).

Young Bear's critical reception reflects the aesthetic differences between him, his supporters, and his critics, such as James Ruppert, who notes that reviewers of *Winter of the Salamander* disagreed about whether or not his poems "worked," claiming that Young Bear's use of images "do not develop out of the poem, that seen from one pole of perception the images do not develop out of that perspective, but seem to be dropped in and then abandoned" (1982, 8). In fact, Young Bear's images usually arise out of his Meskwaki cultural context, a "pole of perception" that critics unfamiliar with Meskwaki cultural symbols are at a loss to understand (8–9). Through the character of Edgar Bearchild, Young Bear addresses his critics' claim that his work does not provide the conceptual tools they need to fully understand it. Speaking to his fellow poetry students at the University of Iowa, Edgar "questioned if anyone had the background knowledge of [his] tribe to see that mythical complexities superseded line structure and rhythm" (Young Bear 1996, 260). He explores the meaning of Black Eagle Child myths within an evolving Black Eagle Child cultural context. Careful not to divulge intimate and sacred tribal knowledge and symbols, and thus to be labeled an "informant," Edgar "cho[se] less intimate symbols for [his] poetry": "Even in my naïveté I knew enough to incorporate misleading themes" (124). He summarizes his position: "Later, literary critics would classify my cryptic work as the 'most puzzling' among the pantheon of emerging or established tribal-affiliated writers. It would bother me that these self-appointed critics of Native American literature would overlook circumspection as the light source that refracted, rearranged, and hid me for reasons pertaining to safety. Essays were published to that regard: that I was one confusing mother" (124). Young Bear's decision to withhold knowledge is grounded in a long-standing Meskwaki stance of cultural preservation through isolationism. He summarizes the implications of his position: "Circumspection is the paradigm of harmony" (1992, 255). *Black Eagle Child* and *Remnants of the First Earth* refuse to explain a tribal metaphysical system for outsiders. Instead they explore the ways Edgar negotiates competing cultural epistemologies within a contemporary context.

Edgar's education into both Black Eagle Child cosmology and the art of writing begins with transcribing his grandmother's Black Eagle Child words into "the Six Grandfathers' Journals," the "twenty-two dusty notebooks, ledgers, and deerhide boxes of rolled parchment" of which Grandmother was the caretaker. These sacred texts were written by the "O ki ma wa ki, or Sacred Chieftains," of whom Edgar is a direct descendant (1996, 74). According to Black Eagle Child belief, the Sacred Chieftains had "living divinity status," and because "writing was deemed too powerful for most people" the Sacred Chieftains were responsible for the "'word-collecting' task"

(74). Edgar's "introduction to Black Eagle Child society and the general workings of the greater world" instills in him an animistic worldview in which the universe is made up of opposing forces, both natural and supernatural (19). These forces are in constant tension and have profound effects on human lives. A chronicle of tribal events dating back to the early 1800s, the Six Grandfathers' Journals contain ominous prophecies concerning the demise of the Black Eagle Child people in a world made hopelessly out of balance through religious negligence. Edgar says, "The passages that most intrigued Grandmother—and later myself—were those that confirmed how we would succumb to the vices of the greater world around us" (76). Although this fate was preventable, as "instructions were given to the Sacred Chieftains on how to prevent this cultural atrophy," Grandmother would insist that prophecy, the "manifestation of undeniable truth, . . . in its rawest form was fatalistic" (76). She describes the world as "a wicked amalgamation of modernity, eventuality, and social change" (87). Within this matrix there is little hope for the future, especially since the imposing of "suzerainty" upon Black Eagle Child, when their tribal "beliefs were granted one hundred / more years to flourish and another / one hundred to subside" (1992, 48).

The reason the world is wicked and the prophecies are fatalistic is because, as both Edgar and his grandmother cannot deny, the Black Eagle Child world has changed. For all of Grandmother's cultural conservatism, her work with the Six Grandfathers' Journals is itself a capitulation to modernity. Faced with the prospect of losing their traditions, the people of Black Eagle Child created the Journals as a means of recording their oral history and religious prophecy in the graphic mode of the Black Eagle Child language in Roman alphabetic script. By graphically recording Black Eagle Child oral tradition, Edgar codifies in the Journals the oral impulse and creates a textual imbalance. This attempt to preserve cultural heritage by actively repudiating cross-cultural contact inevitably leads to a weakening of the critical impulse and the community's ability to create and account for both tradition and the need to adapt to a changing world.

As a scribal "word-collector" whose life had been "prearranged" for the task, Edgar takes on an interpretive role that is not creative, but prescriptive. He is not to actively create with language, but to search for signs that what has been prophesied in the Six Grandfathers' Journals is coming to fruition: "'We are looking for prophecy in its early stages,' Grandmother would forewarn. 'It is all around us. The people themselves, those who reside here with us, are the initial messengers. By their actions we are witnessing the beginnings of what had been said would happen by our grandparents and theirs before'" (1996, 74). Understanding that human beings are largely powerless in this cosmic scheme, Edgar concludes, "Our main purpose, the way I finally perceived it, aside from maintaining ceremonies, was to keep the prophecies of world demise from occurring or at least make note of them" (111).

Understood in the context of balance on the textual continuum, Edgar's embrace of creative writing is a logical outcome of the discursive imbalance Grandmother wills him as a word-collector. In creative writing Edgar finds the interpretive agency that Grandmother's form of divination denied him. She teaches him that time is cyclical, the world is unchanging, and his role as a word-collector is to witness the manifestation of prophecy. But as a modern Black Eagle Child citizen and participant in American life, he experiences the world as changing in dramatic ways from the life described in the Six Grandfathers' Journals. Edgar's capacity to write creatively itself captures this paradox, as language is used artistically to create new meanings with old words. He says, "I became so adept at taking notes that I began jotting down my own observations that had nothing to do with our impoverished plight, like 'drinking the orange skylight' from a Ne-Hi pop bottle" (1996, 19). Aesthetics, however, affect conceptual notions such as selfhood, creativity, and history. Acutely aware of the relationship between writing and cultural survival, Edgar recognizes the epistemological rift his engagement with a foreign cultural conception of art creates in his relationships with the Black Eagle Child community, which is only exacerbated by his relationship with Western education.

In most ways Edgar's Black Eagle Child education and Euro-American education are in conflict. One worldview is animistic, the other mechanistic; one is founded in the Principal Religion, the other owes allegiance to Christianity; one is conducted in the Black Eagle Child language, the other enforces the use of English. What potentially unites these conflicting ways of knowing is the act of writing itself. Comparing himself in junior high to a hunted whale, Edgar writes, "As the youngest of the pod I lagged behind and ended up swimming alongside the very vessel that was hunting us" (1996, 83). If the white whale is Edgar, Captain Ahab is his teacher Mrs. O'Toole, whose "harpoon-laced breath . . . ignited a literary spark in the dimly lit hollowness of [his] immature being" (83). Physically assaulted for speaking their tribal language, Black Eagle Child youth experience education as an organized force of cultural forgetfulness. Writing, however, is encouraged. His older cousin, Luciano Bearchild, tells Edgar that Euro-American education perpetrated an act of "cultural disfiguring": "[He] used to say that being educated meant one was nursed with misinformation and therefore history-blind" (20). Edgar is keenly aware of the influence Western culture has had on his method of interpreting and knowing reality. He was raised to believe in religious principles and stories that would be dismissed as superstition by Western thought, and his contact with the outside world ultimately shakes his epistemological foundations in an unexpected way. Western education does not lead Edgar to become skeptical of traditional beliefs, but, more paralyzing, to become cynical concerning the possibility of a Black Eagle Child future. As a skeptic Edgar might have dismissed traditional knowledge as superstitious. As a cynic he both believes in prophecy and is convinced of the futility of fighting the inevitable dissolution of Black Eagle Child beliefs. Paralyzed into inaction by this intellectual position, he is incapable of fulfilling his traditional duties. Like it or not, Edgar seems reconciled to say, he is a product of both his grandmother's teachings *and* the modern world. This division makes for indecisiveness and deep ironies. Writing, the foundation of Western education, is both the cause of his cynicism and the vehicle through which he may resolve his conceptual impasses.

If Edgar finds a source of forgetfulness in his experiences with American education, it is writing that enables him to recover his own cultural memory. He finally asks himself, "When exactly / did my apprehension and doubt begin?" (1992, 62). In a telling synopsis of his anxieties he asks and answers the questions that ultimately determine the path of

his "Journey of Words": "What is my purpose as a Black Eagle
Child tribal member? What have I done to prolong life-years
of a tribal religion? While there probably ain't a damned thing
wrong with me, I always end up asking half-heartedly: Have I
been irresponsible? What are my priorities? Centuries of history could be blamed, but it's simpler to plead guilty. In the
Cosmic Earthlodge Tribunal I would not contest the charge
of forgetfulness. My rationale is, it is merely a part of 'eventuality'" (1996, 18). In the face of continuing cultural changes, the weight of Edgar's tribal responsibility is heavy to bear.
And though he may plead guilty to an imaginary "Cosmic
Earthlodge Tribunal," the reasons for his dereliction of tribal duty haunt him.

When embracing the Black Eagle Child notion of cyclical time, Edgar is philosophically paralyzed by his inability to live with the changes he witnesses. A Black Eagle Child
Hamlet, he asks, "What is one to say when told a major transgression has already occurred? What is one to say when told
we have already begun to forget?" (1992, 31). He knows where
to cast blame: "Through the polity that subjugated us, we
had splintered apart into factions" (31). He struggles with the
knowledge that his community, though devoted to tradition,
is changing: "Change was unavoidable; / yet we blamed ourselves for creating new mythology / and rituals for the last
traces of the old stories, / our grandfathers' ways" (60). Living in a changing modern world but bound by a static national charter, Edgar comments, "Change is either inescapable
or controversial here" (1996, 281).

There is no template with which Edgar may analyze his
cross-cultural experiences. Instead he must construct one by
analyzing his conceptual development as an artist, a Black

Eagle Child citizen, and a participant in American culture, examining his life as if it were a case study of the effects of cross-cultural epistemological influences. His fascination with the creative power of writing leads him beyond the borders of the Black Eagle Child nation and into an unfulfilling relationship with Western art. He understates, "In terms of poetry, college was a downer" (1996, 260). Ultimately, Western academia cannot offer Edgar an aesthetic framework that will enable him to bridge the gap between the oral and graphic impulses; his flirtation with an aesthetic originating outside of Black Eagle Child culture is a failure because it does not serve his goals as a tribal member and writer. It is only when he returns home that he finds his voice again, "writing 'new stuff'" that many years later becomes *Black Eagle Child* and *Remnants of the First Earth* (225).

The oral impulse of daily Black Eagle Child life is disrupted by Edgar's involvement with writing. His cousin Luciano Bearchild "inculcated the idea that being away from home, whether in reality or dream, was similar to death" (1996, 265). Though writing fosters alienation, even a near-death state, Edgar understands that his art and aesthetic theory are central to his cultural and psychic survival. His very sense of existence is inextricably linked to writing: "There was no greater being than what flowed from the tips of my fingers" (264). But in contrast to those Black Eagle Child members who found artistic expression in their communion with the higher powers represented in religion, Edgar realizes that his devotion is largely personal and secular: "My worship was for the writing instrument—the pencil, pen, and keyboard—and not what the fragile all-pervasive shadow needed" (264).

Approaching the written word from two opposing angles,

one focused on tribal prophecy and oral tradition, another negotiating the world of Western aesthetics and writing in English, Edgar attempts to align his artistic writing with the goals of Black Eagle Child cultural survival. In 1975 he receives a fellowship from the Maecenas Foundation of Athens, Greece, for twelve thousand dollars (1992, 140). Getting this validation from a literary establishment located at the birthplace of Western culture shocks Edgar into the realization that writing in English is a way of engaging the colonial forces that created the "forgetfulness" against which he struggles. Paralyzed by the literary establishment's approval, he likens his sudden self-revelation to a red oak that loses its leaves to reveal "behind it a man deathly afraid of words that were not his" (141). The leaves of excuses finally stripped away by the Maecenas Foundation, Edgar confronts his fear of English and, by extension, colonialism. This is the same fear he has been confronting since the time he committed himself to a Western education that has, in his own estimation, wrought terrible cultural changes to the Black Eagle Child Settlement. Given the economic freedom to write, Edgar instead begins a tortuous quest to understand the role writing may play within a Black Eagle Child cultural context.

It is during this time he calls "The Human Parchment Period" that Edgar makes a choice "to cover every square inch of [his] small-framed body with parchment, glued, resembling Robert De Niro in the movie *Brazil* as he attracts masses of swirling paper trash off the street until he is suffocated" (1996, 165). This Kafkaesque depiction of himself as a "paper cocoon" that his wife, Selene, hung "like a piñata from the ceiling and prodded . . . with a stick to spin and dry, communicating with [him] through a copper umbilical cord," represents Edgar's attempt to gain critical distance from the cultural forces that determine his art and life. His oral body literally covered with the written word, Edgar hopes for a type of linguistic metamorphosis through the unification of opposing oral and graphic impulses. The deep responsibilities he feels concerning Black Eagle Child cultural preservation and religious observation within his clan conflict with his need as a writer, both psychologically and artistically, to distance himself from his subject matter in order to attain a measure of critical insight. Trying to make sense of his life and art, he sees the interpretive process of writing as his best hope: "The long arduous task of pasting paper to every / inch of my body had already begun, and all that / remained was the wait for it to set like a cocoon. / I figured a metamorphosis was my only salvation" (1992, 147).

In the afterword to *Black Eagle Child* Young Bear states of Edgar's life at the settlement, "He finds himself in a unique but precarious 'little earth' where writing becomes the sole means of salvation" (1992, 256). If death is, as Carson Two Red Foot claims, "the return of all memory," Edgar's attempt to recover and make sense of Black Eagle Child history and stories by writing is his attempt to "forestall a cultural death by forgetfulness, keeping memories alive in the living" (1996, 264). Edgar knows the link between writing and isolation: "Inside the paper cocoon I was terribly alone." But he recognizes the concomitant need for such isolation in order to conjure the meaning of the past in the present: "In the blindness / the words from my childhood and past alighted / on my sluggish tongue" (1992, 148–49). He discovers in his artistic metamorphosis an answer to the question of his existence: "How I even came to be confounded me" (149).

Edgar's quest throughout *Black Eagle Child* and *Remnants of the First Earth* is to understand his own history in relation to the Black Eagle Child past and his own experiences with American culture. The problem is that the education he needs to understand the past is not taught by an institution, but can only be created by finding role models from his own culture who have discovered ways of confronting colonialism. Learning how his grandmother, Carson Two Red Foot, William Listener, and Luciano Bearchild dealt with the forces of cultural change brought about by colonialism and modernity, Edgar draws lessons that he can apply to his own unique experiences as a Black Eagle Child member who lives in a specific time and cultural context. His investigation of the possible roles of writing in the survival of a tribal community culminates in his discovery that artistic creativity has been and may continue to be a life-affirming response to colonialism. By reevaluating the past and piecing together the origins of his conceptual dilemmas, he empowers himself to revise his sometimes debilitating concepts of the Black Eagle Child worldview. Reconciling the call to write with his cultural obligations, Edgar creates a useful artistic space in which the tenuous balance between modernity and tradition, forgetfulness and knowledge, eventuality and purposeful change, the Black Eagle Child world and the "Outer World" may continue to oppose one another in ever shifting degrees of textual balance.

Writing the Critical Impulse

Edgar Bearchild identifies the aesthetic roots of, and then constructs, a tribal writing aesthetic that embraces his creativity and cross-cultural experiences while supporting Black Eagle

Child culture. The act of writing itself enables Edgar to recover a history of artistic responses to cultural change, in turn reestablishing a basis for the Black Eagle Child critical impulse to flourish. He creates this aesthetic by *studying* and *writing* about the lives and artistry of particular Black Eagle Child members, each of whom works in particular cultural mediums: Ada Principal Bear is an interpreter of tribal prophecy; Carson Two Red Foot is an oral storyteller; William Listener is a keeper of ceremonies; and Luciano Bearchild is a cross-cultural genius. Through Edgar Bearchild, Young Bear theorizes a Black Eagle Child conception of art that is an expression of community values in a postcolonial context. In imagining an artistic space for self-explorative and creative writing that reflects his experiences, Edgar develops an aesthetic that grounds his artistry in an exploration of the cross-cultural contexts that define his generation of Black Eagle Child citizens. He finds agency through his creative writing and, consequently, a means of escaping the epistemological stasis of eventuality. Writing and reflecting on the epistemological tensions that shape his art become a means of commenting on the tension between tradition and modernity that continues to affect the Black Eagle Child community.

Young Bear shapes Edgar's investigation of Black Eagle Child artistic models in a way that moves from culturally exclusive to cross-culturally inclusive aesthetics. In his twenties Edgar faces an artistic crisis and begins to question his purpose as a Black Eagle Child citizen and artist. His "Journey of Words" involves defining the facets of specific tribal aesthetics associated with the roles particular mentors fulfill. His problem, however, is that unlike the experiences of Grandmother, William Listener, Carson Two Red Foot, and

Luciano Bearchild, initially Edgar's artistry does not ground him in the Black Eagle Child community. In writing about his past and his relationships with these artists, Edgar realizes that his static notions of traditional Black Eagle Child epistemology were in error. As the lives of these mentors suggest to greater and lesser degrees, cultural changes had already been accommodated long before Edgar conceived of "eventuality." His new awareness that change may be accommodated in a healthful way frees him to conceive a useful role for creatively writing about his own experiences in the Black Eagle Child world. Instead of lamenting the loss of culture, Edgar understands the importance and value of representing the struggles of cultural change and adaptation that define his experiences.

Ada Principal Bear teaches Edgar an aesthetic determined by the Six Grandfathers' Journals, which dictate that writing should serve a religious, nationalist, and isolationist agenda to preserve the traditional beliefs of the Black Eagle Child people. Although this aesthetic arises out of an oral traditional context, it is preserved in a static graphic form that is not shared with other community members, and thus reifies Black Eagle Child myths. Cut off from a contemporary critical impulse, it does not support the creation of new narratives, but places great value on a method of exegesis that interprets the world in accordance with Black Eagle Child prophecy. Grandmother dazzles the young Edgar with "awe-inspiring tales of the supernatural past when the forces of good and evil fought a battle which eventually led to the very Creation of [their] lives" (1992, 162). He believes her stories and accepts the "presence of powers who maintained a permanent control and effect upon [their] lives" (163). Grandmother taught that "it wasn't what stretched / endlessly beyond the borders of the sanctuary / that mattered, it was the people themselves / and their cherished woodlands-oriented beliefs" (48). But although Ada Principal Bear is undoubtedly dedicated to the people, her role is as a preserver of cultural beliefs. As he grows older and comes in contact with the world outside Black Eagle Child, Edgar becomes less interested in exegesis and more inclined to explore how writing creatively may free him from his grandmother's static worldview. The adult Edgar remembers his fascination with writing as an escape; his "interest in storytelling began" with Grandmother transporting him "in mind and spirit to another world" (162).

Edgar's artistic concepts are influenced by cultural forces coming from beyond the "sanctuary" that is the Black Eagle Child Tribal Settlement. In spite of his grandmother's attempts to shield him from the world outside Black Eagle Child, Edgar becomes enamored of the way other story forms may also transport a person to a different time and place. While Grandmother works at the laundry and dry cleaner in Why Cheer, Iowa, Edgar and his brother wait for her to finish her shift while watching movies at the Why Cheer Theater (1996, 47). Edgar recounts, "The movies, *ne ne ki sa a ni*, were an ingenious way to see and experience the lives of other people in what was otherwise a faraway, inaccessible world" (47). As a child he embraces his experiences with mainstream American culture, but he is too immature to realize the effects this would have on his aesthetic. Grandmother attempts to keep him from going to the white town's theater: "Without anyone really saying point-blank that my Grandmother was responsible, tree branches at night were made to whip about by themselves, making my demanded walk to the Why Cheer

Theater more frightening" (103). As a child Edgar was dissuaded from walking to town by his fear of the trees, but as
a teenager he ignored the supernatural and "learned how to
prevent the unnerving 'whipping tree branch' phenomena
from taking hold" (103).

Edgar is increasingly drawn to American popular culture for its freedom of artistic expression that Grandmother's exegesis denied him. He is taught from a young age that
"there [is] nothing of value worth learning from white people, not even their language," but the movies contradict this
belief and raise seeds of doubt in his young mind concerning
his grandmother's teachings. Not only are the movies exciting and fun, but they are an escape from life in Black Eagle
Child. The deeper the adult Edgar looks into his artistic development, the more varying and unexpected artistic sources
he finds. Dolores Fox-King, Edgar's first real girlfriend, who
engages in "obsessive / notewriting," introduces him to writing in English as a form of romantic expression (1992, 50). His
uncle Severt provides access to other writings, telling Edgar to
burn Dolores's notes to make room in his dresser for Severt's
MAD magazine collection and his diary, a collection of writings both autobiographical and creative that were to "inspirit" Edgar "just as equally as Dolores's / notes" (51). Edgar says,
"In particular, there was one section / on 'Unearthly Manifestations' which / had an inexorable effect on my dreams / and
fantasies" (51). Whether because Dolores related her romance
with Edgar to the popular songs of the day ("The most memorable was 'Baby Love' / by the Supremes") or because of the
confluence of wry humor, science fiction, and Black Eagle
Child mythology in Severt's diary, Edgar was changed by his
exposure to creative forms of writing (54). As a writer he can

no longer be content with the aesthetics of the Six Grandfathers' Journals.

The tension between Grandmother's traditional aesthetics
and his evolving American popular cultural aesthetic shapes
the young Edgar's notion of art. When he initially approaches this question as a young writer, the choice comes down to
tradition, belief, and certainty or innovation, modernity, and
doubt. His flirtation with academic poetry circles convinces him that he cannot conform to a non–Black Eagle Child
aesthetic, but he also comes to the painful realization that
Grandmother's aesthetic cannot accommodate the influence
of cultural sources outside of Black Eagle Child. If Edgar is
to remain true to himself as a person and an artist, he has
to find an aesthetic that can accommodate his experiences
of both traditional Black Eagle Child culture and American
popular culture. To deny one or the other is to deny a part of
himself and his experience.

Edgar's return to the settlement as a college dropout marks
the beginning of his investigation of other tribal artists who
have also dealt with change in the Black Eagle Child culture.
In an attempt to understand the other sources of his aesthetic roots, he visits Carson Two Red Foot to hear oral historical
stories about the Black Eagle Child past. Edgar writes, "From
1971 to 1975, three to four times a year, I would take a fifth of
Ambrose in a brown bag to Carson. Sometimes I took cigarettes too. His stories were of great interest to me. Blessed in
the sense that he possessed an astonishing memory, Carson
was long thought to be the person who knew the secret of tribal immortality" (1996, 31). The key to "tribal immortality" is
knowing where the "Supernaturals' doorways [are] located
along the mossy riverfronts," for it is through these doorways

that the Black Eagle Child people communicate with sacred
beings, "the Holy Grandfather, His Twin Sons, and Grandmother Earth" (34). Opening "the doorways could reverse
[their] ignorance" (34). Although Carson is silent regarding
whether he actually knows the location of the doorways, he
does offer Edgar an equally valuable source of oral historical knowledge. He believes that "words were powerful, citing
instances where invisible spirits were awakened and angered,"
yet he nevertheless feels compelled to share stories with Edgar:
"Many people around here seek to know what the past was
like. Without me, no one would know" (32). In an era of forgetfulness, Carson Two Red Foot fascinates Edgar because
"where others barely remembered their histories, he could
relive past lives and events" (32). Whereas Ada Principal Bear
preserves oral tradition in a graphic form, Carson's use of
memory is more in keeping with the actual functions of the
oral impulse. He remembers stories that are pertinent to the
lived realities of Black Eagle Child people, and it is these stories that Edgar wishes to hear.

Edgar visits Carson to be transported to a particular point
in Black Eagle Child history, to hear "a story of a young enchant-
ress who stole Carson's father from his family in 1908, a story
replete with romance, witchcraft, and an unsolved murder"
(1996, 32). Edgar is fascinated by the story of the One Most
Afraid and returns time and again to hear it because it provides insights into the development of the Black Eagle Child
people. Unlike his grandmother's myths and prophecies, the
story of the One Most Afraid takes place within historical
memory. At the same time, this story provides a synthesis of
the epistemological conflicts that shape modern Black Eagle
Child experience. Carson's storytelling method lives on the

immediacy of community memory, offering Edgar a tribal storytelling aesthetic that values historical narratives not only for their fascinating content, but as a template with which he can interpret the Black Eagle Child past to better understand himself and the tribal context in which he lives.

The story is about the One Most Afraid's seduction of John Two Red Foot, Carson's father, and his subsequent abandonment of his family. John Two Red Foot fell in love with the One Most Afraid as a "victim of witchcraft," dangerous love medicine used to steal him away from his wife and family (1992, 168). Out of shame over her betrayal, Carson's mother exiled herself and her family outside the settlement and "sought the services of a witch" to murder the One Most Afraid: "Against the One Most Afraid, the strongest night-enemy medicine was unleashed: a trio of cackling owls who had the ability to control the behavior of vulnerable human beings. The three owls, for as long as it is necessary, wear the minds of people who are not mentally in control to accomplish their heinous deeds or requests" (1996, 59). Distraught over these events, Carson's sister committed suicide. According to Carson, his whole family was destroyed by witchcraft. On one hand, this explanation of events is based in supernatural forces that Edgar believes in and can accept. On the other, he is drawn to its "historic implications" and his sense of its being about a "flagrant abuse of justice" as the One Most Afraid's attackers were never caught (57). Apparently not satisfied with Carson's historical interpretation, Edgar turns to Western sources for an alternative explanation.

From the traditional Black Eagle Child viewpoint Carson espouses, the story is about the ramifications of the abuse of witchcraft. But from a Western perspective the story is about an unsolved murder on the Black Eagle Child Settlement. Edgar reports, "'By all appearances,' wrote the Tama County authorities, 'the female Indian subject was about to commit infidelity but someone caught her and punished her swiftly as required by ancient tribal custom'" (1996, 57). Edgar is fascinated with the story because it is irresolvable from either the oral or the graphic perspective; both the Black Eagle Child and Western rationalist interpretations must be accommodated. It speaks to Edgar because it highlights his own lack of proof of epistemological certainty. Unlike his grandmother's interpretations of prophecy, which describe the world with religious certainty, Carson's tale exists in a liminal epistemological space that characterizes this phase of Edgar's artistic and conceptual development. His developing critical impulse enables him to interpret the story of the One Most Afraid from within the interstices of his particular cross-cultural context.

Edgar finds in the story of the One Most Afraid a potential model for his own storytelling form. Like the stories he eventually tells, it is a tale of a particular cross-cultural tribal event that is contextualized in a historical moment. The story portrays with complexity the changes in worldview that Edgar's people were experiencing. His interpretive engagement with the story demonstrates his method of understanding both Black Eagle Child history and its representation in art, and it shows Edgar that his epistemological conflict has historical roots. Knowing this story relieves Edgar of the burden of holding himself solely responsible for being affected by the world outside Black Eagle Child. The irony he learns is that an event need not be understood with epistemological certainty in order to have concrete consequences.

Carson Two Red Foot is a historian of tribal memory, and

his aesthetic differs from Grandmother's because his subject matter and purpose dictate that he employ a different methodology. His stories are concerned with the relationships and motives that drive human beings, not the reoccurrence of mythic events and themes in Black Eagle Child life. At the same time, however, Carson's sense of history is determined by his Black Eagle Child epistemology, including his knowledge of supernatural forces. This epistemological framework is limited because it has no power to explain the workings of the world outside the settlement. He seems aware of the benefits and detriments of his anachronistic worldview. Having experienced firsthand the effects on Black Eagle Child of modernity and the Western world, he tells Edgar that since the time of his "youth and early manhood" life "has been a long uncomfortable adjustment to being an Indian, E ne no te wi ya ni, in the world of the white man" (1992, 167). While Carson teaches Edgar about the value of traditional storytelling in maintaining Black Eagle Child history as understood within the Black Eagle Child worldview, his artistry, like Grandmother's, is limited by its inability to engage the world outside Black Eagle Child. In developing his critical impulse Edgar seeks more applicable forms of placing the oral and graphic into conversation that speak to his experiences.

Edgar finds in William Listener a model of engaging the world through the critical impulse that speaks to his own cross-cultural experiences. Unlike the reclusive Carson Two Red Foot, Listener is deeply involved with both the Black Eagle Child Tribal Settlement and the surrounding American communities, and "move[s] stealthily between the two worlds" (1996, 117). Listener is a "*master plumber and former chair of the Tribal Council*," a "*clan elder*," an orator, and, most important, a "shadow-releaser," one who speaks "The Final Words to the Deceased before Their Journey West," to the Black Eagle Child Hereafter (115). Seeing in Listener a model of how the knowledge of languages and discourses may be used to support the Black Eagle Child people, Edgar marvels at Listener's ability to cross cultural borders that others in his community cannot. To be simultaneously an important religious leader and one who participates in mainstream American life makes Listener anomalous, but Edgar identifies what enables this accomplishment: "William was the first person to aptly demonstrate that one could educate himself in both worlds by first having a thorough command of their diverse languages. Possessing a shrewd, analytical but traditional outlook was also helpful" (116). Actively working for the survival of the Black Eagle Child community, Listener embraces the "diverse languages" of their experience. He embodies the critical impulse: bringing multiple discourses into conversation.

Unlike hard-line traditionalists such as Grandmother, Listener accommodates cultural changes and works cross-culturally with the whites so that the people of Black Eagle Child can flourish (1996, 117). Edgar quotes him: "We'll never get anywhere if we don't make an effort—no matter how shameful or futile—to use them" (117). Listener's pragmatic view of cross-cultural exchange does not advocate assimilation, but self-reliance in a world based on economics: "Through his toothless mouth, he'd discuss the future. 'We've got to do better than the grocery store, barber shop, pool hall, and bread factory we now have'" (117). As a realist, Listener has a strategy for cultural survival that involves proactively working for change: "In Why Cheer he had lawyer friends who wrote up grants for tribal housing needs in return for subcontracting jobs for their own relatives" (117). Edgar marvels that he is "many things to many people" (117). Listener is not hampered by the tensions that his multiple facets of self assuredly create because his purpose in engaging multiple discourses is the good of the Black Eagle Child people.

Unlike Listener, who finds greater tribal belonging through his cross-cultural engagements, Edgar's thoughtful creative writing threatens not only his role within his family, but his sense of self. Though he "rarely" sees Listener, when in his presence Edgar thinks of himself as "an indiscernible face that somehow [stands] out in the Bearchild family portrait as a flaw" (1996, 117). He figures this gradual loss of identity in the depiction of himself as a "blurred movement" in an imagined family portrait. One of his relatives explains his fading presence: "*You can't make him out too clear but that's Edgar Bearchild, esteemed member of the srs—the Society of the Repressed Storytellers*" (130). Unlike Listener's ceremonial knowledge, Edgar believes, his own "repressed" talent as a writer is not useful to the Black Eagle Child community.

According to the models of Black Eagle Child aesthetics that Edgar is defining, only masters of tribal ceremonial traditions and keepers of oral storytelling traditions may approach aesthetic virtuosity. Like Listener's, their art is fully integrated into the traditional tenets of the Black Eagle Child people. Carson Two Red Foot makes concessions to change by breaking a taboo and telling stories about the dead, and William Listener engages the economic world outside the settlement, but neither artist integrates artistic forms from other cultures. The cultural contexts in which Carson Two Red Foot and William Listener move do not accurately reflect Edgar's generation's cross-cultural experiences.

Edgar's older cousin, Luciano Bearchild, models a lived form of Black Eagle Child artistry that is both traditional and cosmopolitan, whose aim is to make "everyone realize there [is] beauty in being human" (1996, 246). Luciano represents to Edgar the type of cross-cultural exchange that is possible. In knowledge, language, hunting skill, and style, Luciano is unrivalled on the Black Eagle Child Tribal Settlement. Before his disappearance at age twenty-five in 1966 "on an errand for earthlodge elders, taking prayers, tobacco, and offerings of food and gifts to the silver metallic UFO that had crash-landed above Liquid Lake, Luciano was blessed manifold" (244). In his "black pinstriped, hand-tailored suits, white silk scarves, Italian shoes, and perforated fingerless gloves," he "would acquiesce to change by tightening his bow tie and shuffling across the concrete floor like James Brown" (241). Luciano knows how to take the best from multiple cultures, literally dancing with change. An addict of soul music as well as a speaker whose "tribal language skills approached archaic perfection," Edgar writes, "He made uncultivated Indians like me cultivated" (241). Refusing the limitations of the settlement boundaries for fear of Others, "at twenty-five he [knows] about the Outside World—Plato, Michelangelo, Degas, Gertrude Stein, Ernest Hemingway, and F. Scott Fitzgerald" (242). What may enable him to shuffle back and forth between multiple cultures with apparent ease, and without any fear that his mind will somehow be contaminated by foreign knowledge, is that having been "raised by the wisest Bearchild elders of the Settlement, Luciano [knows] more than most Indians twice his age" (242). Luciano is open to other cultures because he is secure in his own Black Eagle Child knowledge. A Black Eagle Child genius, he rises above the limitations of the settlement; all knowledge is his to embrace or refuse.

Luciano's cross-cultural expertise leads others in the community to feel "jealousy," which Edgar defines as "admiration that was transmogrified" (1996, 243). In traditional models of behavior Luciano's uniqueness is viewed as abnormal. Edgar reasons that some Black Eagle Child citizens "saw intellect as a curse," and so Luciano is a natural object of scorn. Finding success in everything he does, Luciano breaks with the norm the Black Eagle Child people have come to accept as colonial subjects. Edgar states, "Keep this in mind: To have every facet of life work to one's advantage was seen not as the glorious result of unbounded determination but as the workings of evil. This was—and even today is—the tribal community's mind-set" (242). Rather than recognizing Luciano as an example of what is possible—to be both culturally traditional and cosmopolitan—Black Eagle Child citizens read Luciano from a Black Eagle Child conceptual perspective that interprets his difference as malignant. Although not an artist with a particular medium, Luciano has an approach to living that is as much an artistic creation as the movies Edgar watched in Why Cheer: "What we saw in movies and could only fantasize about, he radiated in living, breathing color" (245). As a teenager Edgar tagged along with his older cousin, keeping him company and fetching "Chesterfield cigarettes and almonds to go with the two Bloody Marys he always started and ended the evening with" (247). Edgar finds in Luciano a hero who is knowledgeable in Black Eagle Child ceremonial life and who has the curiosity to "attend a Navaho Indian anthropology lecture at Grinnell College, a twenty-minute drive south to a foreign country" (242). Like William Listener, Luciano "could sing you to the Black Eagle Child Afterlife," but he could also dance the night away in a Why Cheer bar to the music of Johnny Cash, Glenn Miller, and the Zombies (242, 249).

Edgar realizes that Luciano learned to value different forms of knowledge but that he found the "separation of knowledge, of cultures, gnawed at him" (1996, 251). Luciano's white girlfriend, Angela, would ridicule his "analogies between his successful fur-trapping business and his love life" when he admired that her hand had a "softness greater than a raccoon's paw" (250). Luciano's tongue-in-cheek analogy is also half-serious. Edgar writes, "In the tribal domain where animism and supernaturalism prevailed, he was not off kilter" (250). The fact that Angela does not appreciate his analogy signals that these forms of knowledge, Black Eagle Child and Western, and specifically the way beauty is described within them, have yet to be reconciled by less enlightened individuals. Squarely living in two cultural worlds, Luciano sees himself divided, a "monolithic maple tree beside a river whose roots [are] exposed in the air and underwater, providing a refuge for winged and finned creatures" (251). Luciano tells Edgar, "That's me, helping everyone" (251).

Young Bear states the facts about Luciano's abduction by aliens without any suggestion that it is a metaphor for his death. Instead, as a genius of cross-cultural exchange, perhaps Luciano sacrifices himself for his Black Eagle Child people, offering himself to the UFO's aliens if they left the settlement unharmed. This is what Edgar suggests when he says that Luciano's inability to understand the "separation" of different forms of cultural knowledge "would eventually topple him" (1996, 251). In the end he is dissatisfied with living in multiple worlds, and he makes a choice to leave both the white world and the Black Eagle Child world altogether for an unknown world, in turn leaving Edgar to create his own solution to the same cross-cultural dilemma.

Edgar's artistic metamorphosis creates in him a profound appreciation for the sacrifices and struggles of his fellow Black Eagle Child people. His grandmother, Carson Two Red Foot, William Listener, and Luciano Bearchild stand out among many people who contend with the same colonial forces that affect Edgar's life. Although their approaches to cultural change differ, their effect on Edgar is clear: "My survival was more than a miracle," he says (1992, 149). His artistic "Journey of Words" culminates in a new way of conceptualizing his self-development and his community's development in the context of a recovered Black Eagle Child history: "Contrary to the beliefs / of many, there was indeed a past" (149). His new theory of self and his artistic theory both bloom in this moment of realization, and he seeks to align his artistic yearnings with his Black Eagle Child obligations: "I was in a rage from my inability to find / ways to say thank you" (149). Exploring his self-development in relation to Black Eagle Child history and in an uneasy negotiation with the larger American culture becomes the means for Edgar to express his gratitude to his ancestors and community.

Edgar's conceptual breakthrough comes after years of internal struggle, and still the purposes he assigns creative writing are clearer in theory than in practice. In the chapter titled "The Mask of Seeing" in *Remnants of the First Earth* Edgar examines writing's potential power to influence community in a contemporary context. Unlike his discussion of his aesthetic predecessors, this chapter is situated in Edgar's historical present. He begins the chapter with a not-so-subtle dig on poetry's apparent lack of power to create community action: "It would be good if my self-published book of verse, *The Mask of Seeing* (Hominy Creek Press, 1989), inspired Lorna Bearcap and Claude E. Youthman to write 'The Weeping Willow Manifesto'" (1996, 289). Of course, it has no impact on their actions. Both Black Eagle Child teachers, Bearcap and Youthman somehow "made it through the censors" of the *Black Eagle Child Quarterly*, turning the "community newsletter" into a "glossy tabloid" with their scathing rebuke of the corrupt Black Eagle Child Tribal Council and the Weeping Willow Elementary School Board for its nepotism, for its disregard for law, and for supporting "the unacceptable curriculum of the school, which conformed to the greater society's restraints" (290). Bearcap and Youthman challenge their community, saying, "Instead of developing an institution of tribal learning, we prepared Black Eagle Child youth for an unpredictable and irresponsible tomorrow" (290). After struggling for years with his own artistic purposes, it amazes Edgar to witness how one well-placed "manifesto" may have a profound impact on the Black Eagle Child community.

Edgar realizes that he was mistaken in believing that he alone was concerned with the power of writing to affect his community; that was an effect of his isolation. Once again his static notions of Black Eagle Child culture prevented him from seeing that others of his generation had been struggling with the same problems but attempted to solve them with different methodologies. Scarred from his experiences with education, Edgar assumed that "teachers and writers were different," a belief in which he was "adamant" (1996, 290). Although their cross-cultural education put them in "the same philosophical encampment," Edgar considered Black Eagle Child teachers to be aligned with those establishment "bureaucrats in limbo, no authority to do anything" (290). The "Weeping Willow Manifesto" convinces him that writing can unite disparate Black Eagle Child people in their cause to face a "common enemy," whom he names "ourselves and our relatives" (290). When the effects of colonialism begin to take shape in the greed and corruption of a "grossly uneducated Tribal Council whose members were easily swayed by Twintown businesses with projects that benefited only the whites and themselves—and not the tribe per se," writing becomes an instrument of justice. Just as Edgar accepts blame for his own religious and cultural transgressions, this same forthrightness enables him to critique how his fellow Black Eagle Child citizens never take individual responsibility for their collective future, instead "hoping that someone had the intellectual wherewithal to realign [their] destiny" (296). The words of Youthman and Bearcap provide a pragmatic cultural model for Edgar's aspiration to be not simply a tribal "word-collector" and artist, but a tribal critic who himself is not exempt from guilt, but who nevertheless calls attention to the way tribal politics and life are headed in a destructive direction.

Ray Young Bear asserts in the afterword to *Black Eagle Child*, "[The writing of this book] has been an artistic process for me, the creative emulation of thought through extraordinary, tragic, and comedic stories of an imagined midwestern tribal existence. It has never sought to be more than that" (1992, 261). However, in an artistic engagement with the Black Eagle Child community and the "thought" of people whose experiences speak to his concerns, Edgar reconceives himself through his art. Tribal art cannot be divorced from the tribal communities to which it owes its conceptual origins. At the same time artists cannot deny meaning to their experiences and the historical contexts in which they exist, especially when they conflict with their tribal worldview. In examining the differing ways that key Black Eagle Child artists understand and confront change, Edgar Bearchild comes to understand that the strength of the Black Eagle Child worldview depends on its ability not only to attempt to balance forces of good and evil, but to understand those forces in their multiple cross-cultural oral and graphic forms and complexities.

Conclusion

It is fitting that the last chapter of *Remnants of the First Earth* ends in the future and is written by Edgar and Selene's as yet unborn daughter, Maya Mae Bearchild. Titled "My Summer of 2004" and recognized as "Honorable Mention in Doeting-ham Junior High School's O'Toole Creative Writing Award," the chapter begins with a description of a "grotesque scene": "the hawk, the mud-scooping duck, and the serpent, all clasping one another in the defiant blue sky, all entrapped by differing instincts" (1996, 297–98). The image of a duck caught by a hawk while attempting to eat a snake highlights the tensions inherent in Black Eagle Child existence. Fighting one another, all three end up falling out of the sky, the "Chinese Mig jet" of a hawk crashing "upside down" (298). This fatalistic image of existence, the "macabre scene of a redtail carrying a duck who itself is carrying and fighting with a snake over lunch rights," seems more fitting of Edgar's cynical ambivalence regarding the survival of Black Eagle Child. But as the chapter progresses, Maya's individuality comes to stand on its own, and though her imaginative writing is assuredly influenced by Edgar's wild imagination, her greater ability to fuse tradition and modernity while remaining grounded in her sense of self as a burgeoning Black Eagle Child word-collector expresses hope for the future.

Maya understands that her very existence has a place in a continuum of life and death. She writes,

> I was thinking of the person my parents, Edgar and Selene Bearchild, sometimes talk about: Ted Facepaint. "He is the one that died so that you may be," I was told early on by my father, a troubled artist. "From the Grandfather World, far away from our day-to-day struggle on these minute islands of ourselves," my mother added, "Ted, with the aid of my grandmother and your mother's mother and aunt, arranged it so that you may be here in their place." (298)

Unlike Edgar, the "troubled artist" who struggles to reconcile his art with his Black Eagle Child responsibilities, Maya better understands her role in weaving together an examination of history, artistic expression, and tribal responsibilities.

Maya is precociously self-conscious about her art, wondering out loud about the "aesthetic presentation" of her depiction of the hawk, duck, and snake. She writes, "Hopelessly locked, the tips of the talons acted like fine, curled needles that clamped shut, impaling both victims, who saw an upside-down earth view before Black Heron consciousness waned" (299). Immediately following this sentence, a question asked by a reader of Maya's submission intrudes on the text: "What is the history, you query, of the Black Heron name?" Prodded by this question, Maya explains her allusion: "It is a stat that in our lifetimes one in three of us will meet a murderer. The mud-scooping duck, the serpent, and the hawk incorporate this 'Black Heron' metaphor" (299). Like Edgar's, Maya's tribal aesthetic requires that she explain the very metaphors that give her writing their meaningful depth. But given the tools of Black Eagle Child historical knowledge that Edgar had to discover for himself, she is nonplussed by what one might have interpreted as an ethnographic intrusion. In fact she directs the questioner to further reading in Black Eagle Child literary history: "(Per your request enclosed are the two stories of which I speak: 'How We Delighted in Seeing the Fat' and 'The Great Flood of the Iowa River' by Edgar Bearchild)" (299).

As Edgar's child, Maya represents the next generation not only of Bearchilds, but of Black Eagle Child written art, culture, and life. Her ability to negotiate the tensions that troubled Edgar relies on her deep understanding of Black Eagle Child history, which she recounts for her readers, telling about the murder of Dorothy Black Heron and the One Most Afraid, of Junior Pipestar's beginnings, and of how her great-grandfather, "Jack Principal Bear, as a young man, with the aid of a friend, captured a shawl-wearing sorceress on the first bridge" (300). Far from being a random history, these events are tied together and have given shape to the Black Eagle Child community. As a junior high student Maya sees these connections, which Edgar could recognize only in middle age. Performatively offering a future generation the ability to add their interpretations of Black Eagle Child history, Maya tells readers that the sorceress that was caught by Jack Principal Bear dealt in "powerful 'seeing' medicines," knowledge of which she entrusted to Edgar's grandmother, Ada Principal Bear. These medicines, which could be used for ill or good, included the very stone knife that Edgar wore and that Maya now wears "inside a brass locket necklace" (301). Maya knows where she came from, tracing her genealogy from grandparents to parents:

Edgar Bearchild, upkeeper and maintainer of the Six
Grandfathers' Journals who went on to fall in love with
my mother, Selene Buffalo Husband, in 1973, thereby giving birth to me—after three miscarriages—in 1991, two
years after replacing ceremonially the place once occupied
by Ted Facepaint . . . Ada Principal Bear . . . Pat "Dirty"
Red Hat . . . Luciano Bearchild . . . William Listener . . .
and my lovely grandmother, Lillian Buffalo Husband,
and her ever-present sister, Alice, going back further to
my other grandparents and their own grandparents on
either side, wa wi ta wi. Especially the Sacred Chieftains,
O ki ma wa ki, and the Holy Grandfather who arranged
their rightful return as decision-makers of the Black Eagle
Child Nation, proving that my father was simply a pessimist all along. (301)

In this touching effusion of belonging and connection, Maya
is simply incapable of marking the boundary of her beginnings. The fact that it ends with a rebuff of Edgar as "simply
a pessimist all along" holds out hope that future generations will have a deeper understanding of cultural change
and continuity.

Remnants of the First Earth ends with Maya Mae Bearchild's
invocation: "[I ask] all those before me, including Dorothy
Black Heron and her younger sister, the One Most Afraid, to
partake with me of this journey" (301). But unlike Edgar's
"Journey of Words," which at times seemed to be a journey
toward isolation and figurative death, Maya's journey through
"these ever-circling stories" of Black Eagle Child life are but-
tressed by those spirits caught by colonial machinations, the
workings of evil medicine, modernity, and that which is unex-
plainable, unifying the past and present Black Eagle Child

people in a transcendent community. Though distant in time, these ancestors and events, Maya writes, are as present as the thought that is given them: "[They remind] me every day how imperative it is to realign our destiny, to salvage these cherished but immutable islands of ourselves that tumble aimlessly among the blinding stars" (301).

The cycles that define Black Eagle Child existence do repeat, but they do so with inevitable changes. Through the oral, graphic, and critical impulses, continuity and change may both be accommodated. Maya Mae may have her own voice and artistic perceptions while at the same time knowing her people's history, her place within it, and those ancestors whom she replaces. In their investigation of tribal aesthetics, Young Bear's *Black Eagle Child* and *Remnants of the First Earth* offer readers informed by similar histories and tribal aesthetics that shape Edgar Bearchild's experiences the opportunity to think through their own versions of eventuality—concepts that embrace static responses to cultural change that leave no room for agency. Edgar experiences colonialism as an irreconcilable epistemological dilemma between Black Eagle Child and Western worldviews. Artistry provides the means of negotiating this dilemma. His "Journey of Words" provides a model for how the colonized may reconcile opposing worldviews to achieve a sustainable future. Writing becomes an artistic vehicle of self-discovery, a means of creatively engaging the world and examining one's experiences in relation to multiple worldviews and histories—orally, graphically, and critically expressed. In the artistic growth of Edgar Bearchild, Young Bear shows us how tribal art must change and grow because the languages of our experiences, like the Black Eagle Child people, are continuously made anew just as they are inextricably tied to our pasts.

5

Interpreting Our World

Authority and the Written Word in Robert J. Conley's Real People Series

The summer 2001 issue of the *Cherokee Phoenix* profiles the
Cherokee painter Talmadge Davis, a self-taught artist who
turns for his subject matter to the traditions and history of his
people. The Cherokee journalist Will Chavez writes that Davis
"wants his paintings to teach people about Cherokee history." Chavez describes Davis's depiction of Dragging Canoe, a
Cherokee patriot during the Revolutionary War. Interestingly,
Davis titled his work *Cherokee Dragon*, a title "taken with per-
mission from the book of the same name by Cherokee author
Robert Conley." Davis's Dragging Canoe "bears a striking
resemblance to Cherokee actor Wes Studi because he allowed
Davis to use his image for the painting" (Chavez 2001). In
the creation and naming of Davis's painting, three Cherokee
artists—a writer, a painter, and an actor—converge in the
production of new art representing a Cherokee culture hero

few people outside Cherokee country celebrate. This artistic discourse characterizes an evolving Cherokee aesthetic that seeks to explore Cherokee history, invigorate Cherokee culture, and support Cherokee nationhood. A culturally informed process of critical interpretation that draws on Cherokee oral traditional thought and performance is emerging from these artistic conversations, and at the center of these collaborations are the historical novels of Robert J. Conley's Real People series.

Conley's series of twelve novels depicts episodes of Cherokee history that have never before been fictionalized by a Cherokee. His epic begins in pre-Columbian times in the Appalachian region and covers seminal periods of Cherokee colonial history: first contact with Europeans in 1540, the evolution of trade with the English and Spanish, the American Revolutionary War, the loss of lands through treaty, and the Removal of the Cherokee to Indian Territory in 1838. The Real People series is both painstakingly researched and deeply creative; Conley sets the historical stage and then allows generations of related characters to develop according to their changing circumstances and worldviews. Central in the novels are both fictional characters and important Cherokee historical figures such as Dragging Canoe, the war leader of the Chickamaugas; Nancy Ward, the "Beloved Woman" of the Cherokee; and Sequoyah, the creator of the Cherokee syllabary. Conley brings these historical figures to life and lets their voices speak from a Cherokee worldview in which their actions are rational and justified (Ballard 2001, 332).

Conley's depiction of a Cherokee-centered world may account for the ubiquity of his writings in Cherokee country. Walk into a bookstore in Tahlequah, Oklahoma, the capital of the Cherokee Nation, and Conley's books will be there. They are sold in Cherokee, North Carolina, as well, home of the Eastern Band of Cherokee Indians. His new books are enthusiastically reviewed in the *Cherokee Phoenix*, and the dust jackets of his novels include a recommendation by Wilma Mankiller, former principal chief of the Cherokee Nation. As a citizen of the Cherokee Nation, I have for years been aware of Conley's popularity among Cherokees, but as a scholar I am aware that this anecdotal evidence does not prove a writer's centrality to a community. I wanted to find out if my assessment of Conley's popularity among Cherokees was indeed correct and, if so, what the popularity of his writing might mean to the Cherokee critical impulse.

In the summer of 2004, in consultation with Dr. Richard Allen, the policy analyst for the Cherokee Nation, I initiated a study of Cherokee Nation readers.[1] A survey was published in the September 2004 issue of the *Cherokee Phoenix* newspaper, which, with a circulation of 68,000 in Oklahoma and a worldwide circulation of more than 106,000, is the natural forum for reaching a far-ranging Cherokee citizenry. My initial findings confirm the popularity of Robert Conley's novels among Cherokees and shed light on the reasons for this popularity. Survey respondents reported that they had read works by Native writers such as Sherman Alexie, Louise Erdrich, and Leslie Marmon Silko, and they showed their depth of knowledge of Native writers in referencing works by William Apess, George Copway, Sarah Winnemucca, and Alexander Posey, but the most widely referenced Native American writer was Robert Conley.[2] Conley's popularity rests partially on his accessible engagement with history, the top genre of choice for respondents. When asked "What types of creative works about Cherokees would you like to read or see written?" respondents unequivocally cited historically accurate fiction.

Having published thirty-five novels, including historical fiction, folklore, horror, and westerns, and with a total of eighty-two published books, Conley is undoubtedly the most prolific Native writer of his generation. A member of the United Keetoowah Band of Cherokee and a former long-time resident of the Cherokee Nation capital of Tahlequah, Conley is currently the Sequoyah Distinguished Professor in Cherokee Studies at Western Carolina University in Cullowhee, North Carolina. He is also noted for his Cherokee-specific nonfiction: *Cherokee Thoughts: Honest and Uncensored* (2008), *The Cherokee Nation: A History* (2007), *A Cherokee Encyclopedia* (2007), and *Cherokee Medicine Man: The Life and Work of a Modern-Day Healer* (2005). He has won numerous accolades for his writing, including the 2000 Cherokee Medal of Honor, the 1999 Oklahoma Writer of the Year award, three Spur Awards by the Western Writers of America, and an induction into the Oklahoma Professional Writers Hall of Fame. And yet, despite the widespread recognition of his talent by his fellow Cherokee, his peers, and even the state of Oklahoma, only two critical essays have been published focusing exclusively on his work.[3]

The disjunction between the taste of Cherokee readers and that of literary critics reflects a clash of cultural aesthetics and points to the privileging of specific relationships between oral, graphic, and critical impulses. Conley's straightforward artistic goals are to entertain and educate his audience: "I like people to read my historical novels and stories and first of all say, 'I really enjoyed reading that.' And then say, 'Wait a minute, I think I learned something from it, too'" (S. K. Teuton

2001, 122). Consequently, Conley's insistence on accessibility contrasts with works such as N. Scott Momaday's *House Made of Dawn*, Leslie Marmon Silko's *Ceremony*, and Gerald Vizenor's trickster novels, all of which make use of stylistic approaches pioneered by modernists such as William Faulkner, James Joyce, and Virginia Woolf. These are structurally complex, nonlinear, achronological works that struggle with the effects of modernity on tribal consciousness and communal and individual identity and that presume that readers will have at least some familiarity with the canonical tradition. Conley's novels address similar themes, but they are structured as works of popular fiction, full of action, suspense, and usually at least one happy love story. His omniscient narrator leaves few ambiguities to concern his readers. Instead the tensions that define the action in his novels are readable on the surface. His stories are situationally, not psychologically complex, with multiple subplots that, in the end, come back together. They are largely linear and plot-driven, sometimes poignant, and often very funny. The very aspects of his work that appeal to readers make him difficult for critics to fit into their discussions.

Even scholars concentrating on Native literature have not yet employed the necessary tools to engage that literature critically. Susan Berry Brill de Ramírez summarizes the issue: "To date, many literary critics who study American Indian literatures have been forced either to select among the array of literary criticisms available today (all of which bespeak, in some form or fashion, the Western tradition from which they derive) or to grapple with the inadequacy of these criticisms and theories for American Indian literatures, thereby using those theories provisionally, with a clear sense of that inadequacy" (1999, 7). One reason for this problem is that a growing number of American Indian novels are written from within tribally specific aesthetics. Works such as *House Made of Dawn* and *Ceremony*, which purposefully mediate between Native and non-Native cultural contexts, may circumvent this problem, but writers grounded in the specific traditions of their tribes may be critically ignored because critics lack the cultural knowledge needed to comprehend their work. The application of Western critical traditions to texts such as Ray A. Young Bear's *Black Eagle Child: The Facepaint Narratives* and D. L. Birchfield's *Field of Honor* may generate provocative readings but not necessarily interpretations that are meaningful within each work's tribal cultural contexts.

Conley's Real People novels draw their complexity from the conceptual depth of the oral traditions that provide the critical frameworks for interpreting their plots. Throughout the series Conley presents stories drawn from numerous sources, including his own personal experiences, discussions with fellow Cherokees, the works of the ethnologist James Mooney, the Cherokee folklorists Jack F. and Anna G. Kilpatrick, and many others (Conley 2000b, 171–72). These stories of Jisdu the rabbit, the monster Uk'ten, and Stone Coat, a supernatural eater of hunters, are allegorical tales known throughout Cherokee culture. The stories appear in the flow of the narrative as characters remember and reflect on stories they were told. Following the call of the oral impulse, Conley uses these stories in ways that place characters and readers in conversation with one another.

Conley's juxtaposition of his fiction with traditional stories allows readers familiar with the central function of storytelling in Cherokee culture to read the two story forms across each other as a way of energizing the critical impulse. As Barbara Duncan observes, the contextualizing of stories is a crucial aspect of Cherokee aesthetics: "In traditional Cherokee culture, as in other cultures with living traditions of storytelling, stories are often sprinkled throughout conversation, embedded in the flow of events and casual talk. They make a point or teach a lesson relevant to the events or the conversation in progress" (1998, 15). For Cherokees the inclusion of stories in everyday conversation is an important social event. Depending on what kind of story is told and in what context, it can serve numerous purposes: a storyteller may display his or her humor, wit, knowledge, or rudeness; a listener may be entertained, gratified, reassured, or shamed. Many oral stories are "used consciously to educate children in cultural values and to reaffirm those values for adults" (12). The function of storytelling for adults, Duncan adds, is similar: "Stories provide a way for both outsiders and insiders to understand and to remember the larger worldview of the culture, since stories reflect this worldview while also reinforcing it" (24). Conley's Cherokee novels use oral narratives to teach adult lessons, and readers familiar with Cherokee oral tradition will recognize that his backdrop narratives are in dialogue with the oral stories, just as oral stories are contextualized in everyday conversation. By portraying the way characters think about the meaning of oral traditional stories and the implications of the lessons for their lives, the narratives model a critical impulse methodology. Often the survival of characters depends on their ability to interpret, question, adapt, and relate ideas explored in Cherokee oral tradition to their experiences.

The Real People novels do not presuppose a Cherokee

knowledge base or awareness of Cherokee critical context; rather they are designed to teach the reader a critical impulse grounded in a Cherokee cultural context. The novels use Cherokee words, but each includes a glossary; as readers continue through the series they may develop a small Cherokee vocabulary. The novels also provide maps and dates and even reproduce treaties, which helps readers imagine Cherokee geography and politics. For Cherokee readers the Real People series aids "with the development or recovery of an effective identifying relationship between self and place" (Ashcroft, Griffiths, and Tiffin 1989, 9). Most Cherokee have been displaced from their Appalachian region homelands, so it is crucial that Conley brings those places to life for them in his depictions: readers can imagine the sanctuary town of Echota and Tanasi, the birthplace of Sequoyah, lands the Cherokee lost through treaty and that were flooded in 1976. Part fiction, part history, and part Cherokee cultural encyclopedia, the Real People series strives to represent diverse aspects of Cherokee life as a means of invigorating the critical impulse.

Conley is not self-consciously literary in his approach to style, yet the Real People novels employ several techniques usually associated with metafiction. Patricia Waugh defines *metafiction* as fiction that "self-consciously and systematically draws attention to its status as an artefact in order to pose questions about the relationship between fiction and reality" (1984, 2). In Conley's imagined narrative world, the reader's primary recourse to lived experience is through the oral narratives that exist both in the series and in today's Cherokee culture. Oral narratives form a bridge between the past and the present and show performatively that the Cherokee worldview is shaped by the ideas expressed in oral tradition.

As Waugh states, "If our knowledge of this world is now seen to be mediated through language, then literary fiction (worlds constructed entirely of language) becomes a useful model for learning about the construction of 'reality' itself" (3). Cherokee oral tradition provides Conley's characters and readers the epistemological, ethical, and metaphysical models with which they interpret their worlds, maintaining and reconstructing their realities in the midst of colonialism.

Where most self-consciously postcolonial writers concentrate on the psychological impact of colonialism, Conley is more concerned with the world of action characteristic of oral narratives. As Walter J. Ong writes, "Many, if not all, oral or residually oral cultures strike literates as extraordinarily agonistic in their verbal performance and indeed in their lifestyle. Writing fosters abstractions that disengage knowledge from the arena where human beings struggle with one another. It separates the knower from the known. By keeping knowledge embedded in the human lifeworld, orality situates knowledge within a context of struggle" (1982, 44). Conley could offer an abstract Cherokee history, as he does in his most recently published volume, but it takes him twelve novels to depict half that history "embedded in the human lifeworld." He chooses to tell Cherokee history through the struggle and action of characters, eschewing the approach Ong associates with "literate" forms that "focus . . . action more and more [on] interior crises and away from purely exterior crises" (44). By highlighting the tensions on the textual continuum, Conley's fiction is clearly metafictive in the sense described by Waugh: "The lowest common denominator of metafiction is simultaneously to create a fiction and to make a statement about the creation of that fiction" (1984, 6).

Conley's choice to incorporate the oral impulse in his novels takes on special significance in relation to the long-standing Cherokee interest in literacy. Cherokee cultural traditions remain strong and there are thousands of fluent Cherokee speakers, yet Cherokees long ago embraced a Western-style education system dependent on writing as a means of resisting colonialism. In her analysis of the politics of Indian intellectual discourse, *Writing Indian Nations*, Maureen Konkle writes of Elias Boudinot, who in 1828 became the first editor of the *Cherokee Phoenix*. Sent by his father to a Moravian boarding school at the age of six, Boudinot later used his education in the struggle to preserve the sovereignty of the Cherokee Nation prior to Removal: "The two main points that Boudinot as a Cherokee spokesman tried to get across to whites were, first, that the Cherokees formed a political entity that was separate from and not subordinate to U.S. authority and, second, that the Cherokees and other Native peoples had been misrepresented by whites as static primitives locked in time, when they in fact had changed over time like whites themselves" (2004, 50). A Western education equipped nineteenth-century Indian intellectuals like Boudinot to "reject racial difference, claim history and therefore political equality for themselves, and, often through the use of sustained textual analysis, refute whites' knowledge about them as politically self-interested misrepresentations" (51). Not just literacy, but the use of textual analysis specifically has a historical precedent in the Cherokee Nation as a crucial tool of decolonization.

As Boudinot's example suggests, many Cherokees believed their best hope of preserving their nation lay in educating their citizens. The intent was not simply to assimilate, but to equip them to assert their political rights. After the Civil

War the Cherokee Nation founded "the first free, compulsory public school system in the country, perhaps in the world. (Education was the highest single line item on the Cherokee Nation's budget)" (Conley 2005a, 13). The Cherokee Nation also "built male and female seminaries, the first institutions of higher education west of the Mississippi River." The focus on education had tangible results: "By 1907, the Cherokee Nation had produced more college graduates than the states of Arkansas and Texas combined" (13).

This emphasis on literacy, however, has not destroyed the oral dimensions of Cherokee society. As Conley's own experiences with oral traditional thought exemplify, Cherokees learn oral traditional stories and paradigms from both literate sources, such as the works of James Mooney, and oral sources, such as their grandparents and other elders, and in both English and Cherokee. These sources sometimes differ and conflict but are usually seen as complementary, their contrasts providing fascinating subjects for conversation (Nabokov 2002, 47).

In the Real People series characters perform a similar type of applied epistemological critique as they cultivate their critical impulse. This methodology is characterized by a self-conscious didacticism, including a purposeful repetition of conceptual representations (balance, reciprocity, transformation) and a self-evident goal of providing useful information to the reader regarding ideas about Cherokee history, religion, society, politics, and other facets of a traditional Cherokee worldview (Havelock 1986, 61). Although Cherokee communities are now literate, oral narratives continue to play a crucial role in passing on traditional Cherokee knowledge. The Real People series functions as a supplement to Cherokee oral tradition, recasting in written form narratives that have existed orally for as long as can be remembered.

Scholars of orality and literacy claim that writing down the oral stories, as Conley does, irrevocably distances a once primary culture from its literate incarnation. The shifts in consciousness that the technology of writing creates in the oral mind are profound: the oral as a primary sense is supplanted by the visual; the communal nature of orally supported societies is replaced by the individualism of literate cultures; oral memory is replaced by written records; and the practical didacticism of oral stories becomes in written stories the subject of abstract analysis (Ong 1982, 42). With regard to the differences between listeners of stories and readers of texts, Ong is clear: "Writing and print isolate. There is no collective noun or concept for readers corresponding to 'audience'" (1982, 74). Havelock at least entertains the idea that "texts can supply some sort of image of orality," but his scholarship primarily focuses on the paradoxes that arise when the oral is represented by a "vocabulary and syntax proper to textualization" (1986, 44).

Robert Conley's aesthetics are shaped by his experiences as a member of the Cherokee community of Tahlequah and northeastern Oklahoma. He directs his writing back to that same community. The relationship is not simply felicitous; it is necessary, as it is in community that culture is defined. Speaking of his writing, Conley says, "But yes, it is community based; you're either part of a community or you're not. And if you're not part of a community, if you don't come out of a community, then you are reduced to simply an issue of race" (S. K. Teuton 2001, 122). According to this logic, a Native writer who is not part of a Native community is reliant on social scientific definitions of identity rather than a sense of self gained through communal belonging. In the Real People series Conley addresses his community's desire for historically accurate fiction told from a Cherokee perspective. To create an accurate representation of Cherokee history, his work necessarily must account for the dual influences of orality and literacy that have shaped Cherokee thought and continue to do so.

Conley's Real People series offers Cherokee readers an accessible entry point to engage and recover the history of their people in a critical form that mediates between orality and literacy. Readers get the facts of the past while having those facts constructed as history from within a worldview based in Cherokee oral tradition. The series' discussions of religion, culture, and economics occur in the context of the story of how the Cherokee Nation came into existence, faced threats due to colonization, and has found a means of surviving. As the series argues, however, the ultimate strength of the Nation is dependent on the Cherokee culture's ability to change and adapt through its use of the critical impulse.

Conley is forthright about the political intent of his Cherokee historical fiction. When asked "Is there something about being here in the Cherokee Nation which makes you defend its borders within your writing?" he responded, "Absolutely. I will admit to there being both an educational purpose in my writing and a propaganda purpose in much of my writing, but not all of it. I mean, I've done things which have nothing to do with Cherokee history. But when I do take on those Cherokee subjects, yes, I have those purposes in mind—very definitely. And those were the things that got me started writing" (S. K. Teuton 2001, 118). Conley's view of history as a way of strengthening contemporary Cherokee culture is characteristic of Native American uses of history. In his analysis of Indian historicity Peter Nabokov argues that "Indian representations of the past [are] . . . preoccupied . . . with their stabilizing impact upon the unfolding present" (2002, 46). Nabokov observes that traditional Indian histories are "quite deliberate" in their recitation of "'epitomizing events,' whose combination of notable social and religious elements and historically memorable dramas touched deep cultural nerves and rendered comprehensible to themselves a people's transformation over time" (35). In Conley's work the continued existence of Cherokee oral tradition and the political institution of the Cherokee Nation stabilize the Cherokee present.

The Real People series models an interpretive process in which Cherokee history may be reclaimed as a source of cultural revitalization. A key purpose of the series is to teach its readers a reading methodology that will enable them to understand history as contingent upon the interpretation of narratives, including Cherokee oral tradition and written narratives, of which the series is itself an example. That is how the series works. But the Cherokee concepts that the series thematizes, including ideas such as Duyukta, the Cherokee concept of balance between opposing forces, and the concept of reciprocity as it applies to human relationships, are what give the series its intellectual depth. Conley offers readers no easy, essentialist explanations of how Cherokees thought about the changes their people, religion, culture, and nation experienced in the midst of colonialism. Instead, in keeping with the metafictive nature of the Real People series, the epic begins by foregrounding the epistemological tensions between orality and literacy, offering a Cherokee-centered analysis of the potential benefits and detriments of each mode of communication. The series argues that the very existence of Cherokee civilization has been, and will continue to be, determined by the degree to which Cherokee modes of interpretation are constrained by authoritative literate discourses or liberated by necessarily free-ranging oral-based knowledge systems, for it is through such modes of communication that we know our worlds.

Language and Authority, Stories and Nationhood

The first three books of the Real People series—*The Way of the Priests* (2000b), *The Dark Way* (2000a), and *The White Path* (2000)—are meditations on power and authority in the interpretation of language in the pre-Columbian Cherokee Nation. Interpretive power is exerted in the ways explained by Foucault as arising out of the oppressive control of discourse. Those retaining interpretive power in the series do so with reference to an authority garnered by their ability to read and write, and thus to act as keepers of the principles of the Cherokee worldview and religious traditions. The series allegorizes this epistemological tension with characters wedded to either oral epistemological templates or literate templates. Contextualizing this conflict between oral and literate ways of knowing the world within generations of Cherokee history draws the debate out of the realm of academic discourse and recasts it as something that has profound implications for the Cherokee Nation, both in the past and now.

The central crisis of the first three novels was suggested to Conley by an ancient story recorded in James Mooney's *Myths of the Cherokees*, one that is still a part of Cherokee culture. It tells of the massacre of a powerful priestly class of

Cherokees, the Ani-Kutani, who were destroyed in a revolt against their abuse of ritual power and licentiousness (Mooney 1900, 392). Diverging from written scholarly accounts of the Ani-Kutani, Conley adds an explanation for their betrayal of their subjects: the priests attain too much power through their exclusive ability to write. As keepers of the written ritual traditions, the priests are seduced by their power and brandish their authority to interpret tradition for selfish ends rather than for the well-being of their people.

The moral and ethical theories the Real People series draws on to critique the actions of the priests are in keeping with a contemporary traditional Cherokee worldview, which is founded on the concept of *balance*. Drawn from the Cherokee cosmology in which the universe is structured by tensions between a Sky World and an Under World, with the world humans live on caught in the middle, the striving for balance structures every part of traditional Cherokee culture. The historian Theda Perdue writes of Cherokees, "They conceived of their world as a system of categories that opposed and balanced one another. In this belief system, women balanced men just as summer balanced winter, plants balanced animals, and farming balanced hunting. Peace and prosperity depended on the maintenance of boundaries between these opposing categories, and blurring the lines between them threatened disaster" (1998, 13). Barbara Duncan writes of the contemporary Eastern Band of Cherokee Indians, "The Cherokee believe that stories, along with ceremonies, arts and crafts, and other traditions, help the individual and the culture 'stay in balance.' The Cherokee attribute their survival as a people, a unique culture, to their closeness to the land and their adherence to *Duyukta*. Duyukta is a moral code that might be roughly translated as 'the right way,' 'the right path,' or 'the path of being in balance'" (1998, 25). Duncan continues with a reflection on a Cherokee method of achieving balance:

> One of the medicine people told me: "What does being in balance mean? It is the traditional Cherokee way of living: placing importance on the good of the whole more than the individual; having freedom but taking responsibility for yourself; staying close to the earth and all our relations. And how does one do this? By taking time to dream; by understanding our nature and our needs and taking care of them; by doing ceremonies that keep us in balance like going to water and using the sweat lodge; by listening and praying; by recognizing our dark and light sides; by having the support of family, extended family, clan and tribe. The medicine people say it requires understanding ourselves and our place in the world around us." (25)

Perdue explains, "A communitarian ethic pervaded Cherokee life" (1998, 27). The Cherokee scholar Daniel Heath Justice addresses Cherokee balance in what he identifies as "complementary philosophies" arising out of Cherokee nationhood (2006, 16). Justice names two Cherokee principles that shape Cherokee "literary and cultural expression": the "Beloved Path," which advocates "accommodation and cooperation," and the "Chickamauga consciousness," which takes a position of "physical and/or rhetorical defiance" (16). Whether in the form of ceremonies such as Green Corn, the Cherokee economy, or in colonial conflicts, the ultimate aim for Cherokees has always been a peaceful coexistence between balanced but opposing forces (Perdue 1998, 27).

Rather than binaries, Anne Waters's (2004) concept of nondiscrete nonbinary dualisms informs nearly all facets of the Real People series, from the structure of the narrative, which draws on oral traditions; to the characters represented, who nearly always have opposing figural twins in other characters; to the ideas the series explores, including both the advantages and the disadvantages of orality and literacy. The problem with literacy, the texts argue, is not that it opposes orality in a necessarily abusive way, but that as a tool, literacy may easily be co-opted to perform in an epistemologically authoritative manner, thus upsetting a delicate social balance. Conley tells the story of how the uprising against the Ani-Kutani occurred: "One day a hunter came home after an extended trip and couldn't find his wife. So he was asking around and one of his neighbors finally told him, 'While you were gone the priests came and got her'" (Ballard 2001, 334). The man gathered together his friends and killed the priests for their transgressions against the people, thus upsetting the social, religious, and political balances that sustained the Cherokee. Conley explains, "If the priests are in charge of the ceremonies and you kill all the priests, you've taken a desperate, desperate chance on bringing about the end of the world" (Ballard 2001, 335). By ridding themselves of the Ani-Kutani, the Cherokees attempted to correct an imbalance in the world but were left with another in the form of a hermeneutical vacuum.

Using their written archives, the Ani-Kutani re-create ceremonies based on their interpretations of Cherokee cosmology. Conley admits that his bestowal of the power of writing to the Ani-Kutani is based on academically unsubstantiated stories of an "ancient writing system": "That, of course, flies in the face of the widely held belief that all American Indian societies were preliterate before the arrival of the Europeans. But I believe that the Cherokee syllabary may be an old system, and therefore it exists in *The Way of the Priests*" (2000b, 62). As discussed in chapter 1 in reference to Sequoyah Guess, this claim is well known in Cherokee country. What is crucial about Conley's depiction of writing as a trope for understanding power is that the plot of the Real People series places the responsibility of making meaning out of language squarely on Cherokee shoulders. By imagining that a class of Cherokees, not Europeans or Americans, first abused the written word, Conley decenters the idea that Indians were illiterate prior to European conquest. Like Leslie Marmon Silko, who writes in *Ceremony*, "We can deal with white people, with their machines and beliefs [because] . . . it was Indian witchery that made white people in the first place" (1977, 132), Conley inscribes writing in the pre-contact history in order to grant Cherokees agency in their production of knowledge. *The Way of the Priests* contains two interlocked storylines that offer opposite interpretive methodologies, one authority-centered and the other based on a community-centered interpretive openness. The Aniyunwiya, or Real People, are in the midst of a terrible drought caused by a world out of balance. Charged with maintaining the well-being of the people, the Ani-Kutani have become a kind of oppressive bureaucracy, and their leader, Standing-in-the-Doorway, a dictator. Conley writes of him, "He was the head man of the *Ani-Kutani*, the chief of all the priests. He had more power and authority than anyone among the Real People, but he also had more responsibility" (2000b, 81). Standing-in-the-Doorway was judged by his ability to keep the Cherokee world balanced, and "if the rain did not come soon, he would be blamed. He was the supreme spiritual leader of his people, with all the major religious ceremonies in his charge" (81). Standing-in-the-Doorway has performed all the ceremonies the Ani-Kutani know to bring the rain, but none has worked. In utter desperation he turns for answers to what he considers legend, Cherokee oral tradition, and sends three priests to the West, the home of Thunder, with the hope that they may bring back the rain.

Having handed the Ani-Kutani the power of interpreting tradition, the people have no means of knowing the boundaries of the rights and responsibilities of the priests. Only the old medicine person, Gone-in-the-Water, is able to recount for the Cherokee populace what the Ani-Kutani should actually do and how they should behave. Serving as Standing-in-the-Doorway's oral counterpart, Gone-in-the-Water too serves the people, but has shunned politics: "Gone-in-the-Water had heard the people complaining about the priests lately, but he had kept quiet. It was not a thing for him to get involved in" (Conley 2000a, 16). In the Cherokee way of balance, local medicine people served certain needs, and the priests served others: "Gone-in-the-Water had no problem with the ancient role of the priests. It did not conflict in any way with his own role as conjurer. His job was to deal with individuals on small matters, matters that concerned one person or a few. If a person was sick or hurt, that person would come to Gone-in-the-Water. . . . The roles were clear and did not conflict" (16). At the same time Gone-in-the-Water is secure in his knowledge of a Cherokee worldview characterized by stories and is not impressed by the priestly authority over the people as a whole: "Those priests were no better than anyone else, certainly they were no better than Gone-in-the-Water.

He was good as any *Kutani*. He was sure of that" (16). But, just as Plato argued that writing would do for the Greeks, literacy has for the Cherokee populace destroyed their collective memory (Ong 1982, 24). Gone-in-the-Water comes to the aid of the community and recalls for them that the power and responsibility of the Ani-Kutani is tied directly to their ability to interpret stories and create ceremonies to enact those stories: "From ancient times, the *Ani-Kutani* had been given charge of the public ceremonies of the Real People, the ceremonies designed to keep the worlds in balance and the Real People in harmony with all things. They also had charge of the old stories that explained why things were as they were and how the people should behave" (Conley 2000a, 15–16). The two roles, orally and graphically oriented, were coexistent, each feeding into the other as two important methods for keeping the Real People together politically, socially, spiritually, and culturally. The problem Gone-in-the-Water highlights is that the Cherokee people have failed to fulfill their equally important role as interpreters of tradition and have lost their ability to critically engage oral and graphic discourses. Because of their epistemological dependency, the Cherokee people have slowly relinquished their power to interpret their oral tradition themselves; they have no understanding or control over their knowledge base.

With their world desperately out of balance, Conley offers hope for the Cherokees in the form of two characters who approach the interpretation of stories from opposing oral and graphic modes. In showing the way these characters learn to value the process-oriented nature of oral traditions and the analytical capacity characteristic of a literate consciousness, the Real People series seeks a balance between oral and literate interpretive methodologies. Like-a-Pumpkin, the Kutani scribe who was in the group sent west to find Thunder's house, is very familiar with the stories of the Aniyunwiya. He understands the stories much as a contemporary literate person might. They are not epistemological templates, but legends and folktales, which may be entertaining but ultimately are nonsensical and full of gaps in logic: "Like-a-Pumpkin felt a pang of guilt as he found himself wondering if the stories were true. . . . He had heard the old stories, had learned them, had even repeated them without ever questioning their veracity, but walking the road to the west, going on a journey to seek out the house of Thunder, his mind began to question them" (Conley 2000b, 100–101). Like-a-Pumpkin is bitter about being sent to travel through dangerous foreign lands on the basis of what an old story says. Thinking about a story is one thing, but risking one's life in acting on it is quite another. Only once enslaved by an unknown nation of Natives does Like-a-Pumpkin begin to see the value of oral tradition. Tellingly, his writings have been confiscated, and so Like-a-Pumpkin has only his memory to offer him counsel. He does not remember the complicated ceremonies and rituals he transcribed, but a simple story about Jisdu (Rabbit) that provides the trickster model for his escape: "He thought about Jisdu, the rabbit, the great trickster, and how he had escaped from the wolves" (149).

Like-a-Pumpkin's critical engagement with oral tradition as a source of knowledge models a way of analyzing and interpreting stories, extrapolating from them and applying their lessons in new contexts. Following Jisdu's actions, Like-a-Pumpkin preys on his captor's curiosity. In the story he recalls, Jisdu sings a "new song and a new dance" for the wolves, who admire his skills. Dancing gracefully he moves ever closer to the safety of the woods. The wolves copy his steps and begin singing his song, caught up in the words and movements. Once close enough, Jisdu springs into the forest and escapes the wolves. In a similar way Like-a-Pumpkin sings Rabbit's song: "On the edge of the field I dance about. Ha Nia li li. Ha nia li li" (160). He moves in rhythm with his song, bobbing in and out of the woods, his unworried captor watching lazily from a distance. Suddenly Like-a-Pumpkin feigns a terrible stomach pain and doubles over, leading his captor to come up from behind. When the time is right, Like-a-Pumpkin springs upon his captor and kills him, all the while singing Jisdu's song as he dances out of captivity.

Like-a-Pumpkin survives because he applies an analytical mode of interpretation learned from literacy to his reading of an oral story. Following the example of Jisdu he combines the lessons of the story and his own, new interpretation of it to create a powerful template for not just thought, but action. Like-a-Pumpkin models a form of applied interpretation of oral traditions that the Real People series advocates. Rather than portraying oral traditions as fixed, formulaic modes of expressing traditional thought, Conley's narrative portrays oral tradition as a subject of study and analysis (Ong 1982, 24). This new conception of oral knowledge as that which may be analyzed, abstracted, and categorized is introduced by the literate Like-a-Pumpkin, whose knowledge of writing, as Ong observes, "serves to separate and distance the knower and the known and thus to establish objectivity" (113–14). Thus a story about Rabbit and the Wolves becomes a story about trickery and escape. Of course, the story was always about these themes, but its meaning had been forgotten.

While Like-a-Pumpkin models an interpretive form that mediates between orality and literacy, Standing-in-the-Doorway's dogged privileging of a literate mode of representing and interpreting knowledge results in a deadly clash with the oral impulse tenets structuring the Cherokee epistemology of the common people. In a final attempt to bring rain, Standing-in-the-Doorway orders the sacrifice of a young Cherokee woman, Corn Flower, as an offering to Thunder. Without recourse to an oral tradition that may have helped him decide how to handle a drought, the Kutani leader improvises. The Aniyunwiya are appalled by the brutal action of the Kutani because it is not understood as rational from within an oral Cherokee epistemology. Spoiler, the mother of Corn Flower, asks, "Why did they take my daughter away from me? To make rain? Where is the rain? And what has the blood of my daughter to do with rain?" (2000a, 65). Conley's depiction of the oral Cherokees as having an oral worldview with a violable logic contradicts the position that oral knowledge is formulaic and static. Spoiler looks for a logical reason for the priest's actions, but she cannot find one. Standing-in-the-Doorway misjudges oral culture by assuming that he can placate the nonliterate Cherokee with a dramatic sacrifice. When confronted with injustice common Cherokees like Spoiler begin to reclaim analytical thought from the priests: they ask "Why?"

The orality-based Cherokees revolt against their literate religious leaders and kill all the Ani-Kutani for their misinterpretation of Cherokee tradition and their abuse of power. In a supreme irony writing, which is designed to forestall the death of culture, of tradition, and of the people, actually leads to these very ends through the inflexible use of its authority.

Even after the Kutani are killed writing maintains a measure of power over the Cherokee. Edohi, the leader of the rebellion, has trouble reconciling the fact that the revolt is somehow a repudiation of Aniyunwiya tradition. Edohi is Like-a-Pumpkin's conceptual twin and narrative counterpart; just as Like-a-Pumpkin had to learn the value of oral tradition, Edohi must learn the value of analytical thought. Gone-in-the-Water provides the first lesson in Edohi's conceptual growth. Unlike Standing-in-the-Doorway, whose literacy grants him a measure of objectivity but also distances him from the people he governs, Gone-in-the-Water's knowledge focuses on practical applications "situated in operational contexts" (Ong 1982, 55). He explains Cherokee tradition and in doing so shows performatively that tradition still exists and has returned to oral form. He tells of the world above the Sky-Vault, the Under World below the water, and the world we live upon, Elohi:

> This world on which we walk between the other two is indeed in a delicate situation. The other two worlds are full of powerful spirits, and their forces are opposed to each other. If we lose our balance, we will be crushed, torn apart, when the two opposites meet and mix. We would have no defense.
>
> So we do things in certain ways. We have ceremonies and our rituals and other things we do and don't do. All that is calculated to help us maintain our balance on this middle world. Yes, nephew, I know your fears. (2000a, 137–38)

Central to Gone-in-the-Water's explanation is that nobody can balance the life of another person. Like interpretation, balancing one's world is ultimately the responsibility of individuals acting within the critical impulse of a community context. As Gone-in-the-Water says, "[The literate Ani-Kutani] have led us to believe that they are the ones who keep the balance for us. ... They have created your fears, Edohi" (138). The Aniyunwiya already know the proper ways to keep balance in the world, and Gone-in-the-Water explains that the priests are not needed: "As long as our children are taught to do the right things, there will never be a need for priests" (138). Gone-in-the-Water reasserts the supremacy of orality for engaging the practical needs of life by claiming that an authoritative priesthood is unnecessary if the people live their beliefs, accepting their responsibility to teach their children "the right things." He argues for the necessity of oral notions of knowledge rooted in practice over knowledge rooted exclusively in objective analysis, because the former necessarily operates in a communal context.

Standing-in-the-Doorway's power and authority as the exclusive interpreter of tradition is, in part, structured by the technology of writing. Conley portrays literacy as supporting a hierarchy of knowledge in which those who have read more know more and thus have more power. In contrast, Gone-in-the-Water and Edohi represent a pluralistic approach to knowledge. Gone-in-the-Water is respected because he knows how to apply knowledge practically. Without reference to theory, Conley's texts nevertheless portray the nonliterate Cherokees suffering the effects of what Gayatri Spivak calls "Othering": "These include the assumption of authority, 'voice,' and control of the 'word,' that is, seizure and control of the means of interpretation and communication" (Ashcroft, Griffiths, and Tiffin 1989, 97). The Real People series approaches this question of knowledge as both an epistemological issue and an issue of governance. As Edohi explains, "One man, one town made decisions for our entire nation and issued arbitrary commands to our people. Nothing like that must ever happen again. There cannot be one worldly power over all the Real People" (Conley 2000a, 174).

The White Path, the third novel of the Real People series, uses this evolving conceptual model of a blend of oral tradition and written tradition to theorize a pluralistic Cherokee government. Describing the process of rebuilding their government enables Conley to model a critical impulse method of mediating between oral knowledge and literate analysis. Faced with a crisis that is destroying Cherokee society, Edohi and Like-a-Pumpkin are compelled to create a critical methodology that transforms the formulaic oral tradition into a subject of analysis and contemplation. Gone-in-the-Water provides Edohi with stories and commentary that express fundamental Cherokee concepts, including the notion of balance existing in opposing pairs: "Edohi, everything exists in pairs. There is day and night, light and dark, winter and summer. There is life and death, male and female. There is peace and there is war. Below us is the underworld, and above us is the world at the Seventh Height. Everything in pairs of opposites. This is perhaps the most important thing that we can know" (2000, 75). While he helps Edohi, Gone-in-the-Water will not, or perhaps cannot tell him how he should organize the town leadership in accordance with this understanding of interpenetrating opposites. Conley contends that it is not Gone-in-the-Water's traditional role to explicate stories and use them as models for constructing new systems of government. Nevertheless the old conjurer is aware of what knowledge Edohi may need to fulfill such a mediating role, and so he tells him a story.

Gone-in-the-Water tells Edohi of a tribe of little people, called Tsundigewi: "The Real People learned to talk to these little people, and they learned that these pitiful little people lived in constant fear. Wild geese and other birds came in flocks from the south to make war on them, and the birds carried them away in great numbers each time they attacked" (13). The Real People helped the Tsundigewi fight off the wild birds, but in the end a more powerful enemy came along and killed them off. A surface-level interpretation of the story, one that might have been applicable prior to the revolt against the Ani-Kutani, might imply that some peoples are simply destined to die. But the cultural crisis enables Edohi to offer a new reading of the story. As his counterpart Like-a-Pumpkin once did, Edohi turns in desperation to oral tradition for an applicable model of action. The problem Edohi sees in the story is that the Real People prepared the Tsundigewi for one enemy, but not all enemies: "The young men saved the little people from one danger, but they gave up too soon. . . . They should have stayed longer. They should have anticipated the greater danger and prepared the little people for it as well" (15). Without Gone-in-the-Water's aid, Edohi applies the lesson of the story to the current state of the Real People. He recognizes that the first wave of danger was the Ani-Kutani, and the second wave is the infighting between the people themselves. Analyzing an oral story has enabled him to recognize what actions he should take: "If I quit now, the people will be destroyed" (15).

To a contemporary reader Edohi's rudimentary interpretive skills appear unimpressive. They are designedly so. In charting Edohi's critical growth through his conversations with the oral Gone-in-the-Water and the literate Like-a-Pumpkin, Conley portrays the beginnings of a Cherokee critical interpretive methodology. With the honing of his critical thought, Edohi recognizes that belief systems and governance both depend on the way they are interpreted and for what ends. Speaking of the priests, Edohi determines, "We attacked the men, not our beliefs. We believe the way we have always believed. But now we have no guidance" (30). In contrast to the literacy-based authority of the priest, "guidance" suggests a critical practice of leading by example with an awareness of communal oral traditions.

Gone-in-the-Water models guidance by introducing Edohi to the critical concepts he needs as the young leader contemplates the governance of the Cherokee. He explains, "Edohi, everything exists in pairs. . . . This is perhaps the most important thing that we can know" (75). Relying on the lessons of the oral tradition, Edohi learns from Gone-in-the-Water the appropriate mode of interpretation needed to understand the principles of governance. Edohi does not come up with the solution by himself, but naturally finds it by talking with Like-a-Pumpkin, who has been given the new name Dancing Rabbit.

Edohi and Dancing Rabbit create for the Cherokee a new, decentralized form of government based on an evolving interpretation of the concept of balance. Edohi tells Dancing Rabbit that the people of Ijodi want to make him war chief (142). He is troubled by the responsibilities that come with this position because they are reminiscent of the powers the priests had, and he does not want to replicate that system of power. Together the two reluctant leaders ponder Gone-in-the-Water's statement that everything "comes in twos" (142). Dancing Rabbit comes up with the answer to Edohi's dilemma: "If you become war chief, someone else must be peace chief. Is that it?" (142). Conley writes, "It was a sudden revelation from a former *Kutani*, and Edohi knew right then that he had been right in seeking the help of Dancing Rabbit" (142–43). Building on this concept of balance, the two representatives of orality and literacy theorize their new model of governance.

The system they come up with is simple yet balanced, in accord with fundamental Cherokee values. Both peace chief and war chief "have a council of seven, one from each clan" (143). Government is decentralized and issues of war and peace are decided on a local level by those who are directly affected by the decisions. The chiefs and the council are made up of men, but they are "selected by the women of the clans, and the women should have the power to remove a man from the council if they don't approve his actions" (143). War and peace, all clans represented, men and women in power: the new, pluralistic government is quickly adopted by all Cherokee towns.

Crucial to Conley's depiction of this new system of government in the Real People series is that it completely disassociates itself from the authority of written texts. Writing goes into hiding at the end of *The White Path* and is secretly entrusted to caretakers for generation after generation, reemerging in *Sequoyah* (2002), the twelfth book in the Real People series, as a tool of cultural survival. In *Sequoyah* Conley again uses the story of the written language to argue for the crucial connection between Cherokee storytelling and the political entity called the Cherokee Nation. The famed Cherokee linguist struggles to re-create a nearly forgotten language in order to save his people from the tyranny of the colonizing Americans, whose ability to write plays a key role in their theft of Cherokee homelands.

Conclusion

Robert Conley's Real People series theorizes the tensions between oral and written modes of communication by portraying their effects on an ancient Cherokee world that is part imaginary, part historical. The details of how traditional Cherokee government came into being may differ in some respects from the version told in the Real People series, but the concepts on which that system of government is based and the values through which it is understood remain largely constant. Conley's imaginative telling of history is decidedly aimed at inspiring the responsive imagination of his readers rather than being in absolute accord with principles of historiography. Those values that Conley's depiction of Cherokee governance conjures up, such as the belief in freedom over tyranny, in autonomy over authority, are as pertinent today to the future of the Cherokee people as they must have been when, in ancient times, the Ani-Kutani were overthrown. The popular style of the series serves to underscore one of its central themes: that the preservation of Cherokee oral tradition is crucial to the survival of the Real People. Oral traditions exist in living memory, and if they survive they are necessarily in touch with the needs of the communities from which they arise. At the same time the Real People series argues that society needs guidance in the form of leadership that moves beyond oral thought and draws on critical paradigms that arise out of a graphic approach to knowledge, which interpretation, an embodiment of the critical impulse, will provide. As a potentially static representation of reality, whether it is in the form of stories or of treaties, writing can make the subjective seem objective, the interpretive appear simply as the truth. The egalitarianism of oral tradition regulates the system of hierarchical authority that arises out of literacy. One method of using this tool properly, Conley's novels suggest, is to interpret the written word using traditional oral paradigms to which Cherokee knowledge owes its conceptual health. It is for this reason that oral traditional stories such as those of Jisdu and the Tsundigewi are central to Conley's novels: through our interpretation of these well-known stories we may learn Cherokee cultural concepts that may in turn direct our critical interpretation of the written works. Whether in the form of oral stories placed strategically within a written work, a critic's response to a text, or an artist's rendering of a character from a novel, the guidance of interpretation may lead this evolving critical conversation in new directions. Used critically, oral stories may teach us methods of balancing our literate world.

Epilogue

Building Ground in
American Indian Textual Studies

Dypaloh. A word, an invocation. This one Jemez phrase signals not just the beginning of N. Scott Momaday's *House Made*
of Dawn, but a key moment in the development of a critical
awareness of the relationship between oral and graphic discourses in Native American literature. Since the publication
of Momaday's watershed novel, Native American writers have
responded to that text's call to create literature in relation
to Native community by placing the oral and the written in
conversation. In the twenty-first century, the critical impulse
House Made of Dawn manifested so brilliantly in 1969 is taking new forms in new media and new cultural contexts. How
American Indian textual studies responds to these innova-
tions will determine the future of our field of cultural work.
It is my hope that in this book I have helped further that project in ways that will open paths for future scholars.

Deep Waters proposes a theory of Native American signification that decenters the oral-literate binary and offers in
its place a dynamic tripartite process that accounts for the
relationship between oral and graphic modes of Indigenous
communication in relation to the needs of Native American
survivance. The continued vibrancy of Indigenous knowledge depends on bringing oral and graphic discourses into
conversation through interpretation, what I call the critical
impulse.

It is in the discourse of the novel that the dominance
of graphocentrism is most actively subverted by the critical
impulse. The critical work of the Native American novel serves
a cultural purpose that parallels that described by Milan Kundera in The Art of the Novel. Writing of the "Modern Era" in
Europe, Kundera argues that the Western novel reminds us
of a humanity that is threatened by the conditions of modern life. Viewing the world as "a question to be answered,"
Western societies "reduced the world to a mere object of tech-
nical and mechanical investigation" (2003, 3). Like the rest
of the world, the life of human beings could be understood
through the forces that acted upon them (4). While philosophy and science abandoned the study of humanity's "concrete being," its "world of life," Kundera argues, the novel
has provided a counterbalance with which we may "scruti-
nize man's concrete life and protect it against 'the forget-
ting of being'; to hold 'the world of life' under a permanent
light" (4–5). Echoing Hermann Broch, Kundera argues, "The
sole raison d'être of a novel is to discover what only the novel
can discover. A novel that does not discover a hitherto seg-
ment of existence is immoral. Knowledge is the novel's only
morality" (5–6). Sharing Kundera's sense of the novel's cultural

work, Native American writers have used the form to explore the long-repressed relationship between the oral and graphic impulses, opening up spaces in which the critical impulses of readers may grow. The full articulation of Indigenous knowledge in oral and graphic forms is central to the morality of the Native American novel.

It is my hope that the oral, graphic, and critical impulses will encourage further study of the relationships between oral and other nonalphabetic graphic traditions. The relationships between Indigenous visual art, oral discourses, and written literature deserve immediate attention. For example, how have the aesthetics of visual art and written literature influenced one another? How do their interpretive methodologies relate? Kinesthetic modes of expressing knowledge, such as Plains Sign Talk, dance, rituals, and ceremonies, warrant further study in the context of the impulses. Material culture, such as textiles, basketry, and dress, also function as graphic discourse. As Keith Basso shows in *Wisdom Sits in Places: Landscape and Language among the Western Apache*, landscapes may be marked with story (1996, 7). Not just placenames, but Indigenous rock art, architecture, and geography may be better understood if we approach the study of them as context-dependent forms of recording thought. Exploring the vast array of ways knowledge exists in Indigenous communities in interdependent oral and graphic forms may open new areas of Native American studies to further research. Studying how the oral and the graphic relate will enable scholars to provide clearer, deeper, and more complex Indigenous critical theories will which expand the text world beyond those of Western literary forms.

The critical methodology I advocate in *Deep Waters* has

several implications for the further development of Native literary criticism. My hope is that scholars will reexamine the study of Indigenous texts, both oral and graphic, from within tribally specific Indigenous discursive dynamics. Studying the ways particular Indigenous cultures strike a balance between maintaining knowledge in oral and graphic forms will enable us to understand Indigenous critical discourses not only on a culture-by-culture basis but transnationally. Applying the critical impulse to specific situations will allow scholars to theorize how these discourses respond to particular cultural, social, and historical contexts.

In addition, Deep Waters offers scholars in the social sciences, humanities, and law an explanation of how context-dependent forms of recording thought function to record knowledge. Anthropologists may find in the oral, graphic, and critical impulses a fresh perspective on how Indigenous knowledge is maintained and passed along, changing with the needs of a culture. Historians of Indigenous cultures encounter the graphocentrism of Western historiography, which continues to be dependent on the written word. The textual continuum offers a theory of how Indigenous knowledge is recorded in interdependent oral and graphic forms, thus offering the potential for developing Indigenous historiographies. Similarly, legal scholars such as Robert A. Williams Jr. decry the way racist rhetoric continues to define the ways Native Americans are understood in U.S. law. As Williams writes, "The continuing legal force of a long-established, deeply embedded, and widely dispersed language of racism directed at Indians can be found at work throughout the Supreme Court's Indian law decisions, beginning with the Marshall Court's foundational precedents on Indian rights laid down in the early nineteenth century and continuing in the Rehnquist Court's leading Indian rights decisions of the twenty-first century" (2005, xxv). Referring to the impulses and their function in the textual continuum, legal scholars may better challenge the history of racism against Native Americans that continues in U.S. law. In turn they may be able to make cases for the use of both oral and graphic means of marking territorial boundaries, an issue that arises repeatedly in Indigenous land claims disputes.

In addition to engaging written texts and forms of signification with deep roots in Native culture, Native textual studies is in a position to engage the emerging forms of digital media. Native-centered digital communities have for years served as clearinghouses for Indigenous information, but those forms of text have received very little critical attention. The Web already engages people graphically and orally, and the capacity to construct more complex cyberspace communities will only increase. An understanding of the relationships between the oral, graphic, and critical impulses will prove useful to the study of those discourses.

Indigenous textuality draws its meaning from a social context, and scholars have begun to develop forms that reflect this fact. Craig S. Womack's inclusion of letters from Jim Chibbo to Hotgun between chapters of *Red on Red* marks a new development in Native American literary criticism. The figurative presence of an Indigenous community is given a critical voice in Womack's text through Chibbo's wry and wise commentary, and the text as a whole is stronger for it. Similarly, Taiaiake Alfred includes interviews in his scholarly works, showing performatively how the critical impulse grows in intellectual conversation.

I believe that Native American literary studies needs to continue this work by forging stronger intellectual ties with Indigenous communities outside of academia. In my own way I have attempted to do this by establishing the Denver American Indian Community Reading Group. We range in age from twenty to late sixties, and we come from all over the continent—the Plains, the Southeast, the Southwest, and the Rockies. We are Lakota, Dakota, Diné, Choctaw, Chippewa, Cherokee, and Chickasaw. We read works of Native American literature, and we come together and discuss our ideas about those books and about our world today. In the process we build community.

In writing *Deep Waters* my deepest underlying concern has been to show how the relationship between the oral, graphic, and critical impulses offers scholars and students a theory that explains why the issues and concerns of Indigenous communities should be privileged and foregrounded in Indigenous critical studies. The ideas expressed in Native American literature matter to Native American community, not just to scholars working in academic institutions. Part of the work of scholars is to take the critical impulse beyond the walls of their classrooms. The future of American Indian intellectual discourse depends on building connections between academic and nonacademic communities and grounding the study of Native American knowledge in Native American social, cultural, and political contexts. Being attuned to the diverse voices that interpret Native American literature, we may contribute fruitfully to the critical discourses that enable us to build the world on which we live. *Wado.*

Notes

Introduction

1. In *Survivance: Narratives of Native Presence*, edited by Gerald Vizenor, he writes, "Native survivance is an active sense of presence over absence, deracination, and oblivion; survivance is the continuance of stories, not a mere reaction, however pertinent. Survivance is greater than the right of a survivable name" (2008, 1). Vizenor further explains, "Survivance is a practice, not an ideology, dissimulation, or theory" (11). Related to the word *survival*, *survivance* as used by Vizenor refers to a vibrant form of continuity in the context of ever changing Indigenous worldviews: "Original, communal responsibility, greater than the individual, greater than original sin, but not accountability, animates the practice and consciousness of survivance, a sense of presence, a responsible presence of natural reason and resistance to absence and victimry" (18–19).

1. The Oral Impulse, the Graphic Impulse, and the Critical Impulse

1. The anthropologist Ray Fogelson references the story of the Ani-Kutani: "Nevertheless, the Cherokees possessed a persistent and fairly

widespread historical legend about a priestly class or hereditary clan whose members were massacred in a public uprising in response to their corruption and sexual impropriety" (1984, 255). In *Red Matters: Native American Studies* Arnold Krupat explores the tensions between Western historiography, which is dependent on the facticity of history, and a Native American historiography, which is open to a consensual account of history as it is understood by a group (2002, chapter 3, "America's Histories").

2. See Pearce 1988; Mignolo 2003.

3. See Cook-Lynn 2001, 2007; Alfred 1999, 2005; Wilson 2008; Justice 2006; Weaver, Womack, and Warrior 2006; A. Smith 2005; Adamson 2001; Kelsey 2008; S. K. Teuton 2008.

4. In *The Remembered Earth: An Anthology of Contemporary Native American Literature* Geary Hobson writes, "Traditionally, certainly long before the Europeans came to the Western Hemisphere and even long after their arrival, Native American people have been accustomed to remembering their histories and their ways of life through intricate time-proven processes of storytelling. It is only recently that these ways of storytelling have become designated by scholars as oral tradition" (1979, 2).

5. Elizabeth Boone states, "Archibald Hill, Walter Ong, and anthropologist Jack Goody, too, consider writing as recorded speech, as do historians like Michael Camille and M. T. Clanchy, who have examined the phenomena" (1994, 4–5). John DeFrancis is adamant in his assertion that "all full systems of communication are based on speech" (1989, 7). Florian Coulmas is in agreement: "The decisive step in the development of writing is phonetization: that is, the transition from pictorial icon to phonetic symbol" (1989, 33). David Diringer concurs: "Literally and closely defined, writing is the graphic counterpart of speech, the 'fixing' of spoken language in a permanent or semi-permanent form" (1962, 13).

6. David Diringer defines *civilization* in reference to "ancient Near Eastern and European cultures," which "were based, without exception, on the knowledge of writing, the employment of metals, the cultivation of wheat, the domestication of a variety of animals, the use of the wheel, and the growth of large urban centres" (1962, 95).

7. David Diringer states, "Writing, as we understand it, is a conscious activity, intricately and inseparably bound up with the development,

comparatively recent, of man's conscious intellect. The establishment of stabilisation of a written script—cuneiform, or Chinese, or Hittite hieroglyphic—implies a degree of consciousness towards language so much larger that that of, say, Palaeolithic man, as to amount to a difference in kind" (1962, 16).

8. The anthropologist Brian Street and the cultural psychologists Sylvia Scribner and Michael Cole argue that oral-literate theorists have generalized about the effects of orality and literacy without support from ethnographic case studies and qualitative work. Scribner and Cole claim that differences between literate and oral cognitive skills, specifically the ability to think abstractly, are determined by learning these skills in school, and not by acquiring literacy alone (1981, 12). Street argues that orality and literacy are social processes that cannot be conceptualized as autonomous modes without regard to their applications in societies (1984, 97). When orality and literacy are conceived as a priori categories, literacy is consistently privileged as the more advanced form of communication, what Street calls the "autonomous" model (1–2). The autonomous model "assumes a single direction in which literacy development can be traced, and associates it with 'progress,' 'civilization,' individual liberty and social mobility" (2).

9. For an informative discussion of the relationship between orality and literacy, see Arnold Krupat, "Post-Structuralism and Oral Literature," in Swann and Krupat 1987. For a discussion of Ojibwa worldviews and Euro-American theory, see Vizenor 1998. Bernd C. Peyer discusses the potential implications of oral-literate theory on "linguistic imperialism" in The Tutor'd Min: Indian Missionary-Writers in Antebellum America (1997, 9). As examples of the continued presence of oral-literate theory, see the work of Karl Kroeber and Cheryl Walker. In Native American Storytelling: A Reader of Myths and Legends Kroeber writes, "The form of American Indian storytelling is entirely different from the form of our storytelling. One reason for the radical difference is that all the North American Indians developed their cultures without writing" (2004, 1). In Indian Nation: Native American Literature and Nineteenth-Century Nationalisms Walker writes, "To begin with, one must acknowledge that Native American literature is something of an oddity. Since Indians before contact did not have anything but pictographic writing, written literature emerged, to some degree, as a form of collaboration with the enemy" (1997, 13).

10. See Cook-Lynn 1996, 82.

11. See Arnold Krupat, "Post-Structuralism and Oral Literature," in Swann and Krupat 1987, 115.

12. I recognize that scholars such as Elizabeth Boone (2008) and Linda Martín Alcoff (2008, xi) criticize Todorov for representing Triple Alliance culture as illiterate. I reference him in this passage only to support Carrasco's (1982) argument that the Mexica were bound by a particular interpretation of a myth of the return of Quetzalcoatl, one that supported their claims to power.

5. Interpreting Our World

1. This eleven-question Cherokee readers survey is available on the Cherokee Nation of Oklahoma website, www.Cherokee.org, under the archives section of the *Phoenix*. Nineteen people (eleven women and eight men) responded to the posted survey, and I have personally surveyed four others. They represent a wide range of ages (from sixteen to eighty-two) and come from many different places (from New York to Hawaii) and many walks of life (one is in high school, one in prison). Many are living in Oklahoma. Because this research is ongoing, the preliminary results I share are suggestive rather than conclusive.

2. In the answers to each question concerning Native American writers, more readers cited having read Robert Conley's novels more than any works by any other Native American writer. For example, when asked the question "What books by Native American writers have you read?" two readers cited Conley's *War Woman* and two cited *The Peace Chief*. The third most cited work was the biography of Wilma Mankiller, former principal chief of the Cherokee Nation; two respondents cited that work. The same pattern continued in the other questions relating to reader preferences for Native American literature: Conley was cited more than any other writer.

3. Five works of criticism have engaged Conley's writings to any degree. An earlier version of this chapter was the first essay published exclusively on Conley's work (C. Teuton 2007). See also Berry Brill de Ramírez 2000, 2006–7; Weaver, Womack, and Warrior 1997, 160–61; and Ron Welburn's interesting analysis of the first seven novels of the Real People series, "The Indigenous Fiction of Joseph Bruchac and Robert J. Conley" (2001, 187–221).

Works Cited

Adam, Ian. 1996. "Oracy and Literacy: A Post-Colonial Dilemma?" *Journal of Commonwealth Literature* 31.1: 97–109.

Adamson, Joni. 2001. *American Indian Literature, Environmental Justice, and Ecocriticism.* Tucson: University of Arizona Press.

Alcoff, Linda Martín. 2008. Foreword to *Mestiz@ Scripts, Digital Migrations, and the Territories of Writing,* by Damián Baca. New York: Palgrave Macmillan.

Alfred, Taiaiake. 2005. *Wasáse: Indigenous Pathways of Action and Freedom.* Orchard Park NY: Broadview Press.

———. 1999. *Peace, Power, Righteousness: An Indigenous Manifesto.* Oxford: Oxford University Press.

Allen, Paula Gunn. 1992. *The Sacred Hoop: Recovering the Feminine in American Indian Traditions.* Boston: Beacon.

Ashcroft, Bill, Gareth Griffiths, and Helen Tiffin. 1989. *The Empire Writes Back: Theory and Practice in Post-Colonial Literatures.* New York: Routledge.

Babcock, Barbara. 1985. "A Tolerated Margin of Mess: The Trickster and His Tales Reconsidered." In *Critical Essays on Native American Literature,* ed. Andrew Wiget. Boston: G. K. Hall.

Baca, Damián. 2008. *Mestiz@ Scripts, Digital Migrations, and the Territories of Writing*. New York: Palgrave Macmillan.

Ballard, Sandra L. 2001. "Backtracking from Oklahoma to North Carolina: An Interview with Robert J. Conley." *Appalachian Journal: A Regional Studies Review* 28.3: 326–44.

Barry, Nora. 1993. "Chance and Ritual: The Gambler in the Texts of Gerald Vizenor." *Studies in American Indian Literatures* 5.3: 13–22.

Basso, Keith. 1996. *Wisdom Sits in Places: Landscape and Language among the Western Apache*. Albuquerque: University of New Mexico Press.

Bender, Margaret. 2002. *Signs of Cherokee Culture: Sequoyah's Syllabary in Eastern Cherokee Life*. Chapel Hill: University of North Carolina Press.

Berry Brill de Ramírez, Susan. 2006–7. "Before the South Became the South: Pre-Colonial and Colonial Geographies of Contact in Robert J. Conley's Cherokee Historical Novels." *Mississippi Quarterly: The Journal of Southern Cultures* 60.1: 179–207.

———. 2000. "Walking with the Land: Simon J. Ortiz, Robert J. Conley, and Velma Wallis." *South Dakota Review* 38.1: 59–82.

———. 1999. *Contemporary American Indian Literatures and the Oral Tradition*. Tucson: University of Arizona Press.

Birchfield, D. L. 2004. *Field of Honor*. Norman: University of Oklahoma Press.

Blaeser, Kimberly M. 1996. *Gerald Vizenor: Writing in the Oral Tradition*. Norman: University of Oklahoma Press.

———. 1989. "The Way to Rainy Mountain: Momaday's Work in Motion." In *Narrative Chance: Postmodern Discourse on Native American Indian Literatures*, ed. Gerald Vizenor. Albuquerque: University of New Mexico Press.

Blair, Elizabeth. 1995. "Text as Trickster: Postmodern Language Games in Gerald Vizenor's *Bearheart*." MELUS 20.4: 75–90.

Boone, Elizabeth Hill. 2008. *Stories in Red and Black: Pictorial Histories of the Aztec and Mixtec*. Austin: University of Texas Press.

———. 1994. "Introduction: Writing and Recording Knowledge." In *Writing without Words: Alternative Literacies in Mesoamerica and the Andes*, ed. Elizabeth Hill Boone and Walter D. Mignolo. Durham NC: Duke University Press.

Brooks, Lisa. 2008. *The Common Pot: The Recovery of Native Space in the Northeast*. Minneapolis: University of Minnesota Press.

Brotherston, Gordon. 1992. *Book of the Fourth World: Reading the Native Americas through Their Literature*. Cambridge, England: Cambridge University Press.

Carrasco, Davíd. 1982. *Quetzalcoatl and the Irony of Empire: Myths and Prophecies in the Aztec Tradition*. Chicago: University of Chicago Press.

Chavez, Will. 2001. "Cherokee Artist Captures History with Paintings." *Cherokee Phoenix and Indian Advocate* (Summer). www.cherokee.org/Phoenix/XXVN03_Summer2001/ArtCulturePage.

Coe, Michael D. 1999. *Breaking the Maya Code*. New York: Thames & Hudson.

Conley, Robert. J. 2007. *A Cherokee Encyclopedia*. Albuquerque: University of New Mexico Press.

———. 2005a. *Cherokee Medicine Man: The Life and Work of a Modern-Day Healer*. Norman: University of Oklahoma Press.

———. 2005b. *The Cherokee Nation: A History*. Albuquerque: University of New Mexico Press.

———. 2002. *Sequoyah: A Novel of the Real People*. New York: St. Martin's Press.

———. 2000a. *The Dark Way*. Norman: University of Oklahoma Press.

———. 2000b. *The Way of the Priests*. Norman: University of Oklahoma Press.

———. 2000. *The White Path*. Norman: University of Oklahoma Press.

———. 1992. *Mountain Windsong: A Novel of the Trail of Tears*. Norman: University of Oklahoma Press.

Cook-Lynn, Elizabeth. 2007. *New Indians, Old Wars*. Urbana: University of Illinois Press.

———. 2001. *Anti-Indianism in Modern America: A Voice from Tatekeya's Earth*. Urbana: University of Illinois Press.

———. 1996. *Why I Can't Read Wallace Stegner and Other Essays: A Tribal Voice*. Madison: University of Wisconsin Press.

Coulmas, Florian. 1989. *The Writing Systems of the World*. New York: Basil Blackwell.

Cox, James H. 2006. *Muting White Noise: Native American and European American Novel Traditions*. Norman: University of Oklahoma Press.

Cruikshank, Julie. 1998. *The Social Life of Stories: Narrative and Knowledge in the Yukon Territory*. Lincoln: University of Nebraska Press.

Davis, Lennard J. 1987. *Resisting Novels: Ideology and Fiction*. New York: Methuen.

DeFrancis, John. 1989. *Visible Speech: The Diverse Oneness of Writing Systems*. Honolulu: University of Hawaii Press.

Diamond, Jared. 1999. *Guns, Germs and Steel: The Fates of Human Societies*. New York: Norton.

Diringer, David. 1962. *Writing*. New York: Praeger.

Duncan, Barbara R., ed. 1998. *Living Stories of the Cherokee*. Chapel Hill: University of North Carolina Press.

Eagleton, Terry. 1983. *Literary Theory: An Introduction*. Minneapolis: University of Minnesota Press.

Ellison, Ralph. 1964. *Shadow and Act*. New York: Knopf Doubleday.

Fenton, William N. 1985. "Structure, Continuity, and Change in the Process of Iroquois Treaty Making." In *The History and Culture of Iroquois Diplomacy: An Interdisciplinary Guide to the Treaties of the Six Nations and Their League*, ed. Francis Jennings, William N. Fenton, Mary A. Druke, and David R. Miller. Syracuse NY: Syracuse University Press.

Fogelson, Raymond A. 1984. "Who Were the Aní-Kutánî? An Excursion into Cherokee Historical Thought." *Ethnohistory* 31.4: 255–63.

Foreman, Grant. 1938. *Sequoyah*. Norman: University of Oklahoma Press.

Foster, M. K. 1985. "Another Look at the Function of Wampum in Iroquois-White Councils." In *The History and Culture of Iroquois Diplomacy: An Interdisciplinary Guide to the Treaties of the Six Nations and Their League*, ed. Francis Jennings, William N. Fenton, Mary A. Druke, and David R. Miller. Syracuse NY: Syracuse University Press.

Furniss, Graham. 2004. *Orality: The Power of the Spoken Word*. New York: Palgrave Macmillan.

Gansworth, Eric L. 2004. *Smoke Dancing*. East Lansing: Michigan State University Press.

Gelb, Ignace. 1963. *A Study of Writing*. Chicago: University of Chicago Press.

Griffin-Pierce, Trudy. 1992. *Earth Is My Mother, Sky Is My Father: Space, Time, and Astronomy in Navajo Sandpainting*. Albuquerque: University of New Mexico Press.

Guess, Sequoyah. 1992. *Kholvn*. Kansas OK: Kholvn Books.

Harris, Roy. 2000. *Rethinking Writing*. Bloomington: Indiana University Press.

Havelock, Eric. 1986. *The Muse Learns to Write: Reflections on Orality and Literacy from Antiquity to the Present*. New Haven: Yale University Press.

Henley, Joan. 1988. "Exploring the Ways to Rainy Mountain." In *Approaches to Teaching Momaday's The Way to Rainy Mountain*, ed. Kenneth M. Roemer. New York: Modern Language Association.

Hobson, Geary, ed. 1979. *The Remembered Earth: An Anthology of Contemporary Native American Literature*. Albuquerque: University of New Mexico Press.

Howe, LeAnne. 2008. "Blind Bread and the Business of Theory Making, by Embarrassed Grief." In *Reasoning Together: The Native Critics Collective*, ed. Craig S. Womack, Daniel Heath Justice, and Christopher B. Teuton. Norman: University of Oklahoma Press.

Jahandarie, Khosrow. 1999. *Spoken and Written Discourse: A Multi-disciplinary Perspective*. Stamford CT: Ablex.

Jennings, Francis, William N. Fenton, Mary A. Druke, and David R. Miller, eds. 1985. *The History and Culture of Iroquois Diplomacy: An Interdisciplinary Guide to the Treaties of the Six Nations and Their League*. Syracuse NY: Syracuse University Press.

Johnson, Barbara. 1995. "Writing." In *Critical Terms for Literary Study*, ed. Frank Lentricchia and Thomas McLaughlin. Chicago: University of Chicago Press.

Justice, Daniel Heath. 2006. *Our Fire Survives the Storm: A Cherokee Literary History*. Minneapolis: University of Minnesota Press.

Kelsey, Penelope Myrtle. 2008. *Tribal Theory in Native American Literature: Dakota and Haudenosaunee Writing and Indigenous Worldviews*. Lincoln: University of Nebraska Press.

King, Thomas. 2005. *The Truth about Stories: A Native Narrative*. Minneapolis: University of Minnesota Press.

Konkle, Maureen. 2004. *Writing Indian Nations: Native Intellectuals and the Politics of Historiography, 1827–1863*. Chapel Hill: University of North Carolina Press.

Kroeber, Karl. 2008. *Native American Storytelling: A Reader of Myths and Legends*. Malden MA: Blackwell.

Kundera, Milan. 2003. *The Art of the Novel*. New York: Perennial Classics.

Krupat, Arnold. 2002. *Red Matters: Native American Studies.* Philadelphia: University of Pennsylvania Press.

———, ed. 1994. *Native American Autobiography: An Anthology.* Madison: University of Wisconsin Press.

———. 1989. *The Voice in the Margin: Native American Literature and the Canon.* Berkeley: University of California Press.

León-Portilla, Miguel, and Earl Shorris. 2001. *In the Language of Kings: An Anthology of Mesoamerican Literature—Pre-Columbian to the Present.* New York: Norton.

Li, Victor. 2006. *The Neo-primitivist Turn: Critical Reflections on Alterity, Culture, and Modernity.* Toronto: University of Toronto Press.

Maddox, Lucy. 2005. *Citizen Indians: Native American Intellectuals, Race and Reform.* Ithaca NY: Cornell University Press.

Marcus, Joyce. 1992. *Mesoamerican Writing Systems: Propaganda, Myth, and History in Four Ancient Civilizations.* Princeton: Princeton University Press.

Mohanty, Satya P. 1997. *Literary Theory and the Claims of History: Postmodernism, Objectivity, Multicultural Politics.* Ithaca NY: Cornell University Press.

Mignolo, Walter D. 2003. *The Darker Side of the Renaissance: Literacy, Territoriality, and Colonization.* Ann Arbor: University of Michigan Press.

———. 1994. "Signs and Their Transmission: The Question of the Book in the New World." In *Writing without Words: Alternative Literacies in Mesoamerica and the Andes,* ed. Elizabeth Hill Boone and Walter D. Mignolo. Durham NC: Duke University Press.

Momaday, N. Scott. 1997. *The Man Made of Words: Essays, Stories, Passages.* New York: St. Martin's Griffin.

———. 1975. "The Man Made of Words." In *Literature of the American Indians: Views and Interpretations. A Gathering of Indian Memories, Symbolic Contexts, and Literary Criticism,* ed. Abraham Chapman. New York: New American Library.

———. 1969. *The Way to Rainy Mountain.* Albuquerque: University of New Mexico Press.

———. 1968. *House Made of Dawn.* New York: Perennial Classics.

Mooney, James. 1900. *Myths of the Cherokees.* New York: Dover.

Morgan, William T., Jr. 1997. "Landscapes: N. Scott Momaday." In *Conversations with N. Scott Momaday,* ed. Matthias Schubnell. Jackson: University of Mississippi Press.

Nabokov, Peter. 2002. *A Forest of Time: American Indian Ways of History*. Cambridge, England: Cambridge University Press.

Oandasan, William. 1988. "The Way to Rainy Mountain: Internal and External Structures." In *Approaches to Teaching Momaday's The Way to Rainy Mountain*, ed. Kenneth M. Roemer. New York: Modern Language Association.

Olson, David R. 1994. *The World on Paper: The Conceptual and Cognitive Implications of Writing and Reading*. Cambridge, England: Cambridge University Press.

Ong, Walter J. 1982. *Orality and Literacy: The Technologizing of the Word*. New York: Routledge.

Ortiz, Simon J. 1977. *Song, Poetry and Language—Expression and Perception*. Tsaile AZ: Navajo Community College Press.

Owens, Louis. 2001. *I Hear the Train: Reflections, Inventions, Refractions*. Norman: University of Oklahoma Press.

———. 1998a. Afterword to *Bearheart: The Heirship Chronicles*, by Gerald Vizenor. Minneapolis: University of Minnesota Press.

———. 1998b. *Mixedblood Messages: Literature, Film, Family, Place*. Norman: University of Oklahoma Press.

———. 1997. "Introduction." SAIL, 2nd ser. 9.1: 1–2.

———. 1992. *Other Destinies: Understanding the American Indian Novel*. Norman: University of Oklahoma Press.

Parezo, Nancy J. 1983. *Navajo Sandpainting: From Religious Act to Commercial Art*. Tucson: University of Arizona Press.

Parker, Robert Dale. 2003. *The Invention of Native American Literature*. Ithaca NY: Cornell University Press.

Pasquaretta, Paul. 1996. "Sacred Chance: Gambling and the Contemporary Native American Indian Novel." MELUS 21.2: 21–33.

Pearce, Roy Harvey. 1988. *Savagism and Civilization: A Study of the Indian and the American Mind*. Berkeley: University of California Press.

Perdue, Theda. 1998. *Cherokee Women: Gender and Culture Change, 1700–1835*. Lincoln: University of Nebraska Press.

Peyer, Bernd C. 1997. *The Tutor'd Min: Indian Missionary Writers in Antebellum America*. Amherst: University of Massachusetts Press.

Reynolds, Jack, and Jonathan Roffe. 2004. *Understanding Derrida*. New York: Continuum.

Royle, Nicholas. 2003. *Jacques Derrida*. New York: Routledge.

Ruoff, A. Lavonne Brown. 1993. "Gerald Vizenor: Compassionate Trickster." *Studies in American Indian Literatures*, 2nd ser. 5.2: 39–45.

Ruppert, James. 1995. *Mediation in Contemporary Native American Fiction.* Norman: University of Oklahoma Press.

———. 1982. "Outside the Arc of the Poem: A Review of Ray Young Bear's *Winter of the Salamander*." *Studies in American Indian Literatures* 6.3: 6–10.

Sayre, Gordon M. 1997. *Les Sauvages Americains: Representations of Native Americans in French and English Colonial Literature.* Chapel Hill: University of North Carolina Press.

Schubnell, Matthias. 1997. "Shouting at the Machine: An Interview with N. Scott Momaday." In *Conversations with N. Scott Momaday*, ed. Matthias Schubnell. Jackson: University of Mississippi Press.

———. 1988. "Tribal Identity and the Imagination." In *Approaches to Teaching Momaday's The Way to Rainy Mountain*, ed. Kenneth M. Roemer. New York: Modern Language Association.

Scribner, Sylvia, and Michael Cole. 1981. *The Psychology of Literacy.* Cambridge MA: Harvard University Press.

Silko, Leslie Marmon. 1996. *Yellow Woman and a Beauty of the Spirit: Essays on Native American Life Today.* New York: Touchstone.

———. 1977. *Ceremony.* New York: Penguin.

Smith, Andrea. 2005. *Conquest: Sexual Violence and American Indian Genocide.* Cambridge MA: South End Press.

Smith, Paul Chaat, and Robert Allen Warrior. 1996. *Like a Hurricane: The Indian Movement from Alcatraz to Wounded Knee.* New York: New Press.

Street, Brian V. 1984. *Literacy in Theory and Practice.* Cambridge, England: Cambridge University Press.

Swann, Brian, and Arnold Krupat, eds. 1987. *Recovering the Word: Essays on Native American Literature.* Berkeley: University of California Press.

Tehanetorens. 1972. *Wampum Belts.* Onchiota NY: Six Nations Indian Museum.

Teuton, Chris. 2007. "Interpreting Our World: Authority and the Written Word in Robert J. Conley's *Real People Series*." *Mfs: Modern Fiction Studies* 53.3: 544–68.

Teuton, Sean Kicummah. 2008. *Red Land, Red Power: Grounding Knowledge in the American Indian Novel.* Durham NC: Duke University Press.

———. 2001. "Writing Home: An Interview with Robert J. Conley." *Wicazo Sa Review* 16.2: 115–28.

Todorov, Tzvetan. 1982. *The Conquest of America*. New York: Harper & Row.

Treuer, David. 2006. *Native American Fiction: A User's Manual*. St. Paul MN: Graywolf Press.

Velie, Alan R. 1993. "Vizenor: Post-Modern Fiction." In *Critical Perspectives on Native American Fiction*, compiled and edited by Richard F. Fleck. Washington DC: Three Continents Press.

Vizenor, Gerald, ed. 2008. *Survivance: Narratives of Native Presence*. Lincoln: University of Nebraska Press.

———. 1998. *Fugitive Poses: Native American Indian Scenes of Absence and Presence*. Lincoln: University of Nebraska Press.

———. 1990. *Bearheart: The Heirship Chronicles*. Minneapolis: University of Minnesota Press.

———. 1978a. *Darkness in Saint Louis Bearheart*. St. Paul MN: Truck Press.

———. 1978b. *Wordarrows: Indians and Whites in the New Fur Trade*. Minneapolis: University of Minnesota Press.

Walker, Cheryl. 1997. *Indian Nation: Native American Literature and Nineteenth-Century Nationalisms*. Durham NC: Duke University Press.

Wallace, Paul A. W. 1946. *White Roots of Peace: The Iroquois Book of Life*. Santa Fe NM: Clear Light Publishers.

Warrior, Robert. 2005. *The People and the Word: Reading Native Nonfiction*. Minneapolis: University of Minnesota Press.

———. 1995. *Tribal Secrets: Recovering American Indian Intellectual Traditions*. Minneapolis: University of Minnesota Press.

Waters, Anne. 2004. "Language Matters: Nondiscrete Nonbinary Dualism." In *American Indian Thought*, ed. Anne Waters. Oxford: Blackwell.

Waugh, Patricia. 1984. *Metafiction: The Theory and Practice of Self-Conscious Fiction*. New York: Routledge.

Weaver, Jace, Craig S. Womack, and Robert Warrior. 2006. *American Indian Literary Nationalism*. Albuquerque: University of New Mexico Press.

Weaver, Jace, Craig S. Womack, and Robert Warrior. 1997. *That the People Might Live: Native American Literatures and Native American Community*. New York: Oxford University Press.

Welburn, Ron. 2001. *Roanoke and Wampum: Topics in Native American Heritage and Literatures*. New York: Peter Lang.

Williams, Robert A., Jr. 2005. *Like a Loaded Weapon: The Rehnquist Court, Indian Rights, and the Legal History of Racism in America*. Minneapolis: University of Minnesota Press.

Wilson, Michael D. 2008. *Writing Home: Indigenous Narratives of Resistance*. East Lansing: Michigan State University Press.

———. 1997. "Speaking of Home: The Idea of the Center in Some Contemporary American Indian Writing." *Wicazo Sa Review* (Spring): 129–47.

Womack, Craig S. 1999. *Red on Red: Native American Literary Separatism*. Minneapolis: University of Minnesota Press.

Young Bear, Ray A. 2001. *The Rock Island Hiking Club*. Iowa City: University of Iowa Press.

———. 1996. *Remnants of the First Earth*. New York: Grove Press.

———. 1992. *Black Eagle Child: The Facepaint Narratives*. Iowa City: University of Iowa Press.

———. 1990. *The Invisible Musician*. Duluth MN: Holy Cow! Press.

———. 1980. *Winter of the Salamander: Keeper of Importance*. New York: Harper & Row.

Index

Adams, Ian, 30
African American literature, blues impulse in, xvi
Alexie, Sherman, 149, 185
Alfred, Taiaiake, 51, 219
Algonkin-speaking tribes, flood myths of, 115
alien abduction, 174
Allen, Paula Gunn, 19, 25, 26
alphabet, privileging of, 13
American Indian literature: contemporary works in, xix–xxii; culturalist approach to, 9–10; defining writing of, 8–14; graphic impulse in, xiv, xvi; graphocentrism in, 23–28, 216; history of, xix; Indigenous thought and, 8; literature of resistance, xix; oral impulse in, xiv, xvi; orality in, 8, 10–11; oral-literate binary in, 15, 16, 17, 21, 22, 23, 53, 223nn8–9; relationship of traditional and modern values, xiv–xv; tribally

specific aesthetics in, 188. *See also* critical impulse
American Indian Movement (AIM), 34, 95, 96, 99, 123
American Indians: challenging stereotypes of, 17, 85, 91, 104; graphic traditions of, xv; oral traditions of, xv; origin myths of, 132; political engagement by, 95, 96; struggle of political sovereignty, 6, 7
Ani-Kutani clan: ancient writing system of, 200–201; Cherokee uprising against, 3–5, 198, 200, 206, 207, 213, 221–22n1; as priestly class of Cherokees, 3, 198, 201, 202
animals, xi, xiii
Anishinaabe, xv; dish game played by, 136–37, 140, 142, 143; Evil Gambler, 129, 130, 133, 134, 136, 138, 139; Manabozho Naanabozho trickster, 106, 120, 134, 136, 141, 142
Apess, William, xix, 185

CPSIA information can be obtained
at www.ICGtesting.com
Printed in the USA
LVHW042109120822
725820LV00008B/268

9 781496 207685